UNDERSTANDING FAITH

Understanding Hinduism

W0006079

UNDERSTANDING FAITH

SERIES EDITOR: PROFESSOR FRANK WHALING

UNDERSTANDING FAITH

SERIES EDITOR: PROFESSOR FRANK WHALING

Understanding Hinduism

Frank Whaling

Professor Emeritus, The Study of Religion
University of Edinburgh

DUNEDIN

EDINBURGH ◆ LONDON

First published in 2010 by
Dunedin Academic Press Ltd
Reprinted 2012

Head Office
Hudson House, 8 Albany Street,
Edinburgh EH1 3QB

London Office
The Towers, 54 Vartry Road,
London N15 6PU

ISBN: 978-1-903765-36-4
ISSN: 1744-5833

© 2010 Frank Whaling

British Library Cataloguing in Publication Data
A catalogue record for this book is available from the British Library

Typeset by Makar Publishing Production, Edinburgh
Printed by CPI Group (UK) Ltd., Croydon, CR0 4YY
Printed on paper from sustainable resources

For my wife Margaret,
my children John and Ruth,
and my sisters Joan and Sheila.

Contents

Preface

My thanks go out to a number of people who have been of help in the writing of this book. I am grateful to Hindu friends around the world, in India and elsewhere, for their wisdom and guidance over the years. To my Harvard Professors, Daniel Ingalls and John Carman, I am deeply indebted. My students at Edinburgh University and other places of learning, through their questions and discussions, have been of more help to me than they probably realise. Special thanks are due to my close family and friends, especially to my wife Margaret, who has sustained me through an extended period of illness during the genesis of this book.

We live in a global age with its promise and despair, its hope and fear, its capacity for renewal and destruction, its rapid change and ecological threat. How can we understand it better and live in it more fully? I hope that this book on Hinduism, and the other books in this series on Understanding Faith, will be of help in living creatively in this bewildering, challenging and yet beautiful world.

Timeline of Important Events

BCE

2500–1750	Indus Valley Civilisation
1750–1200	Composition of *Rig Veda* (I–IX)
1200–850	*Rig Veda* X onwards, Brahmanas, Aranyakas
850–500	Composition of Upanishads
599–527	Traditional dates of Jain Mahavira
566–486	Traditional dates of the Buddha; 490–410 in later scholarship
560–325	Magadha Empire
500–200 CE	Composition of *Mahābhārata*, including the *Bhagavad Gītā*, *Rāmāyana* and early Sutras, including Manusmriti and Brahmā Sutras
327–325	Alexander the Great in India
321–181	Mauryan Empire
200–200 CE	Buddhists and Jains spread around India

CE

78–230	Kushana Empire
100–450	Hindu influence in South East Asia
200–300	Composition of *Harivamsha*
250–1200	Composition of Purānas
320–650	Gupta Empire
400–	Rise and spread of Vishnu, Shiva and Goddess traditions and of temple building and iconography. Consolidation of caste, rituals, *Dharmashastra* and Sanskrit literature
500–900	Alvars and Nammalvars lead rise of *bhakti* devotional poetry and religion in South India
600–900	Revival of Brahmin leadership and decline of Buddhism
700–1150	Growth of Shaivite theology
788–820	Life of Shankara and rise of Advaita (non-dual) Vedanta

1000–	Muslim incursions into India and nominal rule until 1858
1013–1137	Traditional dates of Rāmānuja and growth of Sri Vaishnavism and Viśistādvaita (qualified non-dual) Vedanta
1125–62	Traditional dates of Nimbarka and rise of Dvaitadvaita (dual/non-dual) Vedanta
1199–1276	Traditional dates of Madhva and Dvaita (dual) Vedanta
1211–1526	Muslim Delhi Sultanate
1336–1565	Vijayanagar Empire
c.1420	Life of Mīrābāī
1440–1518	Traditional dates of Kabīr
1479–1531	Life of Vallabha and rise of Śuddhādvaita (pure non-dual) Vedanta
1479–1584	Life of Surdas
1486–1533	Life of Chaitanya
1498	Vasco da Gama arrives in South India
1526–1757	Muslim Mughal rule in India
1543–1623	Life of Tulsīdās
1608–81	Life of Rāmdās
1609–49	Life of Tukaram
1650	East India Company formed
1757	Battle of Plassey won by Clive
1772	Warren Hastings becomes Governor-General
1772–1833	Life of Ram Mohan Roy
1774	William Jones founds Bengal Oriental Society
1775	Charles Wilkins translates *Bhagavad Gītā* into English
1781	Sahanand Swami (Swaminarayan) born
1813	Christian missionary work legalised in India
1820–	Swaminarayan Movement begins
1824–83	Life of Dayananda Saraswati
1828	Brahmo Samaj formed
1829	Satī (widow-burning) prohibited
1835	English introduced as official language of India
1836	Indenture system for exporting Indian labourers started
1856–1920	Life of B. G. Tilak
1857	First War of Indian Independence (Indian Mutiny)

1858	Queen Victoria becomes Empress of India
1873	Max Müller completes first critical edition of *Rig Veda*
1869–1948	Life of Mahatma Gandhi
1872–1950	Life of Sri Aurobindo
1875	Arya Samaj formed in India and Theosophical Society in New York
1883–1966	Life of V. D. Sarvarkar, pioneer of Hindutva movement
1885	Indian National Congress formed
1886	Ramakrishna Order formed (Ramakrishna Mission 1897)
1888–1975	Life of President Sarvepalli Radhakrishnan
1891–1956	Life of B. R. Ambedkar
1893	Chicago World Parliament of Religions
1894	First Vedanta Society formed in New York
1896–1977	Life of Bhaktivedanta Prabhupada
1896–1982	Life of Sri Anandamayi Ma
1925	Rashtriya Swayamsevak Sangh (RSS) founded by Savarkar
1930	Gandhi's famous Salt March
1947	Indian Independence and Partition of India
1950–	Significant migration of Indians to the West begins
1950	Indian Constitution drawn up
1955	Untouchability Offences Act
1961	Dowry Prohibition Act (amended 1983)
1966	International Society for Krishna Consciousness (ISKON) formed by Bhaktivedanta Prabhupada: Hare Krishnas
1992	Ayodhya mosque destroyed by right-wing Hindus
1997	A Dalit becomes President of India
2009	A Dalit becomes Speaker of the Indian Parliament

The principal Hindu holy sites of the many hundreds scattered around India.

1

Introduction

The aim of this book is to understand Hinduism or, more precisely, to try to understand Hinduism. The Hindu tradition is very elaborate and bewildering in its complexity. It is also rewarding and energising to engage with. It is one thing to describe Hinduism, it is another to understand Hinduism, yet that is my aim.

The Meaning of Hinduism

An initial task is to grapple with the word 'Hinduism'. In some recent scholarship it has been said that 'Hinduism' is a comparatively new word, coined by westerners at the time of the Enlightenment, to denote a kind of monolithic entity. That is, according to some scholars, a meaningless abstraction that does not accord with reality. There is no such thing as 'Hinduism' or even 'religion' they say – these are empty words. This is given extreme form in Jonathan Z. Smith (1998) whose notion is that religion is solely the creation of the scholar's study. There is an element of truth in this. However, it is significant that this postmodern and post-colonial debate is basically a western debate. Surely if the term is in question, it is the Hindus who should have the most say about who and what they are? I will emphasise the Hindu sense of the word, and the Hindu sense of themselves. Professor Wilfred Cantwell Smith (1964), in his seminal book *The Meaning and End of Religion*, raised a different but allied point to the effect that the modern words for religions such as Hinduism, Buddhism, Sikhism, Zoroastrianism, Daoism, Confucianism and so on, and indeed the word 'religion' itself, are unhelpful in that they make religions and religion into things that can be studied like 'objects'. For Smith 'religion' is to do with persons in religious traditions under transcendence, not with 'religions' or 'religion' as abstract entities. Whilst agreeing with Smith to an extent, it is not clear that the term Hinduism can simply be dropped. It may be misleading but it is in fair measure accepted by Hindus themselves. However, there are alternatives to using the word Hinduism, as I will suggest later.

The term Hinduism is misleading if it suggests that Hinduism is one entity. Hinduism is broad and it contains a number of traditions. The term Hinduism also implies that there is a basic essence that is within all Hindus. This must be debated. The term also dwells upon Hinduism as a religion and whilst that is appropriate to a book in a series called Understanding Faith, Hinduism is a total way of life that includes religion as part of a total world-view. The term also assumes that there is a set of beliefs common to the whole of Hinduism and this is not the case.

There have also been attempts to keep the term 'Hinduism' but to apply it too widely. Hinduism is not coterminous with India nor are all Indians Hindus. The term Hindu appears to have originated in connection with the river Indus, in the north-west of India, which was an obvious invasion point into the subcontinent. Passages in the original *Rig Veda* (e.g. V.53.9) refer to the river Sindhu as early as about 1200 BCE. Later invaders such as Darius I of Persia, Alexander the Great and the Muslims considered the people by or on the other side of the river Indus to be 'Hindus' which amounted to Indians. There have been attempts by the Hindutva Movement in contemporary India to equate Hindus with Indians. Whilst Hinduism has had a profound effect upon other religions and groups in India, there were non-Hindu Buddhists, Jains and Christians in India when the Muslims invaded India and there are many groups in India today, including Sikhs, who are not Hindu. Indeed the Adivasi tribal peoples were in India before Hindus were in existence unless, that is, we call them 'Hindus' also. The Hindu way of life has had a strong influence upon wider India but that influence has not been total. Hinduism is now a global tradition present in other parts of the world. It transcends India. New modes of living and new forms of Hinduism are developing in different countries.

So I prefer the phrase 'the Hindu tradition' rather than Hinduism and I will use it believing that the Hindu tradition describes many strands and groups within its outstretched branches.

What is a Hindu?

Insofar as the Hindu tradition has no founder, no central authority to ordain what is orthodoxy, no set of creeds, a wide variety of sacred texts and no obvious 'big bang' at the beginning it is clear that generalisations about 'what is a Hindu?' can be fraught with problems.

At one end of the spectrum there is Dandekar's suggestion that 'a Hindu is one who is born of Hindu parents and who has not openly abjured Hinduism' (Dandekar, 1979, p. 4). This is pragmatic but it is also slightly negative and takes no account of people who may become Hindus. Dandekar

(1979, p. 7) further suggests that ultimately 'a study of Hinduism would invariably amount to a study of the various Hindu castes and sects'. This makes reasonable sense in that caste has been important at the social level of relationships between people whilst religious traditions (*Sampradāyas*) have been important at the level of relationships between persons and the divine. However, debate about caste has been ongoing for centuries among Hindus, even more so now in Indian cities, universities and amongst Hindus abroad.

Another view of 'what is a Hindu?' relates to the authority of the Veda. According to J. L. Mehta (1984, p. 33), the original Veda has remained the 'animating source of the religiousness that has generated and sustained the Hindu tradition'. However, there has been ongoing discussion about what is the Veda – is it the original *Rig Veda*? Is it the 'wider Veda' including the Upanishads? Should later sacred texts such as the *Bhagavad Gītā* be added to it? Moreover, how should the whole be interpreted?

Yet another view relates to concepts and to the idea that a Hindu is a person who holds certain implicit beliefs. These would normally include the concept of *Brahman* as ultimate reality, the notion of *ātman* as the real self of human beings, the notion of rebirth (*samsāra*) according to one's actions (*karma*) and the notion of final release (*moksha*) from the round of rebirths as one's ultimate destiny. However, not all Hindus accept these beliefs and they are subject to reinterpretation in the light of changing historical situations.

Other views as to what is a Hindu are less universal: for example, the idea that all Hindus are vegetarians and venerate the cow. Any complete view of the Hindu tradition can hardly ignore the fact that India has roughly a third of the world's cattle on 3% of the world's land area, that her cattle represent the largest concentration of domestic animals in the world, that her animal homes are 'essentially religious institutions' and that lying behind them are notions of cow veneration, avoidance of beef, non-violence to living creatures (*ahimsa*) and even ecological echoes (Lodrick, 1981, p. 198). This view is accepted sympathetically by many Hindus although it is also seen from different angles. Moreover, these differing viewpoints are not always compatible. Dandekar (1979, p. 8) states, 'the true glory of Hinduism consists in presenting all these polarities and paradoxes as also the various levels of doctrine and practice as constituting a single well-coordinated religious system'. However, this is debatable and in the Hindu tradition there are many varied traditions in India and elsewhere.

A Model of the Hindu Tradition

The complexities within the Hindu tradition are legion. In order to give structure to this study, a model will be used to help the reader to make sense of the Hindu tradition. The model is universal: it can be used to study any religious tradition. The Hindu tradition, indeed all the major religious traditions, contains eight interlinked elements. The eight links are those of **religious community; ritual; ethics; social and political involvement in wider society; scripture/sacred texts; concepts; aesthetics;** and **spirituality**. Before examining them in depth, it is worth setting the background for all eight elements within the Hindu tradition.

The Hindus lacked a founder and this is one reason why there is no strong sense of a Hindu **religious community**. There is no 'church' and no 'orthodoxy'. Instead there are many *Sampradāyas* (traditions) that focus upon different objects of worship including Shiva, the Goddess and Vishnu with his various *avatāras* (incarnations) notably Rāma and Krishna. Many Hindus belong to no religious community as such, and others owe their allegiance to local gurus often with small followings.

Ritual is accordingly varied and scattered. The main Hindu 'sacraments' (birth, initiation, marriage and death) generally centre upon the home as does daily worship (*pūjā*). Hindus can attend festivals associated with many different deities and they may visit many temples that are open for worship on a daily basis.

Hindu **ethics** encourage good actions and support the maxim of the *Bhagavad Gītā* that one should do one's duty because it is right and without thought of reward (albeit mainly within the orbit of caste). The Hindu notion of *dharma* involves concern for nature as well as for human beings.

Social involvement for Hindus relies fairly heavily upon the question of caste. Hindus are involved in wider society, in the main, through their status in the caste system. Their status in the caste system is determined by their actions, good or bad, according to which they are reborn at the end of each earthly life. The caste system has provided social stability and security to Hindus. It has also raised questions that are now coming to the fore concerning the role of women and the role of the Dalits (former outcastes) in the total scheme of things. Because the caste system has provided security there has been less need for *political power* to rest fully in Hindu hands. Hindus have lived under Buddhist, Muslim and British rule and independent India is a secular state by constitution.

Hindu views of **scripture** are also flexible. In theory, the original *Rig Veda* is the fountainhead of sacred texts containing that which was heard (*shruti*) and revealed. However the *Rig Veda*, together with the other three Vedas and the Brahmanas, Aranyakas and Upanishads, is part of a wider corpus of scripture known collectively as the Veda. In practice the Upanishads are the key to the Veda. Furthermore, later sacred texts, such as the *Bhagavad Gītā*, that are not revealed but handed down and remembered (*smriti*) and are, in theory, subsidiary to the revealed Veda, are often more popular and more used than the Veda itself.

Some key Hindu **concepts**, although they may be differently interpreted, are: *Brahman* as ultimate reality; the *ātman* as the real inner self of human beings; human life as a round of rebirths (*samsāra*) according to one's *karma*; and salvation (*moksha*) as release from the round of rebirths.

Every **aesthetic** approach known to humankind has been utilised by Hindus to represent the diversity of truth within the Hindu world-view. Throughout most of history the majority of people could not read and write, but they could enjoy architecture and sculpture, music and dance, painting and movement. By contrast with the ordered simplicity of a Muslim mosque or the soaring spire of a Christian church reaching up to transcendence, a Hindu temple mirrors Hindu aesthetics and the Hindu vision of life with its ornate structure, its many-crannied complexity, its different levels and its elaborate series of rooms and roofs.

Hindu **spirituality** is also very varied as can be seen in the yoga systems and in the *Bhagavad Gītā* with its 'three ways' (*trimarga*) of inward real-isation through yoga, devotional trust in a personal deity and serving one's fellows and God in the world unselfishly. There is wide variety within Hindu spirituality in its inward as well as its outward sense

When summarising the eight elements in this model it is helpful to realise that Hindu traditions; home worship and worship in Hindu temples; Hindu ethical codes; the caste system; the Veda and later scriptural trad-itions; Hindu concepts of *Brahman*, *ātman* and reincarnation; classical Hindu dance and music; and spiritual modes such as yoga are not a chaotic and separate jumble but are interlinked. They give meaning to each other in the developing organism that is the Hindu tradition. Different Hindus will participate in differing ways at different levels in differing elements. But the model is helpful in providing a framework of understanding what will be elaborated in the rest of this book

Behind the model, however, lies another element of great importance. That element is **transcendence** or transcendent reality. Insofar as it is tran-scendent, transcendent reality is less clear than the eight elements already proposed. The eight elements of the model are directly observable, tran-scendence is not. For Hindus transcendent reality is *Brahman*. However, *Brahman* is made clearer by means of mediating focuses that lie at the heart of the Hindu tradition. Not all Hindus have a sense of *Brahman*, some Hindus are atheists. Many Hindus do have a sense of *Brahman* as ultimate reality but often more immediately clear and available is one of many mediating focuses in the form of personal deities. Some of the main deities are Shiva, the Goddess in her various forms, Vishnu in his own right, and Vishnu in the form of *avatāras* (incarnations) such as Rāma and Krishna. I will consider *Brahman* and the whole panoply of Hindu deities later. One final ingredient is also important. It is difficult to pin down but it is vital: it is that quality and intention within persons and groups of persons that makes a pattern out of life, that responds to mediated reality, that breathes life into a tradition, and makes transcendence real. It is intangible and like transcendence it cannot be seen directly. For it is persons, or groups of persons, who respond to mediated reality and use the eight elements that form the Hindu tradition dynamically, otherwise these elements are lifeless forms. Persons and their intentions matter. Without their '**intentionality**', or even 'faithful intentionality', or the '**faith**' of Hindu men and women, there would be no Hindu tradition to study.

Hindu History

The model described is important in that it provides a structure with which sense may be made of the extraordinarily complex phenomenon that is the Hindu tradition. However, it needs to be complemented by an awareness of Hindu history. Without history the model is becalmed, without the model history lacks context.

It is quite difficult to reconstruct the history of the Hindu tradition. Hindus sometimes call their tradition the *sanatana dharma*, the eternal law. Within Hindu sacred texts very few historical events are mentioned. It is difficult to pin down whether or when the great Hindu heroes and deities, Rāma and Krishna, lived on earth. The considerable interest of Christians and Muslims in investigating the lives of the historical Jesus and Muhammad is something of a mystery to many Hindus. The classical Hindu views of history see it in terms of *yugas* or ages which repeat themselves in enormous cycles in a universe that has no beginning or end. The *yugas* last for vast periods of time and descend through the three golden, silver and copper ages to the final declining iron age (*kali yuga*). During *kali yuga* society reaches a stage where property confers rank; wealth becomes the only source of virtue; passion the sole bond of union between husband and wife; falsehood the source of success in life; sex the only means of enjoyment; a time when outer trappings are confused with inner religion. There are Hindus who for obvious reasons are tempted to apply this notion, taken from the *Vishnu*

Purāna, to today. The Brahmā Kumaris, who began within the Hindu tradition but are now separate, have telescoped the four *yugas*, which last for
aeons of time in classical Hinduism, into a total cycle of six thousand years
divided into four ages of one thousand five hundred years each. According
to the Brahmā Kumaris we are now reaching the end of a cycle and, after a
cataclysmic set of events, the present cycle will end and a new golden age will
immediately begin. So the foreshortened round of the ages will continue.
This view is very untypical. In the light of the eternal view of Hindu historical cosmology it is perhaps not surprising that actual, mundane history has
been relatively underplayed.

The paradoxical background to Hindu history is that most of the great
empires in Indian history were not Hindu. There were a number of small
Hindu kingdoms throughout Indian history but, with a few exceptions,
the largest and best-known Indian empires were led by Buddhist, Muslim
and British rulers. The great Mauryan emperor Ashoka ruled from 273
to 232 BCE and during his victorious reign he inclined to Buddhism.
In the latter part of his reign he ruled equitably, set up a moral political economy, retreated from war, inaugurated helpful public works and
worked for peace and security. He set out his memorable edicts on pillars
and great rocks and built Stūpas for all to see. He did not establish a Buddhist kingdom but, through his influence, the Buddhist tradition spread
to Syria, Egypt and other Hellenistic kingdoms and also to Sri Lanka and
probably Nepal. In India he set up good relationships with the Jains and
with Hindu leaders.

At the end of the first century and the beginning of the second century
CE the Kushan ruler Kanishka set up a Buddhist kingdom in north-west
India stretching from beyond the north-west frontier to Kashmir and Varanasi. He convened one of the great Mahāyāna Buddhist Councils and it was
from his kingdom that the Mahāyāna Buddhist tradition travelled along the
Silk Route into China where it would take hold and become an important
element in the rise of Chinese civilisation.

The next great dynasty, the Gupta dynasty, was Hindu and the only
fairly extensive India-wide Hindu kingdom. It extended from 320 to 540
CE (interrupted by Hun invasions) and, although tolerant to Buddhists
and Jains, it heralded great advances in the Hindu tradition. Great writers
such as Kālidāsa, cave paintings such as those at Ajanta, the six schools of
Hindu philosophy, Buddhist universities such as Nalanda, works such as the
Kāma Sūtra, some of the Purānas and the Laws of Manu, and mathemati-
cal advances such as the notion of zero and nine-digit numbers all emerged
during this period. Hindu influence then spread.

In the Deccan and South India various Hindu dynasties rose and flourished briefly. Of most interest were the Hindu kingdoms of the Chalukyas and Pallavas which had some influence between c.500 and 750 CE. In addition to the extraordinary early stone Hindu temples built in South India during this period, there is evidence of the arrival of Hindu traditions in South East Asia. The Pallavas became involved in Cambodia and Khmer territory in Indochina. They had diplomatic relations with China and were also involved diplomatically in Sri Lanka and had contacts with Indonesia and Java. In addition to temple remains from some of these areas there is the evidence of the architectural marvel of Borobudur in Java, built between around 775 and 840, which probably began as a Hindu temple and was transformed into a Buddhist place of worship after its second stage. Bali remains a place where the Hindu tradition is still important, although South East Asia generally became Buddhist. The present King of Thailand still contains within his title the name of the Hindu deity Rāma.

In the first quarter of the eleventh century Mahmud of Ghazni (998–1030) entered Sind in north-west India. This was the beginning of the Muslim incursion and rule over India that lasted, in theory, up to 1858 when the last Mughal Emperor gave way to Queen Victoria. Al-Biruni accompanied Mahmud of Ghazni's entourage between 1017 and 1030 and he left an extraordinary account of Hindu India at that time summarised by Ainslie Embree in *Alberuni's India* (1971). He learnt Sanskrit and his aim was to explain Hindu civilisation to Muslims. His work was a very early and unusual example of comparative religion. A very different example came much later in the work of the great Mughul emperor Akbar (1556–1605). He established an empire stretching throughout the whole of North India and down into the Deccan. He was religiously very tolerant. He assembled scholars from Hindu, Muslim, Jain, Zoroastrian and Christian traditions to debate and hopefully to agree to differ harmoniously on the basis of Din-I-Illai (Divine Faith). The reality is that, apart from such exceptions as Al-Biruni and Akbar, there is a profound difference between the Hindu and Muslim world-views. There was some significant interaction but in the main the Hindu tradition continued under alien and Muslim rule.

In 1498 Vasco de Gama had looked inside a Hindu temple in Goa and, seeing the image of a Hindu goddess being worshipped, he had been appalled because he thought that it was a Christian church in which the Virgin Mary was being heretically reverenced. What else would he think at that time? There was later cross-fertilisation between Hindus and Christians as seen in the modern work of Ram Mohan Roy, the Tagores, Keshub Chander Sen, Ramakrishna, Vivekananda, Gandhi, Aurobindo, Vinobe Bhave and others.

Thus the Hindu tradition in India has developed, in the main, within political systems run by non-Hindus.

Phenomenology

My task is not only to describe but also to understand. To achieve this we need, insofar as is possible, to get 'inside' the Hindu tradition. We need to try and see that tradition, in some ways, through Hindu eyes. If we are not Hindus, we need to empathise with those who are, and if we are Hindus, it will help us to understand the Hindu tradition more fully. The classical method for doing this is through phenomenology. This involves putting one's own world-view into brackets in order to understand the world-view of others. The technical term for this is *epoché*. The aim is to avoid bias and to understand others in their own right. It is to put our presuppositions on one side in order to see others 'as they are' unhindered by our prejudices. The second arm of phenomenology is empathy. This is the more positive aim of penetrating empathetically into the world-view of others, to see as they themselves see. It is to understand, as far as possible, from within.

This is not easy. It is difficult to become an insider when one is an outsider. The writer happens to be male, white, born in Yorkshire (in Britain, in Europe), an academic and a Christian. It is psychologically hardly possible to put all that on one side. Total empathy, even total objectivity, is very difficult. We come laden with baggage.

However it is possible to exercise a kind of self-reflexive phenomenology. The process can be cumulative. By entering more deeply into the Hindu tradition by study, research, travel and long conversations about findings and observations one is better able to understand Hindus. By talking to Hindus about what their own 'faithful intentions' mean to them one is better able to understand what the Hindu tradition is all about.

Personal Stories

People are important in the study of religion. Some personal stories may illuminate an understanding of the Hindu tradition.

Ambika Datta Upadhyaya and the caste system

I first met Pundit A. D. Upadhyaya when I arrived in Varanasi in 1963 and needed a Hindi teacher. Mr Upadhyaya was a Brahmin, the highest of the four Hindu castes (*varnas*), and he taught Sanskrit at Banaras Hindu University. Every morning he came six miles across Varanasi by cycle rickshaw and between seven and nine o'clock he taught Hindi to my wife and me. He was patient and kind. Upadhyaya means teacher and he was a magnificent teacher. He could safely follow his ancestry back a thousand years or more. Within the Brahmin caste (*varna*) there are many sub-castes (*jātis*) and marriage is only allowed within some of those sub-castes. Not every Brahmin can marry every other Brahmin. One day we were invited for dinner. We never had any chance to look inside the kitchen or to meet and engage with our teacher's wife who did all the cooking. My teacher and his son would only eat food, such as nuts, that had shells on. Otherwise they would have been polluted by sharing food with us as my wife and I were 'prestigious outcastes'. At one point I walked over towards the *pūjā* (worship) room, which is set aside purely for worship in many Hindu homes. When I got near the door my teacher's son shouted in Hindi, asking me to stop. I had no intention of going into the *pūjā* room because if I had done so it would have had to be purified at great length to get rid of the pollution engendered by an 'outcaste'.

Mr Upadhyaya introduced me to a number of Hindu friends from whom I learnt a great deal. He also introduced me to the premier Hindu holy city of Banaras. I learnt much from him and came to know it well. Its true name (before it was corrupted by the British) was Varanasi. The holy river Ganges runs through Varanasi and six miles apart two other rivers run into it, named the Varana and the Asi. These two words joined together in Sanskrit are Varanasi and so the space between the three holy rivers is the sacred place of Varanasi (Banaras). If one dies in Varanasi, according to Hindu folklore, one can go straight to heaven. Along the banks of the Ganges, between the two rivers, are eighty-four ghats (whence sets of steps run down to the river). Two are used for laundry and are covered with brightly covered clothes every day. Two are burning ghats where bodies are cremated daily. Every day processions pass through the streets of Varanasi with four men carrying covered corpses on stretchers. The two front men chant *Rāma nama* (the name of Rāma/God) and the two back men chant *satya hai* (is true). The corpses are laid on a burning ghat and the eldest son lights the funeral pyre and finally the ashes are cast into the holy river to float away towards Calcutta. Some of the remaining eighty ghats are very famous for different reasons and some are venues for great festivals where mighty crowds gather. Varanasi is part of India's sacred geography.

Mr Upadhyaya's father lived alone in a hut a short distance away from his home. He spent his time in meditation and reading Hindu holy books, such as the *Bhagavad Gītā*. He was in the fourth and last stage of life according to the Hindu tradition, after his periods as a student, as a householder who raised a family and as one who had been semi-retired with his wife. Now he was on his own, cared for by his family and waiting peacefully for death which would mean either a better rebirth, or even *moksha*, final salvation. Pundit Upadhyaya and I were deep friends, but of different 'castes', and I learnt a great deal from him.

The outcaste Doms of Varanasi

Through the college in Varanasi where I was manager I met a number of ex-outcastes, now called Dalits who were at the other end of the caste spectrum, indeed outside the four Hindu castes altogether. When I was standing one day in one of their groups of huts (*muhallahs*), I saw pigs grazing around the outskirts. Pigs are unclean to most caste Hindus. There came to my mind the New Testament story of the Prodigal Son who took his father's inheritance into a far country where he wasted it in riotous living and was reduced to eating the food that the swine did eat. It occurred to me that my friends in the *muhallah* sometimes shared some of the food that the swine did not eat, as a matter of course. Poverty was a reality to them. I learnt a lot about other aspects of the Hindu tradition from my outcaste friends. I learnt that, in spite of their poverty, not all Dalits were poor. This group were Doms, the cleaners of Varanasi, who did all the most menial and unclean jobs. But one of them, who organised the wood for the funeral pyres on the burning ghats, was the equivalent of a millionaire. On the other hand, the lowly night-watchman (*chowkidar*) in the compound where we lived was a high-caste Brahmin. Until I stopped him, he woke us in the middle of the night by chanting verses from the Veda! Thus early on it became clear that, although generalisations can be made about the caste system and about the Hindu tradition, they are never fully watertight.

A Hindu householder and holy man

Soon after I arrived in Faizabad I met Ram Kumar Das. He was a Hindu holy man, belonging to a sect called the Rāmānandins who worship the Lord Rāma. We became friends and he told me his life story. His birth name had been Ram Kumar Singh. He had been born in a village north of Faiza-bad into the second caste of Hindus. He had married, at the age of thirteen, a girl aged twelve and he had attended college. He went away to Calcutta to work in a factory and sent money back to his family. He returned home three times a year, on the occasion of three important Hindu festivals. He had three sons who were brought up in the village. One day he received the news that his wife was ill. He returned home, but his wife was gravely ill and she died. Ram cremated her body and decided to stay in the village to be with his sons. Over a period of six months they all died from different causes. He cremated their bodies but he was heartbroken and he decided to commit suicide by walking away from the village until he dropped. He became weaker and weaker, but before he got too far he met an old Hindu holy man who belonged to the Rāmānandins. He was impressed by this man and decided to stay with him. In the end he too decided to become a Rāmānandin and he was initiated into the Rāmānandin tradition which traces itself back to the medieval saint Rāmānanda. My friend then changed his name and became Ram Kumar Das. *Das* means servant and is the name taken by Rāmānandin holy men. He stayed with his preceptor for a while and then he moved on. For a few years he went round India from holy place to holy place, from festival to festival, from Hindu gathering to Hindu gathering. His adventures were many. For a while he joined up with a group of *sādhus* who journeyed together. They were too right wing and worldly from his point of view and eventually he left them and found his way to Ayodhya. Ayodhya, like Varanasi, is in the middle of North India and, like Varanasi, it is one of seven major Hindu holy cities. Ram decided to stay for a while and act as a priest in a Hindu temple in Ayodhya near Faizabad. Ram Kumar Das was very tall, about six feet four in height. He wore white robes and had long black hair and a black beard; he also had beautiful eyes. On his forehead were the red and white marks of a Rāmānandin holy man. One day I asked him what he had done that morning before we met. He said that he had got up at four o'clock. I asked him what he did then and he replied that he had spent four hours in meditation. I asked whether he did that every day and he replied 'yes'.

He had a deep spirituality and we shared many things together at a profound level. Ram had skipped one of the stages of Hindu life. He had been a student and then a householder, but he had missed out the third stage, that of semi-retirement, due to the deaths in his family. He was now, at an early age, in the fourth stage of life as a holy man. He spent his time meditating, teaching and helping people without having to worry about making a living. He was in the world but not of the world. There are an estimated seven million holy men of different traditions, or even no tradition, wandering around the roads and sacred centres of India today. They may be few in number but they matter deeply within the Hindu context.

Anandamayi Ma and the depths of Hindu spirituality

I met Anandamayi Ma at an ashram she used when she came on visits to Varanasi between 1963 and 1966. She radiated a deep spirituality when I met her and, although she answered questions in conversation, her impact was not so much in words as in the aura of realised saintliness she projected. She has been born in 1896 in a village called Kheora in Bengal, now situated in Bangladesh. She was married at the age of twelve to a man known as Bholanath. He would later become the supporter, protector and champion of Sri Anandamayi Ma, as she became known. Although acting as a housewife, from 1918 she became immersed in profound spiritual discipline (*sādhana*) and between 1924 and 1928 she frequently lapsed into deep contemplative experience (*samādhi*), which included intense bliss but also spiritual awareness of other religious traditions. Devotees began to come for audiences with her to Shahbagh in Dhaka, where Bholanath was manager of the Gardens. Later she travelled and ashrams were built for her in Varanasi and other places. Anandamayi Ma was not educated or tutored in particular skills. She had a deep, childlike, spiritual simplicity. She was an exemplar of a profoundly Hindu spiritual way of life that appeals alike to men and women, to people of all religious traditions, to business folk and labourers, to humble and great, to high and low. She did not wander as a *sādhu*, like Ram Kumar Das. She did travel but people also came to her. She had an authentic spirituality that was unmistakable and deeply human, combining earthly and spiritual realms. She was without question a *sui generis* saint whose childlike, beautiful yet commanding serenity was clear to all. The depth and potentiality of Hindu spirituality became obvious to me in Varanasi through Sri Anandamayi Ma.

2

The History of the Hindu Tradition

The history of the Hindu tradition is long, diverse and fascinating. While it is important to see its development over time, I will place more emphasis upon the recent history of the Hindu tradition which is changing before our eyes. But the present can only be understood by glancing at the whole history of the Hindu tradition in order to identify the rocks whence the Hindu tradition was hewed and the historical background whence it came.

Early Hindu History: Prehistory to 1500 BCE

Its beginnings are unknown in that the artefacts and records that might describe those beginnings are absent. The original human inhabitants of India were the Negrito people who are still present in the Andaman Islands and parts of South India. They appear to have shared ideas of the passage of the dead to a kind of heaven that was guarded by a demonic creature. Later, the proto-Australoids came to India and they were interested in the phases of the moon. They used them to map out what were to become some of the days (*tithis*) of the Hindu calendar. Early Stone Age settlements have been found in parts of India where stone weapons, painted and unpainted pottery and bronze and copper ornaments have been discovered. It appears that corpses were burned and that there was some worship of mother deities and trees. Although facts may be surmised only with difficulty, it seems not unreasonable to suppose that the animism, fertility cults, mother goddesses and worship of natural elements found partly transmuted in later popular Hinduism had their origins in this earlier period.

More concrete evidence comes from the Indus Valley Civilisation dating back to approximately 2500–1500 BCE. Our understanding of this era is not complete in that the Indus Valley script and writing have yet to be deciphered. The main urban centres of this quite extensive civilisation, Harrapa and Mohenjodaro, were in what is now Pakistan. The people of the Indus Valley may have been related to the Dravidian tribes of South India. Debate rages as to the nature of the Indus Valley Civilisation and this has been heightened by the desire of the present nationalist Hindutva movement to locate the beginnings of the Hindu tradition within India with the Aryans. Until recently, they were seen as invaders into India. This theory of an Aryan presence and importance in India before the Indus Valley Civilisation arose has not been fully validated (Feuerstein *et al.*, 1995, offer seventeen arguments why the Aryan invasion never happened). However, Brockington (1996, p. 24) comments 'it must not be forgotten that the religion of the Vedas was an alien culture brought into India by the Aryans'. This view has by no means been disproved fully.

Various buildings or artefacts of the Indus Valley people have elements that lingered on in the Hindu tradition. The great bath at Mohenjodaro was elaborate and clearly important. Later Hindu traditions contain large bathing ponds outside temples; they stress ritual bathing, the importance of sacred rivers and various procedures connected with water, and they place emphasis upon purity and pollution. Other buildings excavated in the Indus Valley may well have been temples of reasonable size containing statues and these are suggestive of later Hindu places of worship with their cult images. Other Indus Valley stone statues include a standing female figure that is reminiscent of later goddesses. Some terracotta figurines, mainly female, are also suggestive of later cult goddesses. In addition to the Indus Valley great bath, buildings, statues and terracotta figurines, there are also important sets of seals. These contain symbolic patterns, human and animal figures and larger scenes. Especially interesting is the prevalence of bulls among the various animals represented and also the presence of a horned figure surrounded by animals that is suggestive of the later Hindu deity Shiva whose favourite animal was a bull and one of whose names was 'lord of the animals'. The structures of the cities of Harrapa and Mohenjodaro are well-organised in their overall plan and execution and, together with the great bath and ordered buildings, they are at least partly indicative of the later Hindu sense of structural order in regard to edifices and wider matters, such as the caste system.

This discussion of early Hindu history raises ongoing questions. First, did the Hindu tradition arise in India among the Indus Valley people and Vedic Aryans who were already there? Alternatively, did it come to India around 1750 BCE with the Aryan tribes from Mesopotamia? Did it arrive from outside like the Buddhist, Christian and Muslim traditions that became prominent in South East Asia or was it in India from its beginning? Second, to what extent is the Hindu tradition a fusion of Aryan and Dravidian and other elements? And if so which predominates? Is it a mixture of different traditions that shelter under the umbrella of the 'Hindu tradition'? Debate continues. There is evidence in the Veda, the set of Aryan sacred texts, of spirits and deities known as *yakshas* and of snakelike figures known as *nāgas*, which later appear as symbols or stones in village worship and even in Hindu temples. Thus, difference and fusion are abiding elements within the Hindu tradition.

The Veda Tradition

The Veda later became an umbrella term for a series of texts including the four early Vedas, the Brahmanas, the Aranyakas and the Upanishads. The Veda became known as that which was revealed to and was heard (*shruti*) by the early Vedic seers. The authority of the Veda as the scriptural source of the Hindu tradition is widely accepted by Hindus today. The Veda tradition began in oral form and indeed there are still teachers (*pundits*) who know it by heart and chant it. The language used in the early Vedic tradition was an ancient form of Sanskrit and by the time of the Upanishads this had developed into classical Sanskrit. Due to the lack of evidence from other sources our knowledge of the early Hindu tradition is taken from the Veda. Recent attempts to modify Hindu history would date its origins to the Aryans who supposedly lived in India *c.*4000 BCE, in contrast with the earlier notion that the Aryans invaded India around 1750 BCE and produced the Veda after they had entered India. In any event it is mainly from the Veda that we know about the early Hindu tradition.

The four early Vedas that are part of the total Veda were the *Rig Veda*, consisting of 1028 hymns in ten books, followed by the *Sāma Veda*, *Yajur Veda* and *Atharva Veda*. A second layer of the Veda are the Brahmanas that are priestly works composed in prose rather than in verse and centred upon ritual and sacrifices. The third source are the Aranyakas, which are more reflective works composed in forests (*aranyas*) that attempt to tease out the meaning of rituals and sacrifice. As the fourth and most important part of the Veda, the Upanishads explore the meaning of life, the nature of ultimate reality and the truth behind the universe. The whole Veda is taken by Hindus to be revealed (*shruti*), whereas later sacred texts are seen as remembered (*smriti*). However, some later texts such as the *Bhagavad Gītā*, theoretically less important, have in practice become more important in Hindu life. This may be because they are written in easier Sanskrit or in modern languages that offer greater intelligibility, as well as because of their relevance to everyday life.

The tremendous development within the Veda gives an idea of the nature of the early Hindu tradition. A significant deepening of understanding occurs in the Upanishads and the evolution from the three earlier layers of the Veda through to the Upanishads offers an insight into early Hindu history.

A New World-view: the Upanishads

The earlier tradition stressed worldly matters, including the notion that humans had one life in this world followed by death. By contrast, in the Upanishads there appeared the notion that there is more than one life. There is reincarnation through a round of rebirths (*samsāra*): individuals will be reborn according to their actions (*karma*) until liberation from rebirth is reached through *moksha* (release, salvation).

In the *Rig Veda* there are a variety of deities to whom praise or sacrifice can be offered. Important ones included Indra, Soma, Varuna and Agni. Different layers of meaning can be read into the role of these deities. For example, there is the god Agni. *Agni* means fire, both in the sense of a fire that warms and one used for cooking. Agni is important in rituals and sacrifices. Agni is also a kind of link between earth and the higher realms, rising through smoke as a kind of messenger into the heavens. Agni is also a deity in his own right. These levels of meaning (often three) remain not only in regard to gods but also in regard to the whole of life. Hindu life is not black or white, it is multifaceted. This sense of correspondence between different levels would be deepened in the Upanishads.

Within the early Veda we sense the development of four kinds of people to accommodate the advance of the Vedic tribes across the northern part of India. Priests (*brahmins*) were needed to superintend the Vedic prayers, rituals and sacrifices; gradually rulers (*Kshatriyas*) arose; in addition farmers and early craftsmen (*vaishyas*) began to emerge to provide for the communities that were evolving whilst a 'servant' (*shudra*) group also emerged to serve the other groups. Their lives and their religion were accommodated to this world. By the time of the Upanishads the later caste system was anticipated in greater depth.

The early Veda represents a worldly sense of activity implying three stages of life, which evolved more clearly later. These stages were the life of a student, the life of a householder (who was married with children) and the life of retirement within the family. The Upanishads added a fourth stage of life that opened up the possibility of renouncing life in the world and moving beyond life in the family. This might involve leaving the family and becoming a 'renouncer', who left the family home to engage in meditation as a wandering holy person, or it might involve staying near the family but abandoning family duties to focus upon a higher aim in life.

The early Veda presupposes three aims of life which were spelled out in later centuries and which centre upon life in the world. These threefold aims were that of *kāma* involving aesthetic or sensual satisfaction (hence the later Kāma Sūtra), that of *artha*, centred upon satisfaction in daily work and success in life, and that of *dharma* involving right living in a more general ethical sense. In early Vedic times these three aims were more related to the Vedic sacrifices with *kāma* being the pleasure received from the sacrifices, *artha* being the work done to fund the sacrifices, and *dharma* being the merit received from performing the sacrifices. The Upanishads added a fourth aim of life (related to the fourth stage of life), namely *moksha* or seeking directly for release from the rounds of rebirth in order to achieve 'salvation'.

The stress of the early Veda is on hymns of prayer or praise and on rituals and sacrifices. For example:

> I pray to Agni, the household priest who is the god of the sacrifice, the one who chants and invokes and brings most treasure...To you Agni, who shines upon darkness, we come day after day, bringing our thoughts and homage to you, the king over sacrifices...Be easy for us to reach, like a father to his son. Abide with us, Agni, for our happiness.

Alongside the hymns were the sacrificial rituals (*yajnas*) that were of central importance in the *Rig Veda* and the Brahmanas. In the Aranyakas and especially in the Upanishads, the hymns and sacrifices became, so to speak, internalised so that the stress was placed upon knowledge and contemplation. It was not the outward chant or ceremony that remained paramount. The emphasis upon ritual was accompanied by or replaced by an emphasis upon inwardness.

Discontent with the externals of religion – characterised in the early Veda by emphasis on deities, hymns, prayers, sacrifices and ritual – found expression in two key terms that emerge and deepen in the Upanishads. Those terms were *Brahman* and *ātman*. The sacred power, located in the sacrifices that maintain the world in the early Veda becomes, in the Upanishads, the sacred power that lies behind the world. It becomes *Brahman*. Meanwhile the 'breath' (*prana*) within humans, that upholds the five organs of the self and corresponds to the five natural forces, becomes the *ātman*, the ongoing self, which is reborn when the body dies and is the permanent self within. The Upanishads bring together the notions of *Brahman* and *ātman* in different ways. In *Chāndogya Upanishad* (ch. 6), Uddālaka teaches his son the identity of *ātman* and *Brahman* in the famous phrase *tat tvam asi*, 'that art thou', *Brahman* is *ātman*. The meaning of such terms lie at the heart of the Vedanta philosophies.

The new world-view of the Upanishads opened up new ways of being religious that moved beyond the world-view of the early Veda. The way of yoga and the way of asceticism made their appearance in the Upanishads, especially in connection with the fourth stage of life, and were destined to become very important.

In the Veda a plethora of deities of different kinds appear. They are plentiful in the early Veda whilst some disappear and others emerge in the Upanishads and the later Hindu tradition. Three key points should be made in connection with this abundance of gods. The first is that the Hindu tradition is not monotheistic. There are many deities and, although one god may be a Hindu's own chosen deity (*ishta-devata*), others may be worshipped also. Secondly, prominent divine figures are beginning to emerge in the Veda. Vishnu is present in the *Rig Veda* and he is important as he is benevolent towards the human race; he is a solar deity who can cover the universe in three strides and is thus all-pervasive. In the later Mahānāryana Upanishads, Vishnu is portrayed as a supreme personal deity. The second great deity to emerge in the Veda is Shiva. He is present in a preliminary way in the *Rig Veda* in the form of the somewhat destructive Rudra, but in the Śvetāśvatara Upanishad he is the supreme Lord who is the creator of the universe. Thus already Vishnu and Shiva are seen as important personal deities to whom devotion (*bhakti*) can be given.

Thirdly, *Brahman* as the impersonal power behind the universe is present in the Veda. The development of the Hindu sense of the relationships between *Brahman* and *ātman* and between *Brahman* and the great personal deities Vishnu and Shiva is a core theme.

Social Developments and Archaeology

The sociological and archaeological background of the Veda is not easy to trace. The Finnish historian Asko Parpola (1994) has observed that the Vedic tribes appear to have been different from the Indus Valley Civilisation in that they had horses and chariots whilst the Indus people did not; they did not use seals as the Indus people did; and, insofar as the Indus Valley language has been 'guessed at', it appears to be more Dravidian (like Tamil and Telugu) than Aryan. Whether the Aryans entered India before 1750 BCE or after 1750 BCE, better evidence comes from 1750 BCE onwards and it comes mainly from the Veda as archaeological evidence is very sparse. Three eras can reasonably be traced: 1750–1200 BCE (*Rig Veda* I–IX) when the Vedic tribes were advancing in north-west India; 1200–850 BCE (*Rig Veda* X to the Brāhmana texts) when the Vedic tribes were advancing in the Upper Ganges Valley; and 800–500 BCE (encompassing the early Upanishadic period) when the Vedic tribes were advancing along the lower Ganges plain. These advances encompassed many changes: growing settlements, a rising priesthood, a system of rulership, some administrative machinery, new trading arrangements and the emergence of small luxury items. In parallel, especially in their latter stages, there is a growing sense of inwardness, scepticism and desire for change revealed in the Upanishads that took the Hindu tradition into deeper realms of philosophy, mysticism and spirituality.

The Wider Religious Context

To place these developments in the context of wider religious trends around the sixth century. In China, the beginnings of the Daoist (Taoist) tradition were evident and Confucius was alive. In the Middle East, some key Hebrew prophets such as Jeremiah, Ezekiel and the later Isaiah were prophesying. In Greece the Ionian philosophers were preparing the way for Aristotle, Plato and western philosophy. In Persia, Zoroaster's dates have been placed around 1000 BCE but his thought was still relevant in the sixth century. In India, some of the key Upanishads emerged. Also in India, the Buddha and the Mahavira (the fountainhead of the Jain tradition) were alive. This period is known as the Axial Age and although the term can be questioned, it is clear that something important was happening. In all these four great civilisations – China, the Middle East, Europe and India – radical changes were occurring which had resonance for the world.

In India the resonance was twofold. In the first place, from the Axial Age onward, the Hindu tradition in India had two competitors, the Buddhist and Jain traditions. Some modern nationalist Hindus suggest that Buddhists, Jains and followers of other religious traditions born in India, including the Sikhs, are all in some sense 'Hindu'. In fact there has long been rivalry, sometimes severe, between Hindus and other Indian religious traditions. For a few centuries Buddhists were as popular as Hindus in parts of India and in the rest of Asia they became more popular. The Buddhist reaction was to basic tenets in the Upanishads. They opposed the notion of *Brahman* or indeed any notion of 'God' and they opposed the notion of the *ātman* or indeed any notion of a 'self'. They opposed the endemic caste system and they did not accept many of the outward rituals that remained central to the Hindus. Nor did they accept the Vedic sacrifices, nor indeed the Veda itself which for many Hindus became the touchstone of orthodoxy. Likewise the Jains did not accept the Upanishadic notions of *Brahman* and *ātman*, or the endemic caste system, or the Vedic sacrifices and they had a deep concern for non-violence (*ahimsa*). There is a case to be made that the 'Hindu tradition' emerged after the time of the early Veda, in the Upanishads and afterwards. The difference is that it emerged in continuity with the Veda whereas the Buddhist and Jain traditions were radical departures from the Veda.

A Period of Definition: 500–200 BCE

The period from roughly 500–200 BCE was an early defining moment for the Hindu tradition. Sixteen kingdoms appeared centred upon the Magadha Empire (560–325 BCE) in the eastern Ganges area and the Mauryan Empire (321–181 BCE) in Central and Northern India. Farming techniques were improving and there were food surpluses; writing began and merchants and wider trade developed, as did money. Urban elites emerged and there was scope for individuals to soul-search and for communities to explore spirituality in new city environments. The Buddhists and Jains began to spread around India and into further Asia.

Architectural remains from around this period are mainly Buddhist, such as the Ashoka inscriptions and the great Stūpas. However, Hindu Vedic Brahmanism continued and also grew in what K. M. Panikkar (1962) has called one of three determining periods of Indian history from 350–250 BCE. At this time the Mauryan Empire extended as far as Mysore and the notion of India as an entity (*Bharata Varsha*) arose. Importantly, Sanskrit emerged from coexistence with Prakrit and Pāli (originally the preferred Buddhist and Jain languages) to a position of such dominance that eventually Mahāyāna Buddhism used Sanskrit as well. The great Sanskritists, Pāninī, Kātyāyana and Patañjali, formed a purified and stabilised Sanskrit with a rich, unified and varied language that guaranteed its future influence.

Hindu law and domestic rituals became more organised during this period. The Code of Manu, which gave an early framework to Hindu *dharma* in its legal sense, began to emerge and paved the way for the more far-reaching systematisation of Hindu law. Of equal importance was the development of domestic rituals which were written down in the *Grihya Sutras*. These set out rituals to be followed by householders from the conception of a child, through to birth, initiation, marriage and death. These rituals lie at the heart of Hindu society.

At the level of religious practice there is evidence from this time of greater interest in Shiva and Vishnu as objects of worship and the emergence of Krishna as a figure of importance. The two great epics, the *Mahābhārata* and the *Rāmāyana*, had begun with Krishna being prominent in the first and Rāma in the second. Krishna and Rāma would later become the key *avatāras* (incarnations) of Vishnu. Around the second century BCE the *Bhagavad Gītā* was written, as part of the *Mahābhārata*, and in it Krishna emerges as a devotional Lord. In the *Bhagavad Gītā*, Krishna opens up the three ways of salvation (*trimarga*), namely the ways of devotion (*bhakti*), inward spiritual knowledge (*jnāna*) and of doing one's duty (*dharma*) in the world without thought of reward. A fourth way was implied, that of ritual worship. This was developing beyond Vedic sacrifices into new areas of worship and practice that were becoming matters of social etiquette.

Thus, alongside the growth and spread of the Buddhist and Jain traditions, the Hindu tradition was growing and developing in important directions which included the adaptation, reinterpretation or abandonment of some of its early Vedic background. The inward spirituality of the Upanishads had been supplemented with new devotional patterns and a greater sense of involvement in the world.

The Classical Hindu Tradition: 200 BCE – 1100 CE

From 200 BCE to 1100 CE was the time of what may be called the classical Hindu tradition. There was more contact with other cultures from about 200 BCE to 320 CE. The later Gupta Empire (320–650 CE) is recognised as the high watermark of the classical Hindu tradition The downfall of the Gupta Empire was followed by a period of smaller kingdoms ending with the Muslim invasions in the eleventh century. This was the zenith of the classical Hindu tradition.

There were foreign influences in Northern India from Greeks, Scythians and Kushanas from Central Asia, Parthians from Iran, and Huns. Particularly important were the reverberations of Alexander the Great's arrival in 327–325 BCE and the entry of the Kushanas who were inclined to Buddhism and dominated North India from about 78 to 230 CE. The emerging Hindu tradition came into contact with Greek, Iranian and Buddhist cultural elements by which it was influenced.

As time went there were also contacts with other cultures including trade with the Roman Empire, with South East Asia from the first to fifth centuries CE, with central Asia through the Silk Route from the second century CE and contact with Tibet in the seventh century CE. There was a start towards the Indianisation and even the part Hinduisation of wider Asia through trade and friendly contact. There are still some traces of Hindu elements in wider Asia.

However, the social and ritual reasons for the Hindu spread and triumph in India made it less likely that the Hindu tradition would be successful abroad. The evolving caste system and particularistic rituals were not easy to apply abroad, and even at the level of sacred texts, architecture and ideas the Buddhists were far more able to indigenise in China and further Asia. The brilliant translation of key Sanskrit Mahāyāna Buddhist sūtras into Chinese by Kumārajīva in the fourth century CE was a premonition of the Buddhist triumph in China and South East Asia. In India the Buddhist tradition was still strong when Fa-hsien visited early in the fifth century to collect Buddhist sūtras and take them back to China. It was less strong in the seventh century when Hsuan-tsang left an account of his visit to India from China. By the time of the Muslim invasions into India in the eleventh century the Buddhist tradition was weaker still.

The Gupta Empire (320–650 CE)

By the time of the Gupta Empire the major building blocks of the Hindu tradition were falling into place, including the eight elements of the model used as a structure for this book. Although the authority of the Veda remained, much of the old Vedic religion was taken in new directions or replaced. Temple building began. The extraordinary South Indian Gupta temples at Aihole and Deogarh, dedicated to the goddess Durga and the deity Vishnu respectively, still remain with their distinctive towers, their niches for the main and other deities and their anticipation of later temples. In literature this was a golden age. The two great Hindu Epics had reached their final form. The *Mahābhārata* (which means 'Great India') has nearly 100,000 couplets in eighteen books and the *Rāmāyana* ('Life of Rāma') has 24,000 couplets in seven books. They tell the partly mythological early history of India. Krishna is important in the *Mahābhārata* and Rāma lies at the centre of the *Rāmāyana*. These deities would later be seen as incarnations (*avatāras*) of Vishnu and worshipped in their own right as major divine figures. They would also stress the key Hindu principle of *dharma* (righteousness).

The Purānas came into prominence in the Gupta period. They are a storehouse of Hindu mythology and of the Hindu gods in their increasing variety and significance. There are eighteen major Purānas and a number of minor ones. They are in metrical Sanskrit and represent elements in popular Hinduism. The so-called Hindu trinity (*trimūrti)* of Brahmā the creator, Vishnu the preserver and Shiva the destroyer emerged in them, although mysteriously the worship of Brahmā faded while that of Vishnu and Shiva grew. The *Bhāgavata Purāna* brought out many more details of the life of Krishna. The *Devi Māhātmya* ('Glory of the Goddess') section of another Purāna opened up a female theology of the Goddess. Elsewhere the Purānas showed how Vishnu became 'incarnate' in order to save the world in the form of ten *avatāras*, namely as fish, tortoise, boar, man-lion, dwarf, Rāma with the Axe, Rāma in his own right, Krishna, the Buddha and Kalkin, the tenth *avatāra* who will wind up the world.

Other forms of literature emerged also. The Tantric Agamas centre mainly upon the goddess Shakti and were important in setting out rules for the building of temples and the installing of images. They were also effective in recommending the use of pithy sayings (*mantras*), mystical diagrams (*yantras*), bodily postures (*asanas*) and hand gestures (*mudrās*). India's key writer and poet Kālidāsa was active in the Gupta Age writing important works such as *Shakantala*. Elsewhere drama, science and crafts also prospered. Instruction for daily living in connection with various rituals, rites of passage and legal matters became consolidated in the extensive *Dharmaśāstra* law books. After the seventh century this was almost complete, so that later law writers could only comment on existing law rather than make new law

The Caste System

Key elements of the caste system emerged. One of the words for caste is *varna*, the four varnas were the Brahmins (priests and intellectuals), Kshatriyas (rulers and warriors), Vaishyas (farmers and traders) and Shudras (servants). *Varna* means 'colour' and there is some accuracy in its application, insofar as the high-caste Brahmins tend to be fairer and the low-caste Shūdras darker than the other castes. But the key to the caste system lay in the sub-castes (*jātis*) of which there were thousands. In the key matters of eating with others and marrying others, only certain *jātis* could eat together and intermarry. For example, not all Brahmins could intermarry or eat with all other Brahmins but only through the relevant sub-castes. This system, together with the allied notions of the four stages of life (student, householder, semi-retirement and renouncing the world), the four aims of life (*kāma*, sensual living; *artha*, working and earning money; *dharma*, living morally; and *moksha*, seeking release from the round of rebirths) became more developed, along with connected rituals of worship, sacraments and festivals. Other elements were beginning to appear: outcastes, who were excluded from the caste system, and changes leading to the less exalted role of women. Child-marriage appeared, as did the burning of women on the funeral pyres of their husbands (*satī*) and the remarriage of widows was frowned upon.

Further Developments and Expansion

The final stage before the advent of Islam into India in the twelfth century came with the collapse of the Harsha Empire (606–47 CE) that had encompassed Bengal, Bihar and Malwa. Smaller kingdoms appeared in the east, south-west, north-west, west and north, including the Chalukyas and the Pallavas. However, it was an age of semi-fragmentation, which was fruitful for the wider Hindu tradition. In general this final age of the classical Hindu period involved further expansion into other parts of India, especially the Deccan and the South. It also involved the building of major temples and the rise of new languages, new regions, new groups, new rivalries and new opportunities for diversity within the wider Hindu tradition. Alongside the continuing growth of 'Vedic-type' Hindu traditions there was also the emergence of anti-Vedic elements within the Hindu tradition. Coterminous with the Hindu spread came the decline of the Jain and Buddhist presence in India which had been so strong, and this was partly due to the work of the great Shankara who inaugurated major developments within Vedanta, the key philosophical/theological system in Hindu life.

New temples were built in many parts of India including big temples in the major pilgrimage centres that were growing in significance during this period. These great temples included Mahabalipuram in the south in the seventh century, Bhubaneshwar in Orissa and Ellora near Bombay in the eighth and ninth centuries, and Tanjore in the eleventh century. Meanwhile Varanasi and Mathura, which had been influenced by the Buddhist tradition, began to re-emerge as two of the key Hindu cities and pilgrimage sites.

The Buddhist tradition went into obvious decline, and this decline deepened with the Muslim entry into India, so that Buddhism virtually disappeared in India until modern times. There were various reasons for this decline. There was growing weakness within Indian Buddhism as monks retreated from the villages, where they were needed, into great monasteries or monastic universities, such as Nalanda and Sarnath. Moreover, divergences arose between Buddhists themselves as Hindu rulers removed their support for Buddhists. Finally, great thinkers such as Shankara attacked Buddhist thought whilst absorbing elements from it into Hindu thought.

Shankara

Shankara (*c.*788–820) inaugurated the rise of Vedanta philosophy through his great commentaries on the Upanishad, the *Bhagavad Gītā* and the *Vedanta Sūtras* in which he promoted non-dualism (*Advaita*) which contended that ultimately our own self (*ātman*), which seems to be different from *Brahman* (Ultimate Reality), is in fact identical with *Brahman*. As he put it, partly borrowing from the Buddhist notion of two levels of truth, at the highest level of truth *aham brahmāsmi*, 'I am Brahman'. Shankara is also credited with founding a monastic order, the Dashanamis, and with setting up important monasteries in the four corners of India.

Shankara came from South India, which now became more prominent for the Hindu tradition, and the two outstanding later Vedanta thinkers, Rāmānuja and Madhva, also came from South India. Outside Vedic Hinduism, in the south in the seventh century, two important devotional movements blossomed that used the Tamil language rather than Sanskrit as their medium. The Nāyanmārs worshipped Shiva and the Alvars worshipped Vishnu in language of deep devotion, penitence, love and mystical piety. Companies toured around singing, dancing and radiating an emotional love for Shiva or Vishnu. Some were women and some from lower castes. This was devotional religion (*bhakti*) in earnest, and the combination of non-Sanskrit language with profound emotion was redolent for the future. So was the rivalry between languages, castes, cults and regions.

The Tantric movement emerged into greater prominence during this period. Many of the Tantras were composed in Bengal, Kashmir and Nepal, and they could be related to Vishnu, Shiva or the Goddess. They were all opposed to the Veda as the main authority for the Hindu tradition. More importance was given to women and the main focus of worship was the Goddess in the form of Shakti. Ritual practice was important in Tantra including the use of mystical circles (*mandalas*), mystical centres (*chakras*), worship (*pūjā*), visualisation, meditation and the liberation of *kundalini* power.

Towards the end of the period of 'classical Hinduism', as well as these innovations, there was also a paradoxical increase in conservatism and an interest in basic values which would stand the Hindu tradition in good stead as it faced the Muslim invasions that were to come.

The Advent of Islam (*c.*1100–1800)

During the period from roughly 1100–1800 Islam provided the main background to the development of Hindu history. From 1192, when the Rajput Hindu ruler of the north was killed by Muhammad Ghuri, to the end of the Mughal dynasty in 1858 the Hindu tradition lived against a background of Muslim rule and was deeply affected by it. Hitherto it had succeeded in fending off or assimilating invading elements so that the Nestorian Christians (who had been in India from the fourth century), Jains and Buddhists had accommodated to the caste system or had been partly assimilated theologically; as when the Buddha was adopted as an *avatāra* of the Hindu deity Vishnu. The Muslims were stronger militarily and more organised. They were not willing to adapt to Hindu customs. They laid great stress upon their one book the Qur'an, their one God Allah, their prophet Muhammad, their basic community the Ummah, their legal system the Sharīa, and they found the Hindu tradition alien.

The main group of Hindus became more rigid. Socially, they strengthened the caste system and ostracised the Muslims under the reviving leadership of their own Brahmins. Thus, the basic Hindu movement took a more conservative direction.

However, some Hindus were attracted by the stress upon equality and monotheism they saw in Islam and new Hindu/Muslim or Muslim/Hindu groups appeared.

Mystical Islam could find similarities with the mysticism of some Hindus and Hindu–Muslim interaction took place. Kabīr in the fifteenth century combined Sufi Islam with Bhakti Hinduism and equated Rāma with Allah. Dādū (1544–1603) dreamed of unifying the Hindu and Muslim traditions. Guru Nānak (1469–1538) also combined elements from devotional Hindu and Muslim teachers in his movement which became the Sikh tradition. Some Hindus, especially in the low castes, converted to Islam and their successors provide the core for Islam in India today. Modern India has the world's second largest Muslim population.

Resistance to Islam was stronger in the south, in the impressive Vijayanagar Empire (1336–1565), and in Orissa and Nepal. The stronghold of what remained of 'progressive Hinduism' retreated to the south. The best-known commentary on the *Rig Veda* was written by Sayana in the Vijayanagar Empire whilst three important Vedanta leaders Rāmānuja, Madhva and Vallabha came from the south and their philosophy gave an inspirational impetus to the growing sectarian devotional movements.

Many devotional groups formed under great Hindu leaders using vernacular languages and these helped galvanise Hindu devotion. The leaders included Tulsīdās (*c*.1543–1623) who wrote the famous *Rāmāyana* in Hindi, the *Rāmcaritamānas*, centred on devotion to Rāma, whilst Chaitanya (1486–1533) sang ecstatically about Krishna and was a forerunner of the Hare Krishna Movement of recent times. Many new devotional (*bhakti*) sects appeared around India during this period. Some later *bhakti* leaders remained deeply devotional whilst glorifying the Hindu past in a more militant way. Tukaram (1609–49) and Rāmdās (1608–81), who wrote in Marathi, supported the militaristic ruler Shivaji in his resistance to the Muslim Mughals. The Brahmins too began to eulogise the Hindu past and to collect or write engaging chronicles (*māhātmyas*) to publicise famous Hindu sites such as Varanasi and Mathura. This tendency to 'resymbolise Hinduism' was accelerated by a growing veneration of the cow as being in some way symbolic of the Hindu tradition.

The occasional severe persecution of Hindus by Muslims, including the iconoclastic destruction of their treasures and buildings, was not inclined to ingratiate Hindus to their conquerors. Alberuni suggested, in the early period of the Muslim conquest of India, that Hindu sciences were retiring far away from those parts of the country conquered by the Muslims and had fled to places that the Muslims could not reach, to Kashmir, Varanasi and other such places (Embree, 1971). Later Varanasi itself would have to be rebuilt after being partly destroyed by Muslims. When on 6 December 1992 modern Hindu militants dismantled the mosque in Ayodhya, which is said to have been built by the Mughal Emperor Babar in 1528 over the birth-place of the Lord Rāma, were they 'gaining revenge' for the wrongs of the period of Muslim rule or were they betraying their own heritage of peaceful assimilation as told in *Rāmāyana*?

British Overlordship (*c.*1770–1947)

The penultimate era of Hindu history is that of the British overlordship over India from roughly 1770 to 1947. This was a different kind of rule from that of the Muslims. It did not come by planned invasion. It did not aim (except perhaps in the minds of some early Roman Catholics in Goa and Kerala and some later evangelical Christians) at the conversion of India to Christianity. It happened almost by chance whilst the British Raj was maintained by a small band of administrators and soldiers. Yet it was a very important period for India and for the Hindu tradition.

The background facts are well known. Clive's victory at the Battle of Plassey in 1757 gave the British, first through the East India Company and later more directly, control over Bengal and then over most of the rest of India, although it was not until 1858 that Queen Victoria became Empress of India. English became the official language of the ruling hierarchy in 1835 and British education was introduced. Industrialisation began and from the nineteenth century Indian transport was transformed with rail-ways, roads and waterways. Medical provision was improved. The economy grew. In time the population increased markedly as well. This promoted the rise of an all-India middle class that would eventually provide the fulcrum for the rise of the independence movement.

At first the East India Company steered clear of religious matters to the extent that Christian missionaries such as William Carey had to locate at Serampore in Danish territory. It was not until 1813 that missionary soci-eties were allowed in. This change of policy was partly due to concern in Britain about elements in the Hindu caste system, such as widow burning (satī), child marriages and untouchability. There was relatively little inter-ference by the British in the affairs of the Hindu or Muslim traditions. However, inevitably, there was occasional unrest about the British colo-nial presence in India and a sense that the British were playing the Hindu and Muslim populations off against each other. The First Indian War of Independence of 1857, otherwise known as the Indian Mutiny, arose out of concerns by Hindus that the cartridges for newly introduced rifles were greased by 'unclean' cow fat whilst Muslims feared that they were greased by 'unclean' pig fat.

Reform and Nationalism

There were differing reactions to British rule in India. Hindu reformers were influenced by the West in their attempts to reform the Hindu tradition. These neo-Hindu reformers took the incoming western trends of science, secularism and humane values seriously. They saw merit in some facets of Christianity. This neo-Hindu movement went through three stages of development. The work of Ram Mohan Roy (1772–1833) was central to the first stage. He turned to the West, especially to Britain, in the areas of social reform, education and interest in science, Hindu reform and the English language. He saw the need for Hindus to take the stronger western culture seriously in respect of social reform; he supported the abolition of satī, education in the English language and modernisation of Hindu theory and practice. He founded the Brahmo Samāj to reform Hinduism on the lines of Upanishadic theism. The second stage was symbolised in the work of Ramakrishna (1836–86). He saw that the Hindu tradition had things to offer to the Christian West, as well as things to receive from it, and his work helped to revive Hindu self-confidence. His extraordinary spiritual experience, including aspects of Sufi Islam and Christ along with devotional, Tantric and Advaita Hinduism, provided a corrective to the materialism and spiritual shallowness of the West whilst his Hindu universalism queried the need for conversion and offered hospitality within a wide spiritual perspective. The final stage, symbolised by the work of Swami Vivekananda (1863–1902) and Mahatma Gandhi (1869–1948), saw Hindus embracing the nationalist movement for independence from Britain. Whilst recognising that the Hindu tradition could still learn from the West (Gandhi spent his formative years in Britain and South Africa), the West was open to influence by Hinduism, as happened with Vivekananda's charismatic presence at the Chicago World Parliament of Religions in 1893.

Another reaction was that of nationalist communalism in the Hindu tradition. Nathuram Godse shot Mahatma Gandhi on 30 January 1948 for being too tolerant of other religions and for acquiescing in the partitioning of India into two nations. Movingly Godse bowed in reverence as he fired and Gandhi, though dying, indicated his forgiveness. Dayananda Saraswati (1824–83) had founded the Arya Samaj in 1875 to reform the Hindu tradition without relying on the West and B. G. Tilak (1856–1920) had interpreted the *Bhagavad Gītā* on militant l80ines. Later political bodies, such as the Hindu Mahāsabha and the Rashtriya Swayamsevak Sangh (founded in 1925), were created to heighten awareness of the Hindu heritage and to work for a Hindu nation based on Hindutva (Hinduness).

Secular Hinduism

The development of secular Hinduism was also important. It was typified by Nehru who would eventually lead India to a secular constitution. However, it was viewed lukewarmly by Gandhi who took religion seriously and who was engaged in interfaith activity. Gandhi's ideal, which he had to compromise, was that of independent India as Rāmarājya (the Kingdom of Rāma) based upon the ideal kingdom set up in the *Rāmāyana* by Rāma on his return to Ayodhya. But pragmatically this vision was too 'Hindu' and not secular enough.

Revival of the Veda and the *Bhagavad Gītā*

Conversely, other Hindus looked back to the Veda. They were helped by a group of British scholars under Sir William Jones (1746–94) who encouraged a group of British Orientalists to rediscover Vedic and other early texts. From 1849–73 Max Muller of Oxford edited the *Rig Veda* for the first time. There were different reactions to the rediscovery of the Veda which had been kept secret by Brahmins from people of lower castes and from foreigners. Neo-Hindus such as Ram Mohan Roy went back to Vedanta monotheism to justify their reforms. Hindu nationalists such as Dayananda Saraswati went back to the Veda as the fountainhead of the Hindu tradition, since corrupted by later works: it became his supreme authority. Deeply spiritual leaders such as Ramakrishna exalted the importance of spiritual experience as being paramount and yet they still utilised the Vedas. Sri Aurobindo revalorised the Veda. Pundits memorised the Vedas and passed them on to disciples. Thus the importance of the Veda was reaffirmed.

Having rediscovered the Veda, Hindus began to single out the *Bhagavad Gītā* for study and action. This small insertion into the *Mahābhārata*, which is *smriti* (remembered) rather than *shruti* (revealed), became venerated by Hindus. It is probably the most read Hindu text from school to scholar to guru. Its interpretation has taken different directions. For Gandhi, it was his favourite text as a spiritual classic of non-violence. The battle at its core was an allegory, relating to the battle in the soul of all people between good and evil, between righteousness and unrighteousness. For B. G. Tilak, it was the opposite. For him the battle was real and it related to the conflict with the British. Insofar as the *ātman* or soul is reborn after death, if a British soldier was killed that was not the end of his sojourn on earth. Clearly the shortness, the easy Sanskrit, the Hindi and other translations of the *Bhagavad*

Gītā, contribute to its popularity. Another reason may be that it is a kind of equivalent, for shorthand purposes, to the single scriptures of the Christians and Muslims.

Amidst all the change and vibrancy of the Hindu tradition during the British period a comment about the famous deity, the Lord Jaggarnath of Puri, comes to mind: 'He majestically stands there on his throne graciously smiling down to his devotees: stands as a unique symbol of the great flexibility and dynamics of Hinduism, of its capacity to absorb integrate and remodel' (Tripathi, 1978). For many Hindus India remained a sacred land with symbolic holy places at the four corners of the subcontinent, with sacred natural features such as the Ganges and Himalayas, with holy cities such as Varanasi and Mathura, with itinerant holy men (*sādhus*), with Hindus worshipping at home or going to 'see' and 'be seen' by their local deities, with ritual worship, sacraments and festivals and with homespun spirituality. At local level the Hindu tradition continued and adapted, it was not deeply affected by what was happening at government level.

Post-Independence and the Rise of Hindu Nationalism

The present is, in some ways, the most dynamic period within the Hindu story. With Independence on 15 August 1947 changes came into being that would affect India and the Hindu tradition. The British left, democracy was established and the Indian native states were abolished and merged into the new India, a new and independent legal entity. Nehru stressed science, technology and secular advance; industrialisation grew and the green revolution improved agriculture and food supplies. The population grew, tourism increased, globalisation continued, whilst television, video and the internet emerged as potent forces. These changes have had a deep effect upon the Hindu tradition.

With partition India became a secular state. For Nehru, India was a secular state because he had a secular, non-religious view of life. For Gandhi, insofar as all religions were relevant and basically equal, India was a secular state that could hold the fort between all religions and treat them equally. Because the Hindu tradition has no controlling body, the state became involved in reforming Hindu affairs through measures such as the Hindu Marriage and Divorce Act and through the organising of Hindu Endowments. After three small wars between secular India and Muslim Pakistan, the former East Pakistan became Bangladesh, an independent secular state in 1971; it later became a Muslim state. Sri Lanka had in effect become a Buddhist state and for a while the Punjab threatened to become a Sikh state. So to some Hindus in India the situation appears to be that of a subcontinent with three religious states and the possibility of another one forming. Furthermore, in the secular state of India, Hindus felt restricted by their own government, whilst the government provided rights to minorities that were withheld from Hindus.

Against this background Hindu political militancy appeared with the Vishva Hindu Parishad in 1966 and the rise of the Bharatiya Janata Party in 1979, which for a short time achieved the leadership of India and remains politically strong. Part of this process included the very public demolition of the Muslim mosque in the Hindu holy city of Ayodhya in 1992. It is unclear where this militant Hindu nationalism is progressing, but it is clear that it is here to stay. It is a jolt to the general Hindu perception that theirs is a tolerant religion and it is something new in Hindu history. However, it is unlikely that India will surrender its proud title as the world's largest democracy.

Diaspora

The Hindu tradition is the third largest in the world, outnumbered only by the Christian and Muslim traditions, and there are 900 million Hindus alive on the planet, roughly a seventh of the world's population. Gandhi had been warned by his caste leaders against leaving the sacred shores of India to go to Britain to study law, but he had gone anyway. However, Hindus had already migrated into Nepal (until recently the only Hindu nation in the world), into South East Asia and into what are now Bangladesh, Pakistan, Sri Lanka and Mauritius. There are Hindu populations in Bali and Fiji. In the West Indies and in South America there are Hindu populations in Trinidad, Guyana and Suriname. In South Africa there is an important Hindu constituency. There has been a significant influx of Hindus into Britain and into many parts of the western world. Alongside this general emigration there has arisen a kind of Hindu global ecumenism. What is it that holds Hindus together around the world? Global Hindu institutions such as the Virat Hindu Samaj led by Dr Karan Singh and the Vishva Hindu Parishad under Maharana Bhagwat Singh have attempted to address this question. In doing so, and helped by the close contact of Hindus with people of other religions in other parts of the world, they have attempted not only to unify Hindus but also to interact with other faiths.

Interfaith initiatives are established also in India itself, between Hindus and others. Although there has been a temporary local pause in Christian–Hindu and Muslim–Hindu dialogue, due to the Hindutva movement's recent persecution of Christians and Muslims in Orissa and elsewhere, the general dialogue includes Hindu leaders in global dialogues.

Post-War Hindu Leaders

The influence of three post-war Hindu leaders upon wider developments in the world has also proved to be important. Vinoba Bhave, born in 1895, followed Gandhi's ideas in the social and economic spheres, and like Gandhi he stressed the religious foundations of his work. Thus for him *seva* (service) became service by all persons to all persons, *karma* (works) became serving all others through good works without thought of reward, *bhakti* (devotion) became devotion to human beings. He called on others, especially the rich, to give to others gifts of land, labour, wealth, intelligence, love and life. His principles of Sarvodaya consolidated Gandhi's influence upon the wider world through national liberation uplift movements following Gandhian principles, such as those of Ariyaratna in Sri Lanka, the Sarvodaya Movement in Japan, the efforts of Martin Luther King in the USA, the work of Desmond Tutu and Nelson Mandela in South Africa, and the work of the Dalai Lama.

Sarvepalli Radhakrishnan was born in 1888 and was President of India from 1961 to 1967. A great scholar, his process of reinterpretation engaged Hindu thought with recent notions of history, the importance of this world, the role of the individual, the world process, religious experience, national development and the march of science. As a committed Hindu he argued that Vedanta is not a religion, but religion itself in its most universal and deepest significance (Whaling, 1984, pp. 401-6). He had a profound influence on Hindu philosophical thought and he outlined what its place might be in a future global culture.

Sri Aurobindo (1872–1950) was a deeply spiritual philosophical thinker who retired from active life as leader of the early independence movement to settle down in Pondicherry where he set up his famous ashram. He applied the theory of creative evolution to Hinduism and he emphasised what he called integral yoga as a synthesis of all yogas. He used as his sources a wide variety of Hindu scriptures (not just one or two like a number of Hindu thinkers) and he set up the new town of Auroville to articulate more spiritually a Hindu view of future humanity. He, together with Vinoba Bhave and Radhakrishnan, took the theory and practice of neo-Hinduism into a new era.

Stemming in part from the work of Sri Aurobindo, another facet of the recent Hindu tradition has been the rise of charismatic gurus. There are said to be tens of thousands of gurus in India today and that may be a conservative figure. Some are charlatans, but most are not. Some of them are proselytisers for Hinduism, others are open to all, like Sri Anandamayi Ma. Some go out to seek disciples, others wait for people to come to them.

Well-known figures include Ramana Maharshi (1879–1950), Shivananda (1887–1963), Jagadguru Sri Chandrasekharendra Saraswati (1894–1994), Krishnamurti (1895–1986), Bhaktivedanta Prabhupada (1896–1977), Maharishi Mahesh Yogi (1911–2008), Saccidananda (1914–2002), Sathya Sai Baba (1926–) and Rajneesh (1931–90).

Let us look at three who set up well-known movements. Bhaktivedanta Prabhupada founded the International Society for Krishna Consciousness (ISKCON) in 1966, better known as the Hare Krishnas with their well-known *mantra*. His movement swept around the world and he made fourteen world tours, wrote more than eighty books and founded many centres and temples. His was a missionary organisation but it also has a strong educational and service role among Hindus.

Sathya Sai Baba is the best-known among contemporary Hindu Gurus with his black hair and ochre robes. He has only left India once, although he has a world following of millions, and he argues that only in India can Gurus constantly experiment and practice. He claims to be an incarnation of Shiva and Shakti, and his own Guru was Sai Baba (1856–1918). He has the confidence of Indian leaders, performs miracles and has founded many hospitals, educational establishments and a university.

Maharishi Mahesh Yogi founded the Transcendental Meditation Movement in 1960 by means of which followers meditated upon a personal *mantra* that he gave to them. His contact with the Beatles made him well known. Although his movement has an Indian Guru and uses Hindu *mantras*, it has become partly removed from its Hindu roots. It functions as a means to better health, increased efficiency of living and a more rewarding lifestyle.

Of the three Gurus instanced, two were staunch Hindus. One lived almost exclusively in India, while another worked mainly abroad. The third, although Hindu, promoted wider than Hindu concerns. It is clear that Hindu Gurus differ but the best of them are genuine saints with a genuine influence both on the Hindu world and, more generally, on the wider world.

Popular Hindu Religion

The growing body of work done by scholars since Independence provides much more information about popular Hindu religion than was previously known. Past evidence about the Hindu tradition was derived mainly from classical 'High Hinduism' and was based mainly on literature, on converse with Brahmins and on the great deities. Local research is remedying the lack of knowledge about Hindu village life. Radio, television, films and popular literature have become ubiquitous in India and they have affected contemporary Hinduism. The popularity in North India of a new goddess, Santoshi Ma, who is especially attractive to women, derived originally from a film. Perhaps even more importantly television serialisations of the two great epics, the *Mahābhārata* and the *Rāmāyana*, broadcast over many months to huge audiences, have swayed nationalist opinion because of the way the epics were interpreted as precursors of Indian nationalism.

The rapid growth of the Indian population to over 1.1 billion people, the developing rich and progressive capitalist oligarchy and the accelerating rise of cities have raised a number of issues for Hindus and have partly contributed to the rise of the Hindutva Movement.

Questions about the caste system are increasing. On the one hand, there has been considerable discussion while, on the other, some of those disenfranchised by the caste system have taken action. This is particularly evident among the ex-outcastes, including the group named by Gandhi as Harijans (People of God). They have renamed themselves as Dalits (Broken Ones). Under B. R. Ambedkar (1891–1956), himself an outcaste, the Mahar caste in Maharashtra converted together to Buddhism, and elsewhere Hindu Dalits have become Christians or Bahá'ís. If Dalits desert the Hindu tradition, Hindu numbers and prestige are impaired but if they stay they remain subject to discrimination. If they convert they become liable to persecution. A similar issue relates to the primal tribespeople (*Ādivāsī* or old inhabitants), living mainly in forests, who, due to isolation, are even more deprived and discriminated against. A different kind of question relates to the position of women who have improved their position somewhat (Indira and Sonia Gandhi are symbols of this advance) but who still have a long way to go.

Capitalism and Modernity

A deeper matter for Hindu concern is the increasing disparity of wealth engendered by the rise of city-dwelling, super-rich, capitalist moguls, who are tempted to try to impose on India their contemporary ideas, beautiful artefacts, lifestyles and religious views influenced from abroad. The temptation exists for younger people to adopt a secular lifestyle, thus abandoning Hindu joint families, leaving aside the elderly, neglecting Hindu rituals and losing contact with rural India.

At the intellectual level, contemporary genetic concepts, subatomic theories, astronomical discoveries and evolutionary models present probing questions for the Hindu world-view concerning such questions as rebirth, traditional cosmology and cyclical views of history. A key question is whether India can modernise, not in a predominantly western way but in a Hindu/Indian way. Will India become a great power on its own terms whilst the Hindu tradition modernises itself on its own principles? Are the variety, adaptability and assimilative power of the Hindu tradition sufficient? Can the Lord Jaggarnath of Puri still remain majestically on his throne smiling down on his devotees as a unique symbol of the great flexibility and dynamics of the Hindu way, of its capacity to absorb, integrate and remodel?

3

Transcendence and the Gods

Within the Hindu tradition there are many manifestations of the divine, too many to describe them all. This chapter deals with the topics of transcendence and the divine.

Brahman, Humanity and the World

A key Hindu word for transcendence is *Brahman* or **Absolute Reality**. *Brahman* is unique and ineffable. In the Taittiriya Upanishad, *Brahman* is described in transcendental terms as truth (*satya*), knowledge (*jnāna*) and infinity (*ananta*). Elsewhere three allied words, existence (*sat*), consciousness (*cit*) and bliss (*ananda*) form a single word *Saccidananda*, which summarises *Brahman* in ineffable terms as existence, knowledge and bliss combined.

In his theory of creative evolution, Sri Aurobindo suggested that the eternal *Brahman* became involved in the world by involution from the Absolute Reality of *Saccidananda* through various levels until the transcendent was involved in matter and the material world. The process is being reversed now through the process of creative evolution whereby matter evolves back into the pure transcendence of *Saccidananda*.

There is a sense in which, for some Hindus, *Brahman* is indescribable at all, except perhaps in terms of what it is not. Indeed in the Advaita Vedanta system of Shankara, *Brahman* is without attributes (*nirguna*) and cannot be confined to human thought or language. *Brahman*, although being ultimate Reality, is beyond human comprehension.

The question then arises within Vedanta thought as to what the relationship is between the ultimate godhead *Brahman* and the human self (*ātman*). They seem to be separate. Shankara uses the Chāndogya Upanishad's story of a father telling his son to experiment by putting salt into water. They seem to be separate but in fact the salt dissolves into the water. So, says the father, *Brahman* and *ātman* are one in a similar manner. As the famous Upanishadic phrase puts it: *tat tvam asi*, 'Brahman (tat) art thou (tvam)'. Therefore, in a sense, ultimately transcendence is all. Not only humanity but also the world itself is part of *Brahman*. There is an *advaita*, a-dvaita meaning the opposite of twoness (*dvaita*), within the godhead. There is an *advaita* (non-twoness) between *Brahman*, humans and the world. All are ultimately one.

However that, of course, is not the end of the story. In the other Vedanta schools of thought *Brahman* is with attributes (*saguna*). *Brahman* is separate from humans and the world in Madhva's dual (*dvaita*) Vedanta and is partially non-separate from humans and the world in Rāmānuja's *viśiṣṭādvaita* Vedanta. This leaves open the possibility of many representations of the godhead in Hindu thought and life.

In another passage in the Upanishads, Yājnavalkya is asked how many gods there are. He replies that there are three thousand and three and then three hundred and three. He is asked again how many gods are there? The answer this time is thirty-three. He is asked again how many gods there are and the answer this time is six. The same question is asked yet again and this time the answer is three. In answer to the self-same question, the answer is one and a half. Again the question comes of how many gods there are and this time the answer is one. The ineffable may be the Ultimate One but most Hindus consider that the godhead takes many forms, many names and many powers. Far from being beyond male and female and beyond one and many, the godhead with attributes can be expressed in a legion of ways.

Hindu Deities

To attempt to explain this multiplicity of gods and goddesses from the viewpoint of Hindu worshippers: for some worshippers there are many different deities that can be accepted and acknowledged but one of them is the supreme godhead who is higher than the others and is thus the one to be worshipped. Others are willing to accept that there are many gods and goddesses that are all equal. However, in practice one of these deities may be selected as a personal favourite or chosen deity (*ishta-devata*) and thus the personal focus of worship.

Hindu gods and goddesses are often worshipped in the form of an image (*mūrti*) These images are found in temples and in homes. They are seen also in stores, in cars, in hospitals, in government and business offices. The images are manufactured in workshops in Varanasi and various other places. In temples they are consecrated in a special ritual ceremony (*prana pratiṣṭa*) after which they become, in the eyes of some worshippers, a living form taken by a deity in order to receive worship. For others, images are symbols of a deity rather than the living presence of the deity itself. Some communities, such as the Vīraśaivas (Lingāyats) founded by Basava in Karnataka in the twelfth century, saw images as unnecessary, as were temple worship and the full caste system. Their own symbol was a small Shiva *lingam* tied round them to remind them of their own immediate contact with Shiva. However the use of images is common throughout the Hindu tradition. Going to have *darshana* of a god or goddess, that is to say to 'see' or to 'be seen' by a god or goddess, is common in Hindu life. Images of all the gods and goddesses, whether major or minor, are found in large towns or small villages throughout India.

Natural phenomena have also been seen as in some way divine. A holy river such as the Ganges was venerated as a goddess in the Purānas, and this is especially true of the Ganges in Varanasi where pilgrims go to bathe in its waters, purify themselves, cremate their dead and take away its holy water (it is called *jala*, as opposed to ordinary water which is called *pāni*). Other rivers are personified also as mother goddesses. The earth itself, or part of the earth such as Mother India (*Bharat Māta*), or a particular place such as Varanasi, have also been divinised. In Varanasi one temple contains an enormous sculptured map of India which many people visit and reverence. In parts of South India images of the planets, especially the *navagraha* (nine planets), are revered and even propitiated as heavenly bodies.

Humans too can be seen as 'divine' in a way that might seem odd to unwary onlookers who are unaware of the symbolism. Especially at the level of popular Hinduism there is no total separation between deities and humans or even an absolute distinction between them. A wife may 'venerate' her husband as in some way divine. In wedding services the couple may be 'worshipped' for once in their lives and in wedding rituals in some places the bride and groom are dressed in the likeness of particular deities. In parts of North India 'virgin worship' (*kumari pūjā*) is occasionally offered to virgin girls. In great temples priests may perform a ritual to 'be divinised' in order to lead worship. Moreover, Hindu holy men and holy women who are recognised to be genuinely holy Gurus, such as Ramana Maharshi, Sathya Sai Baba, Anandamayi Ma and the four Shankarācharyas, are revered as 'divine' at the same time as they are also recognised to be human beings. The point is that there is a closer connection between the human and the divine than in most religious traditions. The historical survey highlighted a number of gods in the original *Rig Veda*. They included Indra, Mitra, Varuna, Agni, Rudra and Soma as relatively important deities. Minor ones included Dyaus, Pṛthivi, Sūrya, Vayu, Ushas, the two Asvins and Yama. In the interim period before the emergence of the Upanishads, other deities, such as Prajāpati, became important. Subsequently, two other deities who had been relatively minor gods in the *Rig Veda*, namely Shiva and Vishnu, become important in the Upanishads. In contrast, most of the major gods in the *Rig Veda* decline, with the partial exception of Indra, some of whose qualities are later absorbed by Rāma and Shiva. Ushas, the minor goddess of the dawn, was the only goddess to appear in the *Rig Veda*, while the Goddess as a major deity appears later in the Purānas.

The Major Deities

In the later development of the Hindu tradition three 'great deities' emerge, namely Shiva, Vishnu and the Goddess. It is important to remember that they are often known under different names, are often present in localised forms and are often connected to village deities who have narrower powers. In the case of Vishnu it is also important to remember that he came to earth in the form of ten *avatāras* (incarnations), two of whom – Rāma and Krishna – are very important deities in their own right. Indeed there is a real sense in which it is more accurate to say that there are five 'great deities' in the Hindu pantheon including Rāma and Krishna. Brahmā, is seen in some earlier Puranic literature as part of a kind of Hindu trinity. He is the creator and 'activity', alongside Vishnu who is the preserver and 'light' and Shiva who is the destroyer and 'darkness'. Although important in classical mythology, in the actuality of myth, ritual and worship Brahmā is unimportant and only one major temple is dedicated to him at Pushkar in Rajasthan.

Shiva

Shiva is in many ways the most unique Indian god. He has many different characteristics and many names. The title of O'Flaherty's book, *Asceticism and Eroticism in the Mythology of Shiva* (1973), points to bewildering opposites (to the western mind) in the character of Shiva. On the one hand, he is the great ascetic, the incarnation of chastity, the burner of Kāma (the goddess of desire), the world-renouncer, the one who undergoes austerities, the one with matted locks who is the model for ascetics. On the other, his favourite symbol is the Shiva *linga* which represents his phallus and it is often accompanied by, or indeed placed in, a base representing the female *yoni*. In other words erotic power and even adultery are not absent from Shiva's being. Moreover, the fierce endeavour generated by his ascetic austerities generates a tremendous heat (*tapas*) which can be applied to sexual creativity, and so he is a kind of combination of opposites. To take the contrasts within Shiva further, on the one hand he is the destroyer of the world, while on the other he is the 'auspicious' one who helps the world. On the one hand in his horrid form as Bhairava and in his earlier form as Rudra he was wild, destructive and ferocious, but on the other he is the Protector, the Beautiful Lord (Sundareśwara), the Gracious One (Shankara) or the Beneficent One (Shambhu). To continue the contrast, the great ascetic, the dedicated world-renouncer Shiva is still chivalrous to his wife Parvati with whom he has sons, unlike Vishnu who has no children but comes down to earth from time to time in the form of incarnations (*avatāras*). Shiva's sons are Ganesha and Skanda who are lesser but important deities in their own right. One final contrast is that of Shiva who, in his famous symbol as Lord of the Dance (Nataraja), dances both the dance of destruction and the dance of bliss. Devotees of Shiva differ from one another in that they see Shiva from different viewpoints, in their own way and according to their own sect, their own family tradition and their own area. They also see him under different names but all agree that he is a 'great deity'.

In order to understand these contrasts within Shiva it is important to recognise that he is mainly outlined in the Purānas through the medium of mythology. And in India mythology is not make-believe but neither is it hard fact. It matters. As Ernst Cassirer puts it: 'a nation's history is determined by its mythology' (Cassirer, 1955, p. 10). Although the monotheistic traditions have stressed the notion of one God and have been attacked by atheists for doing so, Hindus have held together contrasts within their godheads, and also polytheism. Western modernity finds it hard to understand this, as do the Buddhists who reject godheads of any sort. There are ranges of opinion in the Hindu tradition ranging from *Brahman* as Absolute Reality to virtual monotheism, to an extraordinary proliferation of deities, to a kind of Hindu atheism.

Vishnu

Vishnu is very different from Shiva. He also has many names, one of which is simply 'great god' (Mahādeva). Vishnu is represented mythologically as more mild and benevolent than Shiva. He preserves and helps and protects the world. He 'pervades' the world. He is sovereign over the world and he upholds righteousness (*dharma*) in the world. He is a celestial deity who maintains the order of the world. Indeed he is relevant in regard to kingship. Unlike Shiva whose favourite symbol is the *lingam* and who is portrayed in some ways as being indifferent to the world, Vishnu is often portrayed as a monarch who carries a conch, a discus, a lotus and a mace and wears a crown and diadem.

Vishnu is popular not only in his own right but also as sending incarnations, known as *avatāras*, into the world. Many of them are mentioned but ten of them are recognised to be classical. Vishnu comes to earth to save the world at crucial times, and it is fascinating to see how his *avatāras* are part of evolution and relevant to impending catastrophes in evolution. Thus, he descends to earth as a fish, as a tortoise, as a boar, as a man-lion, as a dwarf, as Rāma-with-an-axe, as the Lord Rāma, as the Lord Krishna and (later) as the Buddha, and he will descend as Kalkin at the end of time.

Two points are worth noting. First, this process covers an immense amount of time in Hindu mythology from the golden age down to the iron age. Secondly, Vishnu's descents are seen to evolve through a process of ascending evolution from simple to complex whereas the Hindu ages work the other way round by declining from the best age to the worst. Sri Aurobindo suggests a possible way of looking at this: there is first an involution of the divine from the complex to the simple, followed by an evolution of the divine in the opposite direction to help the world at its time of greatest need.

The Goddess

A short passage in the *Mārkandeya Purāna* sums up both the might and the gracious mercy of the Goddess (Devi):

> O Goddess who removes the suffering of your supplicants, have mercy! O mother of the whole world, be gracious! O mistress of the universe, protect the world! Have mercy! You are the mistress of all that moves and moves not! You alone are the foundation of the world, residing in the form of the earth. O you whose prowess is unsurpassed, you nourish the world in the form of the waters. (Dimmitt and van Buitenen, 1978, p. 219)

This passage refers basically to the Great Goddess (Mahādevī). Other goddesses, of whom there are many, can be seen as different forms of the Great Goddess or as separate goddesses in their own right.

At one level, important goddesses can be seen as consorts of Shiva and Vishnu. Thus, Pārvati and Umā are seen as amiable consorts of Shiva. However, Durga and Kali are seen as unamiable consorts of Shiva. Moreover, Durga, who lies at the centre of the great Durga Pūjā festival, becomes in that context an independent goddess who kills the world-threatening buffalo-demon Mahisha and stands on his chest thrusting her spear into him. Kali, who gives her name to Calcutta (Kalighat), is sometimes portrayed independently as being black, wearing a garland of skulls and even standing on the chest of her husband Shiva.

Saraswatī is at one level the consort of Brahmā, but she is much more worshipped in her own right than Brahmā and is the much-loved goddess of the arts and sciences, of learning and music. Lakshmī, or Shrī, is the ever-faithful consort of Vishnu and they are often worshipped together, but she is also seen independently as the goddess of business, wealth and good fortune and is thus worshipped by businessmen at the beginning of the new financial year.

At another level the Goddess is often given the epithet Shakti, which means power. She is sometimes seen as the female energy or power of Shiva; thus, he may be regarded as the passive consciousness who, through her power, performs his five acts of making, supporting and destroying the universe, giving grace to devotees and hiding himself from them. In the Tantric tradition Shakti becomes more important in religious practice than Shiva, and in Kashmir Shaivism and other Tantric traditions she is personified in various gentle or ferocious forms. At this level Shakti becomes a kind of primordial power, more active and in a sense 'embodied' than any male deity. As Michaels (1996, p. 334) puts it:

> goddesses reflect, in sharp distinction to western concepts of identity, the Hindu belief in the power of pre-verbal, preconscious experiences of reality...What makes goddesses powerful is beyond words, theories, analysis, separations, boundaries – beyond identity.

During the Durga Pūjā festival in Varanasi the great actual power of the Goddess is represented by men who dance round for minutes holding a great container of burning coals that ordinary men could scarcely hold up for seconds.

Rāma and Krishna

The two main *avatāras* of Vishnu are Rāma and Krishna who become deities in their own right. The western question would be, do they remain manifestations of Vishnu or are they in fact separate deities in their own right? This question is not vital to the Hindu mind. Krishna first appears in the *Mahābhārata* as a human adviser and astute ally of the Pāndavas in the conflict between the Pāndavas and the Kauravas that lies at the heart of the longest epic in the world. Little is portrayed of Krishna's own intimate life and in most of the *Mahābhārata* he is not seen as God. Much more detail about Krishna appears in the *Bhagavad Gītā*, which is a later insertion into the *Mahābhārata* dating from around 200 BCE. At the human level he is the charioteer of Arjuna, one of the Pāndava leaders, in the great battle at the heart of the epic. However, Arjuna has qualms about fighting because he realises that some of his own kinsfolk are in the opposing army and he will probably have to kill them. In the *Bhagavad Gītā* Krishna tries to answer

Arjuna's qualms. He reveals himself to the startled Arjuna as the cosmic Lord and he displays his supernal form to Arjuna in a great vision. Moreover, he reveals himself to Arjuna as the loving Lord who responds in love to surrender and devotion. In the course of doing all this he also lays before Arjuna important teaching that remains important to the Hindu world to this day. However, the *Bhagavad Gītā* reveals nothing about the intimate details of Krishna's life, nor is he yet seen to be an *avatāra* of Vishnu.

The *Harivamsha*, a later appendix to the *Mahābhārata* from the early centuries CE, brings out more details of Krishna's birth, childhood, youth, life as a cowherd and death. It also stresses that he is an *avatāra* of Vishnu.

Much more of Krishna's story is portrayed in the *Vishnu Purāna* and especially in the tenth and eleventh books of the *Bhāgavata Purāna* dating from around the ninth century. We hear about his being saved as a child from his tyrant uncle Kamsa and being taken from Mathura to be brought up as a foster-child in a peasant village. We see his childhood pranks and how he revealed his divine element to his startled foster-mother. We also see his youthful miracles. There are stories too about his life among the cowherds and his relationships with the cowgirls (*gopis*) at Brindaban, including his dancing with the *gopis*, stealing their clothes, playing his flute to them and dancing to make each of them think that he is dancing with them alone.

The story continues with Krishna killing his tyrant uncle and returning to Mathura as a prince to rejoin his natural parents, after sadly leaving his foster parents. Eventually he moves on to Dwaraka and marries Rukmini and other wives, in formal and 'respectable' fashion. Eventually he dies. Throughout the *Bhāgavata Purāna* Krishna is seen as both a deity and a human being. The places where he lives – Mathura, Brindaban and Dwaraka – become centres of Krishna worship. The basis for deep Krishna devotion (*bhakti*) is truly laid.

It was further reinforced by later Krishna poetry, for example, in the twelfth-century *Gītā Govinda* of Jayadeva, in the poetry of Mira Bai, a western Indian princess, in the work of Vallabha born in 1478, in the work of Vallabha's disciples, especially Surdas (1479–1584), and in the work of Chaitanya (1486–1533). Here the focus moves to one of the cowgirls, Rādhā, with whom Krishna shares a deeply passionate love, and the language switches from Sanskrit to Bengali and Hindi. Strictly speaking their love is adulterous. However, their love is symbolic of the union of the soul with God, of the need for a passionate love for God, and of the mystical and philosophical depths possible in *bhakti* devotional religion.

By contrast, Rāma is an exemplary figure, a great hero, an ideal king, a figure who chooses the way of suffering because it is right, an embodiment of *dharma* (right living) and eventually a chaste, loving Lord. He is similar in many ways to the great deity Vishnu of whom he is an *avatāra*, whereas Krishna is more similar in some ways to Shiva.

Rāma is at the centre of the great epic *Rāmāyana* which is named after him. In it he is viewed first as a heroic successor to the Vedic deity, Indra, but later he is seen to be an *avatāra* of Vishnu. In the *Rāmāyana*, Rāma is an example of human relationships. He is an ideal son to his father, the king of Ayodhya; he is ideally married to his wife Sītā; he is an ideal brother to his brother Lakshmana; he is an ideal ally to others in his battle with the demon king Rāvana; he is an ideal protector to those in need. Moreover, he is also a great hero who bravely defeats Rāvana's army and the forces of evil to recover his kidnapped wife Sītā. He is portrayed as a kind of Messianic figure who after victory in battle returns to Ayodhya to set up the ideal kingdom, Rāmarājya (the kingdom of Rāma), wherein humans are at peace with themselves and with nature. Later Gandhi's ideal for Indian independence would be not just freedom from the British Raj, but even more importantly the hope that India, when independent, could be like Rāmarājya, the kingdom of God on earth.

A number of later *Rāmāyanas* fill out the story of Rāma. They are not commentaries. They pick up and develop the basic story of the *Rāmāyana* and they also bring out the divinity of Rāma in striking ways. In the fifteenth-century *Adhyātma Rāmāyana* (Spiritual Rāmāyana), written against the background of a Rāma community, Rāma remains an example at the phenomenal level. However, he has also become a devotional Lord. More than that, he has become Vishnu and yet more than Vishnu. In the *Adhyātma Rāmāyana* he is now seen occasionally as *Brahman*, Absolute Reality, as in Advaita Vedanta philosophy.

Probably the greatest *Rāmāyana* of all was written in Hindi, not in Sanskrit, by Tulsīdās in the sixteenth century. It is rather like the Bible and Shakespeare combined – that is to say great religion and great literature under one cover. Tulsīdās's stress is upon Rāma as a devotional rather than a philosophical Lord. His genius achieves continuity in the Rāma story by integrating the original *Rāmāyana*'s human Rāma with the *Adhyātma Rāmāyana*'s Rāma as *Brahman* into a basic and glorious emphasis upon Rāma as loving Lord.

Rāma and Krishna are very different, rather like yin and yang. Rāma is an example whereas Krishna is not. Rāma chooses suffering whereas Krishna does not. Rāma is an obviously kingly figure; Krishna is not. Love for Rāma, as human and divine, is mainly through service and friendship, whereas love for Krishna, as human and divine, is more mystical and erotic. They mirror and exemplify the extraordinarily varied views of deity within the Hindu tradition. Insofar as they tend to have a more 'human face' than Shiva, Vishnu or the Goddess, Krishna and Rāma retain a strong attraction for many Hindus.

Other Gods

Some deities who are not major gods are nevertheless important at the level of religious practice. Three examples are Ganesha, Skanda and Hanuman. Ganesha is, with Skanda, one of the two sons of Shiva. In parts of South India, especially in Maharashtra, Ganesha (the elephant-headed god) is very popular. There are only a few largish temples devoted to him but he has cult standing among the people. His brother Skanda is unimportant in most of India. However, in the south, and especially in Tamilnadu, where he is called Murugan, Skanda is often the main and presiding deity in prestigious temples as well as being a clan deity. In parts of North and Central India, Hanuman is an important deity. He has a monkey form and is sometimes known as the 'monkey god'. His loyal devotion to Rāma and his tremendous strength in the battle with Rāvana invite devotion to him, especially in villages, as a helper in times of danger and as part of the Rāma and Vishnu entourage.

Scattered throughout village India there are a myriad of 'small gods and goddesses' who are related to particular villages or kinship groups in an important way. A study by Mayer (1960) of the village of Ramkheri in Madhya Pradesh describes forty-four shrines. They include two Vishnu temples, one Shiva temple, three Sai Mata shrines, six 'village Lord' shrines, eight Mata shrines, thirteen Bhairava shrines, eight other minor deity shrines and three other special but unspecified shrines. Another study by Rein-iche (1985) in the village of Mel Ceval in Tamilnadu describes thirty-five temples and shrines. They include a large Shiva temple, a fairly large Shasta temple and a number of local shrines. Village goddesses (*grāmadevatās*) are especially important in South India.

These gods and goddesses may be separate from the 'great gods' or they may be subordinate to or derive their powers from them. Some local deities have human origins, having been local heroes or heroines or even ghostly spirits who had suffered a bad death and were later deified. It is difficult to catalogue Hindu local gods because they are so different and so numerous. Yet, in practical terms, they are sometimes of more immediate significance to ordinary people.

4

Hindu Rituals

Much of Hindu life revolves around practice rather than theory. Much of it is a way of life as well as being centred upon purely religious matters and can be examined under three headings: rites of passage (or sacraments), worship, festivals and pilgrimages.

Rites of Passage

The key Hindu rites of passage are the same as in other religious traditions, in the sense of sacramental activities to do with birth, initiation, marriage and death, and they are age-old within the tradition of the Brahmins. Traditionally there were sixteen ceremonies relating to five different stages of life. All are intricate in regard to detail.

Pre-birth to birth

There were four rituals connected to this stage: first, the original conception of a child; then the development of a foetus within the womb; then the parting of the hair of the pregnant mother; and finally the birth itself. Clearly there is trial and error in the actualities of pre-birth, but the desire was to ritualise each stage.

Childhood

Five ceremonies were connected to childhood. They centred upon the naming of the child; the child's first outing; the child's first eating of solid food; the tonsure of the child; and finally the ear-piercing of the child. In the early stages of life Hindu children, especially boys, are extremely close to their mothers.

Puberty

At the stage of puberty and youth, there were five more ceremonies. They focused upon initial learning; the initiation; the beginning of formal study; the first shave; and the end of study. The sacred thread received at initiation (*upanayana*) by men of the three upper castes is a symbol of being twice-born and is worn next to the body throughout life and replaced when it wears out.

Marriage

When the period of youth and study were over, there came the stage of being married in a traditional wedding service. The marriage ceremony includes elements that date right back to the *Rig Veda*.

Death

Finally, there came a ceremony to do with death centred upon the ritual burning of the corpse of the dead person, hopefully on the funeral ghat of a holy river. At times in Hindu history this ceremony could include the burning of a widow on the funeral pyre of her husband in the satī ritual and also ancestor rituals (*śrāddha*) at various intervals after death.

These ceremonies are not performed generally now. Clearly, the satī widow-burning ritual is outside the law. However, this classical scheme gives a vivid picture of the importance of life-cycle rituals in the Hindu scheme of things. The rituals are limited to the three 'twice-born' castes. Thus, the fourth (Shūdra) caste and the outcastes are outside the scope of these life-cycle rituals; so too, in theory, are converts to the Hindu tradition from other cultures. This raises the question, what is Hinduism? In practice it is the initiation ritual that is especially important for Hindu life.

Worship

This is mainly performed in homes or in a temple. A number of Hindu homes have a *pūjā* room (worship room) that is holy and reserved for worship. In it there are the chosen deity of the householder and other gods in image form. In some poorer homes with few rooms there is no space for a *pūjā* room, and so the gods are organised neatly on a mantelpiece in a family room for worship. The worship may be very simple or at other times complicated.

Worship at home

Home worship is very important for Hindus as there is no obligation to worship in temples. The full ritual of home morning worship involves eleven stages and is modelled on the impressive morning worship at the river Ganges in Varanasi. Not all are performed in every home but they give an idea of the sensitivities involved. Firstly, there are ablutions to get ready for worship followed by a short time of breath-control. This is followed by ritual washing of the mouth and further ritual (as opposed to ordinary) washing

using, if possible, holy Ganges water. Guilt is wiped away and there is iden-
tification with godhead. The sun is then worshipped and the Vedic *gāyatrī
mantra* recited: 'we meditate on that shining light of the divine Sun; may
he stimulate our thoughts'. Gāyatrī is then worshipped with hand gestures
(mudrās). Libations and prayers are offered to gods, seers and ancestors and
further libations are offered to the sun. Finally the worship is brought to a
fitting end. Sometimes, after the ritual, marks are applied to the forehead,
usually three horizontal yellow marks to represent Shiva and two white and
one red vertical marks to represent Vishnu. There may be also a *tilaka* mark
for women

There are other forms of home worship and they are often led by women.
An important variant is the worship of five deities which are usually Vishnu,
Shiva, the Goddess (usually Durga), Ganesha and Sūrya (the sun) in image
form. This is an ecumenical choice of five of the main divinities and it originated in the sixth century. The five-god worship is often strong and fervent,
involving chanting and devotion and the use of incense, lights and flowers.

Worship in the temple

Another form of morning worship is to visit a temple and on the way to
offer small gifts to animals, beggars and holy men. This is an alternative way
of performing the traditional five daily sacrifices to gods, seers, ancestors,
animals and humans. Most of the rituals mentioned so far are part of preparing oneself, psychologically and spiritually, for the life of the day.

Temple worship is not a weekly matter but a daily phenomenon, but
there is no obligation to attend. For monotheistic traditions worship will
normally be on a particular day each week. For Hindus it can be on every
day or on no day. Daily worship in temples is punctuated by great festivals
that take place in favourite temples. Otherwise it is up to the worshipper as
to whether he or she wishes to go and worship in a temple, or not. There is
no obligation.

Darshana

The main act of worship in a temple is to stand before a deity, in the form
of an image, and to 'see' the deity and 'be seen' by the deity. Hindus will say
that the deity is giving *darshana* (sight) and the worshipper is taking *darshana*. Sight is important and the 'language of the eyes' is important for the
process of seeing and being seen. There is a sense in which divinity is visible
for Hindus outside the context of a temple – in the earth, in other people, in
life and in death. However, *darshana* is most clear in worship in a temple.

Such worship came into its own with the building of the great temples
in Mahabalipuram (7th–9th centuries), Ellora (8th–9th centuries),

Bhubaneshwar (8th–11th centuries), Khujaraho (11th century), Tanjore (11th century), Konarak (13th century), Vijayanagar (16th century) and Madurai (17th century). Elsewhere, in places like Varanasi, great temples had to be rebuilt after being torn down by Muslim invaders. Temples in smaller towns and in villages keep their routine of worship whereby people come at any time to give and receive *darshana* from the local deity or deities.

In addition to giving and receiving *darshana*, the worshipper sees an embodiment of godhead in image form as a focus of concentration. He or she is also participating in a visible theology seen with the eyes rather than being read as words, wherein the story of the godhead becomes alive in the image and surrounding temple designs. As the great philosopher Rāmānuja put it, in the case of Vishnu, the god of grace had become finite, bound, dependent, seeable, available, touchable even, in image form, through a sacrificial act of condescension. He allows himself to be woken, dressed, fed, reverenced by worshippers, allowed rest, fed again and finally put to sleep. He has humbled himself for the sake of *darshana*.

The deity, looked after by a priest, is the *raison d'etre* for the temple. Communal worship is not the point of the temple. There is a sense in which visitors to the temple are secondary. Nevertheless, the temple is helpful to the community as well. The presence of the deity and the blessing received from the deity feed into the welfare of the community.

The usual term for Hindu worship is *pūjā*. In its simplest sense it involves entering the presence of the godhead, honouring the deity, offering presents of water, food, flowers, incense and money, giving and receiving *darshana*, and finally receiving a present, often of sanctified food called *prasāda*, before departing. *Prasāda* is sometimes the return of the devotee's own gifts blessed by the deity. More complicated and ornate kinds of *pūjā* can also be offered. These might include offering many more gifts, often as many as sixteen, known as *upacāras* (honour offerings).

The Minakshi temple in Madurai seems like a maze of buildings that go from lightness at the entrance towards the darker part where the central temple shrine is situated. Before entering the temple it is necessary to negotiate the area outside, in order to find one's way in. A long road leads up to the temple where gifts may be bought to offer to the deity as well as guidebooks, pictures of the deity, bangles and trinkets, food and clothing. These purchases honour the deity, help visitors and support the city. The road is also used to process the image of the deity at festival times. The image is not taken out of the temple except during festivals, although in some places a separate festival image may be taken out on procession instead of the image in the temple.

Inside the gateway the buildings may include images of deities to be honoured, small exhibitions and even an indoor pond. In other courtyard buildings, or in buildings inside the outer wall of the compound, there may be other shrines, offices, accommodation, storehouses for musical instruments, ritual clothing and festival paraphernalia. There may even be temple elephants. Visitors may find it helpful to look round the compound, but it is essential to make one's way towards the central shrine of the main deity by walking in a clockwise direction. To do otherwise would be frowned upon. Eventually the devotee approaches closer to a group of halls (*mandapas*) surrounding the central shrine. They are open and columned and offer shade. They provide rest and somewhere for devotees and pilgrims to congregate. There is often a wait in order to proceed to *darshana* of the deity. From there one prepares to enter the innermost sanctuary. The atmosphere by this time is somewhat dark and awesome. It is possible in some temples, at this point, to walk auspiciously in a clockwise direction around the sanctuary. Finally one enters the sanctuary and offers gifts to the (usually) Brahmin priest that he in turn offers to the deity. The role of the priest is important. Gifts are then received back from the priest as *prasāda*. The priest may offer incense and light to the deity and then offer them on to the devotee. While all this is happening, the devotee exchanges *darshana* with the god.

Other things may also happen. The worshippers may also honour the deity and keep him cool by fanning him with a flywhisk. They may slowly circle a camphor lamp around the deity and honour him or her with songs or bells in an *arathi* (light) ceremony. The arathi ceremony is often done in a simpler form by Hindu women at home when they light the lamps in the early evening. They will wave them around the deity in simple acts of worship. Worship in temples or in wealthy homes is often conducted by priests (*pūjārīs*) but it can also be conducted in homes by laymen and in certain contexts by women.

The actual images of the deities are made by workmen in the workshops of Varanasi and elsewhere who follow ancient texts. They are not impresarios who do the job as an expression of their own genius as in the case of much western art. They follow age-old instructions. There may be many ways of representing a divinity in image form. For example, Shiva can be seen in the form of a *lingam*, as the lord of the dance (Nataraja), as the killer of demons, as an ascetic meditator, as the husband of Pārvāti, or with his wider family of Pārvāti, Ganesha and Skanda. The creators of images see their task as a religious as well as an artistic endeavour. In consecration rituals images are then purified with appropriate sweet substances, then they may be ritually touched. Finally, and most importantly, they are 'made alive' in a ceremony called *prāna pratiṣṭa* which establishes the breath of life in an image so that the deity becomes 'enlivened'. A particular sacred saying (*mantra*) may be intoned as the deity is transformed from wood or stone into worshipful form. After this the eyes of the image are opened (after having been sealed) and, as they are crucial to the *darshana* (seeing) at the centre of *pūjā*, this is the climactic act.

A similar process takes place, on a more extensive level, in the building of a temple. An auspicious place is found and cleared. A plan (mandala) is drawn up as a kind of minuscule map of the universe that the temple will represent. Building follows ritual prescriptions and when it is finished the priest and main architect will ritually 'open' the 'eyes' of the temple that is then itself 'alive' for worship.

As a group of pundits of Varanasi explained to a seventeenth-century French traveller, Bernier:

> we have indeed in our temples a great variety of images...To all these images we pay great honour; prostrating our bodies and presenting to them, with much ceremony, flowers, rice, scented oil, saffron and other similar articles. Yet we do not believe that these statues are themselves Brahmā or Vishnu; but merely their images or representations. We show them deference only for the sake of the deity whom they represent and when we pray it is not to the statue but to that deity. (Humphrey, 1914, p. 243)

Festivals and Pilgrimage

Hindu festivals are often spectacular affairs that contain more than ritual performances. They are times of merriment and joy as well as times of solemnity.

However ritual and worship are part of festivals as temples are usually involved in festivals. In a wider context festivals can sometimes be interpreted as rituals writ large. Festivals, including *pūjā*, are often part of pilgrimages to the important holy places that Hindus desire to visit at special times in their lives. Many thousands of local festivals take part in the half-million villages of Hindu India but the following examples indicate the widespread importance of festival.

Hindu festivals occur at variable times as they follow the Hindu calendar with its own months and its own agenda in regard to the dark halves of the moon and the waning halves of the moon. The following dates for Hindu festivals only approximate to their actual dates.

Calendar of festivals

The **Navarātri** festival begins in mid September or early October. The word means 'nine nights' of celebrations for the goddess Durga and other goddesses. A special Durga Pūjā day is held on the tenth day and on that night an annually-made image of her slaying the gigantic buffalo-demon Mahiṣāsura is thrown into a nearby river with great light and acclaim. On the final days of the Navarātri festival, another very important festival occurs named Rāmlīlā to commemorate the victory of Rāma over Rāvana, the demon-king of Lankā (which may or may not be the present Sri Lanka). In parts of North India, especially in Varanasi, the festival lasts for longer and re-enacts the wider story of Rāma in nightly spectacles that draw enormous crowds, including the Maharajah of Banāras on the main nights. The Rāmlīlā festival is also known as Dussehra and the conjunction of the Navaratri, Durga Pūjā and Rāmlīlā/Dussehra festivals is a joyous and climactic time in the Hindu year.

The beautiful **Diwālī** festival begins in late October or early November, coinciding with the darkest night of the lunar month. It is a New Year festival marking the beginning of the financial year in India. It is a festival of lights that can be either very simple or majestically glorious. Fireworks are exploded, sweetmeats are eaten and the festival has different connotations around India. It is often associated with the goddess Lakshmī who is the patron goddess of prosperity and wealth. In Varanasi it coincides with the ritual return of Rāma and his wife Sītā to rule in their capital city Ayodhya at the end of a long exile. Thus October is a great month for Hindu festivals.

The beginning of the Spring (around 31 January) is celebrated by the festival of **Vasant Panchamī**, especially in North India. Saraswatī, the goddess of learning and the arts, is worshipped at this festival.

In February Shiva takes the centre of the stage in the **Mahāśivarātri** (Great Night of Shiva). Every night of the new moon is said to relate to Shiva, but this one is set aside for all-night prayers and worship, for fasting and for special veneration of Shiva. His cosmic dance as Nataraja (Lord of the Dance) is remembered, when he was both creator and destroyer of the cosmos. Milk is poured ritually on his symbol, the *lingam*.

The flamboyant **Holi festival** begins its five-day course in late February or the beginning of March. It combines different features. It is an end-of-Spring festival. It is associated with Krishna in his deep love for Rādhā and his flirtatious love with the cowgirls. Coloured dyes and paints are thrown around and there is a kind of reversal of roles across social boundaries for a short time. Bonfires are also lit in connection with a myth about Holika, who was immune to fire and saved the life of her princely cousin Prahlāda. In spite of this she is burnt as part of the festivities!

April is a prime month for Rāma festivals. **Rāma Navami** (the Birth of Rāma) recalls the birth of Rāma. It falls on the ninth day of Shukla Paksha (waxing phase of moon) in the month of Chaitra (March–April). In addition to normal *pūjā*, a candle (*aarti*) is also ritually waved over pictures of the baby Rāma or 'dolls' of Rāma in a real cradle. Later comes the **Hanumān Jayantī** (the birth of Hanumān) festival. Devout Hindus get up at sunrise to celebrate the birth of Rāma's most faithful devotee, Hanumān, at the start of an auspicious day, namely the full-moon day of the important lunar month of Chaitra.

A different kind of festival dedicated to Krishna is held in June or early July (in 2010 it falls on 13 July), mainly in Puri in Orissa state. This is the famous **Ratha Yātrā** ('Chariot Journey') when thousands of devotees become involved in pulling enormous chariots through the streets each containing images of Krishna. Krishna is represented as Jaggarnath (Lord of the World). It is a time of great emotion, great devotion and occasional accidents. At other times images of Krishna as Jaggarnath remain in the temple at Puri and *darshana* takes place in the temple. However, on this special day Krishna goes out into the streets to offer *darshana* in the open air to his devotees. This festival is sometimes celebrated in Britain, mainly by Hari Krishna devotees, who organise Ratha Yātrā processions in London.

August marks a climax in the festival year. The festival of **Rakshā Bandhan** (binding of the demons) takes place on the full-moon day of an auspicious month, Shrāvana. The festival is a moving family affair, when sisters and sometimes other female relatives bind amulets (*rākhīs*) on the right wrists of brothers to protect them from all harm. Krishna's birthday is celebrated eight days later in the **Krishnajanmāshtami** festival. Many Hindus fast until midnight, the time of Krishna's birth. In temples there is worship but also singing and dancing. Special sweets, such as *panjiri* given to women after childbirth, are distributed and shared and, as in the case of Rāma's birth, images of the baby Krishna are put in cradles and celebrated. Finally, the birthday of Ganesha, the son of Shiva, is honoured in the festival of **Ganesha Chaturthi** (Ganesha's Fourth). Ganesha is the god of good fortune and new beginnings and is thus a popular deity. His festival is especially celebrated in Maharashtra and the great city of Mumbai where it can last for up to ten days and may end with the image of Ganesha being immersed in water.

Pilgrimage

Pilgrimage plays an important role in festivals and ritual worship. Pilgrimage to holy places gives devout Hindus the opportunity to increase their merit (good *karma*), and can raise worship to a more exalted level. Although ordinary worship is beneficial there is a more 'luminous' quality to worship experienced on a special journey away from ordinary life. The classical list of seven Hindu holy cities, the favoured places for pilgrimage, includes Varanasi and Hardwar on the Ganges, Ayodhya (Rāma's capital), Mathura and Dwaraka (of Krishna fame), Kanchipuram (the only city not in the north, known as the 'southern Banaras') and Ujjain. There are special pilgrim routes around such cities with several stops for worship.

The seven great rivers of India offer well-known places for pilgrimage, especially the river Ganges, and in particular the city of Varanasi. One 600-mile 'Great Ganges' pilgrimage, undertaken in May, June and July, begins at Hardwar and Rishikesh where the sacred river meets the plains and then goes up to the three sources of the Ganges high in the Himalayas. The long journey involves hardships as well as profound ritual experiences. The biggest festival in the world takes place every twelve years at Allahabad in North India where the Ganges meets the river Yamunā (Jumna). A third river, the Saraswatī, which was connected with the union of the rivers at Allahabad, has recently been discovered underground and is not mythical, as originally supposed. In sites adjacent to the swirl in the waters where the rivers meet, the Kumbha Melā occurs every twelve years and, on the main day, a million people meet to try and 'step in the swirl'. During the month-long festival millions of people descend upon Allahabad for the course of the festival which affords many opportunities for *pūjā* both at the site and on the way. At three-year intervals smaller Kumbha Melās are held at Hardwar, Ujjain and Nasik.

In 2001 an attempt was made to organise a combined Hindu right-wing leadership for India during the Allahabad Kumbha Melā. This was opposed by many religious figures, leaders, orders and organisations who objected to the great festival pilgrimage being perverted for political ends.

Personal Stories

In other places, and especially in the West, religious festivals have partly lost their sense of communal celebration. I remember my best suit being spoiled when brightly coloured water was thrown over it in the festival of Holi when normal behaviour can be overturned for a day. I was fooled again in a pleasant way when, as honoured guest at a festival centred upon the deity Rāma, I was given a prestigious seat in a packed outdoor auditorium in Varanasi on the night of the great battle between Rāma and Rāvana. I realised when I sat down that I was in front of the army of the arch-villain Rāvana! On another occasion I walked into a great temple in Varanasi and found a large model train chugging round the floor of the temple full of people cheerfully sitting on it. As I walked out of the side door I felt myself being attacked by a lion. It turned out to be part of a set of lights of animals fixed on trees that went on and off every two minutes and, as I walked out, the tree with the lion on its branches suddenly lit up!

Finally, while I was a Visiting Professor in Bangalore in 2002, I taught for four days a week but spent the other three days touring South India. Travelling by coach to famous Hindu centres, I was often the only white person involved. Despite such quick trips there was a real sense of pilgrimage and ritual worship devoutly performed by my Hindu friends and sensitively shared with me.

5

Hindu Religious Traditions

There is no monolithic 'Hinduism', nor indeed is there a monolithic 'Hindu Tradition'. Instead there is a congeries of Hindu traditions, especially so in regard to particular groups of Hindus. Even those associated with a particular deity may use different names for those deities and differ among themselves as to their key features. As examples of this diversity it is possible to look at two extremes. The Smārta Brahmins worship an ecumenical set of five deities, whilst two unorthodox groups, the Bauls and the Lingāyats are at the other end of the spectrum. We will also examine various groups who worship Shiva, Vishnu, Rāma and Krishna. (We will look at the Goddess Devi's groups in a later chapter.)

Smārta Brahmins

The Smārtas appeared as a kind of ecumenical force who followed a non-sectarian way. They wanted to go beyond the sometimes deep differences between the followers of individual gods by offering devotion to five deities combined, namely Shiva, Vishnu, Devi, Surya (the sun) and Ganesha. The great Advaita Vedanta philosopher Shankara, while stressing the non-dual nature of *Brahman* as Absolute Reality at the ultimate level, composed hymns to the five deities within the Smārta pantheon at the phenomenal level. They could all be worshipped simultaneously as well as separately. Moreover, the members of the religious order organised by Shankara, named the Dashanamis, were also Smārta in their outlook. According to tradition, Shankara set up monasteries in the four corners of India, and the present-day leaders of those monasteries are the nearest thing to 'Hindu leaders' at this point in Hindu history. They take the name of Shankarācharya. The great sixty-eighth Shankarācharya of the Kanchi monastery took office in 1907 when he was seventeen and handed over to his successor in 1970. He was considered to be a Jagadguru (world leader). He was a strong advocate of intra-religious harmony within the Hindu fold but also of interreligious harmony at the world level: 'He whom the Shaivas worship as Shiva, the Vedantins as Brahman, who is worshipped as Creator by the Naiyayikas, and as Arhat by the Jains, may that Hari give you the fruits that you desire' (Sivaraman, 1989, p. 384). In other words, the Smārtas are strong advocates of harmony within and between religions, while at the same time encouraging people to have their own chosen deity (*ishta-devata*).

Bauls of Bengal

At the other extreme come the Bauls of Bengal. As one of their songs puts it:

> This is why, brother, I became a madcap Baul. No master I obey, nor injunctions, canons or custom. Man-made distinctions have no hold on me now. I rejoice in the gladness of love that wells out of my own being. In love there is no separation, but a meeting of hearts forever. So I rejoice in song and I dance with each and all. That is why, brother, I became a madcap Baul. (Sen, 1961, p. 103)

The Bauls recognise no divisions in society, whether to do with caste or class, with particular gods, with worship, with scriptures or with temple and mosque. They tend to be from the lower strata of Hindu and Muslim society, they are not ascetics and they have a high regard for their gurus. They are known for their beautiful songs which focus on direct present contact with God. They have no deep sense of history or of general knowledge as such. They are virtually adrift from every tradition although they sometimes claim to have been founded by Chaitanya. And yet are they or are they not Hindus?

Lingāyats

Very different again are the Lingāyats, or Vīraśaivas. They were founded by Basava in the middle of the twelfth century and they play an important role in parts of the state of Karnataka. Basava was born into a traditional Shaiva Brahmin family but he rebelled against the social and religious practices of his time and threw away the sacred thread given to him at initiation. He went to a town named Samgama to renew the Shaiva tradition but eventually he discarded his own inherited beliefs and took a new direction, abandoning distinctions of caste or sex and working for the betterment of the lower castes. He, and reputedly two hundred others, wrote *vacanas* (prose praises of Shiva) asking people to put their faith in Shiva and decrying any stress upon wealth, ritual and learning. An academy and organisation were set up that evolved into the Lingāyat/Vīraśaiva tradition.

Basava's reform was a radical one. A *lingam*, worn in a kind of amulet around the neck, became the symbol of Shiva, which was given at initiation and worshipped daily. It came to be the main object of devotion and worship. Later it was given to a child soon after birth, in place of the normal Hindu birth ceremonies. There was thus no need for the normal paraphernalia of *pūjā*. Fasts, penances, pilgrimages, priests, rites and sacrifices became superfluous. Sacred texts of Hindu scripture were of value only in regard to their personal relationship with Shiva, and the Veda was rejected. Moreover, Basava went to the length of establishing a new kind of priestly leadership called *jangamas*, later divided into householder and ascetic orders. According to Lingāyat tradition, the jangamas became organised around a number of institutions known as *mathas*, and each Lingāyat was able to have his or her own hereditary guru from among the jangamas.

Equally radical was the Lingāyat stress upon equality between men and women, allowing women to marry when mature, to have a say in the choice of their husbands and to remarry after the death of a husband. Basava also criticised cremation as being unnecessary since, after death, one's destiny is to go straight to Shiva without the necessity of funeral rituals. Caste was also rejected although, in India, this proved difficult to put into practice. It is interesting that a number of the early Lingāyats were converts from the Jain tradition, and the strict vegetarianism that is important among the Jains became part of Lingāyat practice. Despite the Lingāyats being close to the Jains, they are still regarded as part, if a slightly unorthodox part, of the Hindu tradition.

The Five Major Traditions

Minor local Hindu traditions are manifold. At village, town and city level many small groups organise fairs, festivals or bazaars and they may be only vaguely connected with any major tradition. Further complexity comes from groups within the five major traditions – the Shiva, Vishnu, Devi, Rāma and Krishna traditions – who have followed different sets of sacred texts at different times.

Moreover, the Hindu tradition has many sets of sacred texts in Sanskrit and other languages. Unlike the monotheistic traditions which their holy books for guidance, Hindus have many sets of sacred texts. Further, the composite Veda, which is in theory 'revealed' and paramount, has in practice been replaced by later texts which are 'remembered' and human, and therefore supposedly less important.

Shaivism

Traditions worshipping Shiva have been present in India from early times. Early sources were the possible Shiva image of the Indus Valley civilisation, the Dravidian roots in Tamil South India where Shiva became strong, possible Shiva/Rudra-like gods in tribal areas, and the personal theistic Shiva of the Śvetāśvatara Upanishad. The oldest Shiva group seems to have been the Pāśupatas in the second century CE. Their aims were to abolish suffering and find union with Shiva (Pāśupati) by progressing through five stages wherein past *karma* could be purified and good *karma* could be built up. A subgroup of the Pāśupatas, the Lakula, took a direction of unusual behaviour but a further subgroup, the Kālāmukhas developed from them to become dominant in Karnataka from the eleventh to thirteenth centuries. Another Shaiva group named the Kapālikas exercised devotion to Shiva in his Bhairava being. This was a more horrible side of his being that the Kapālikas attempted to both follow and atone for. We know about them from their orthodox opponents according to whom the Kapālikas were prone to extreme ascetic penance for untoward acts such as murder or illicit sex. It is possible that they were overly imitating the Puranic version of Shiva's own beheading of Brahmā and Shiva's own blissful sexual union with his consort. There is a sense that some of the early Shaivites would follow Shiva's asceticism or his eroticism.

Around the seventh century in South India a strong Shaiva devotional movement began to emerge. It was led by the Nāyanmārs using the Tamil language. This was a deviation from the Sanskrit used by other groups, and later the works of sixty-three of their leaders were brought together into a collected resource of devotional writings. Tamil Shaivite *bhakti* stressed the importance of a deep personal faith in Shiva that was exercised at a fervent devotional level. This was not a personal achievement but was developed in response to the caring grace of the godhead. In fact, a favourite godhead was Murugan, who strictly speaking was Shiva's son Skanda. However Shiva himself, as his loving and beneficent self, was also prominent in this important movement. The four best known among the Nāyanmārs were Campantar, Cuntarar, Appar and Mānikkavācakar. Between them they helped to strengthen the cause of Shiva against the Buddhists and Jains. They opened up the possibility of lower castes having a place within the worshipping Shiva fold, emphasised the depth of sin and the need for redemption from it, stressed the importance of humility, and produced a deep religious response to their poetry. Especially in the mystical poetry of Appar and through Mānikkavācakar's *Tiruvacakam*, they have influenced Tamil Shaivite devotion in South India down to our own times and their beautiful poems still evoke an ecstatic search for and desire for union with Shiva in Tamil homes and temples today.

The main Shaiva school in North India was Kashmir Shaivism. Its main written evidence dates back to the eighth century. It flourished for many centuries but is now depleted in numbers. Although it contained two main schools, they have much in common. Kashmir Shaivism was monistic with similarities to Shankara's Advaita Vedanta put into a Shiva framework. Thus Shiva was the *ātman* dwelling in all persons and things as well as in the universe as a whole. The supreme reality was Shiva who was pure consciousness pervading everything. There were five 'faces of Shiva', five aspects of his pervading energy, namely consciousness (chit), bliss (ānanda), desire, knowledge and activity. Although Shiva is eternal and pure consciousness he conceals himself by the power of illusion (*māyā*). Thus, through *māyā*, people are ignorant of reality and they require the grace of Shiva to escape from bondage. To do this they need a guru who can initiate them and set them on the journey to enlightenment. According to one of the most famous figures in Kashmir Shaivism, Abhivinagupta (950–1020) and his disciple Kshemarāja (975–1050), *māyā* does not mean the absolute unreality of the world (as in Shankara) but its mistaken separation from Shiva. Thus all that matters is that, through one's guru, one recognises the Shiva who is present in all beings. Liberation (*moksha*) is recognising or 'remembering' one's identity with Shiva. Will and effort are important in the process of salvation so that although all exists through the will of Shiva, will and effort are necessary in order to 'recognise' Shiva.

Shaiva Siddhānta

The most important Shaiva tradition has been that of Shaiva Siddhānta which rose out of the poetry of the Nayanmars, the 28 Shaiva Agamas, the 14 Shaiva Siddhānta sūtras and, theoretically, the Veda. It is predominant in South India. By the thirteenth century it had developed a set of centres in a more settled organisational system modelled on the monasteries (*mathas*) of the Brahmins. Non-Brahmins could be gurus in this organisation, including Shūdras (who were not twice-born in the view of the three higher castes). Shaiva Siddhānta does not reject the caste system completely, neither does it reject the Veda fully. In practice Brahmins have a part to play in the movement. Umapati wrote, at the beginning of the fourteenth century, a basic summary of Shaiva Siddhānta ideas. In it he stresses that Shiva is love and he emphasises the centrality of the grace of Shiva. Out of love he comes to his people as a guru to save them from *samsāra* (the round of rebirths). Shiva himself is eternally free and incomparable, and human souls (jivas) are liberated by his compassionate grace.

Shaiva Siddhānta makes great play with the principles of *pati* (Shiva as Lord), *pasus* (souls that are bound) and *paśa* (the fetter binding the soul). The path of salvation begins with personal discipline, observing ritual and yoga. At a more advanced level a guru makes use of a variety of methods to take the soul away from its binding fetters into enlightenment, through the grace of Shiva, and into the personal salvation that brings release from rebirth. The road to salvation goes along four stages of devotion (*bhakti*). In the first place, service to the sanctuary and to others makes one a servant within the sphere of Shiva. Secondly serving the godhead, through offerings, makes one a child within the presence of Shiva. Thirdly, loving intelligent concern for the deity makes one a friend who can attain the form of Shiva. Finally, direct intuition of the deity brings about loving unity with Shiva. Mystical union with Shiva is combined with surrender to and dependence on Shiva. Immanence and transcendence are combined.

Alongside the rise of Shaiva Siddhānta in Tamilnadu arose a strong temple culture of great regional temples such as Cidambaram (where there is a famous Nataraja, or Dancing Shiva). These became centres of learning and political power. Thus, in an extraordinary fashion, Tamil Shaivism came to combine an association of royal power and temple authorities with popular devotion outside the control of Brahmins.

An important part of the Shiva tradition in most areas was the significance of the guru, and this was often more important than the significance of the textual background. In effect the grace of Shiva was mediated in practice through the teacher-pupil relationship and this opened up flexible possibilities for the exercise and transmission of 'faith in Shiva'. Thus Puranic and Vedic Shaivism existed side-by-side with non-Puranic and Tantric Shaivism.

Other Shiva Traditions: Gorakhnath Yogins

Amongst other Shiva traditions are a northern group known as the Gorakhnāth Yogins. Gorakhnāth himself (dates uncertain) was the outstanding guru of this tradition and he serves as a kind of patron godhead of the Gurkha people. Later Indian traditions consider him to be an incarnation of Shiva who, unlike Vishnu, does not normally send forth incarnations. The aim of the Gorakhnāth Yogins is to aim for the perfection of the body through yoga and to gain some control over death. The goal is to develop an immortal body through which a divine body may be built and thus progress to union with Shiva. As the inward discipline of bodily yoga is the only means to work towards this end, scriptures, elaborate doctrines, caste distinctions, rituals and other usual religious practices are viewed as superfluous. Nevertheless, the Gorakhnāth Yogins are reputed to have occult powers that enable them to perform miracles. They have a number of subsects and a number of monasteries, including one at Gorakhpur. The Gorakhnāth Yogins illustrate diversity within the Shiva tradition.

Vaishnavism

This is the largest branch of mainstream Hindu life and is present today in a multitude of Hindu temples, places of pilgrimage and festivals dedicated to Vishnu. The tradition is well-organised and is theologically well-led. It is more straightforward in traditions, rules, rituals and outlook than most of the Shaiva tradition. This makes it less spectacular than the Shaiva tradition but it is also probably stronger in character, norms and ethos.

Vishnu appeared in the Veda as a benevolent figure and this continued in the traditions that bear his name. In the Mahānārāyana Upanishad, Nārāyana, as an early form of Vishnu, is praised as dwelling within humans, as the highest Lord, as the one who pervades all and as the Absolute *Brahman*. In the two epics, the *Mahābhārata* and the *Rāmāyana*, Vishnu emerges as a supreme deity. The *Bhāgavata* movement, which appeared early, had begun to recede and two other movements developed in which Vishnu was prominent, namely the Pāncarātra and Vaikhānasa sects. In three of the key Pāncarātra texts, Vishnu manifests himself in the form of four *vyūhas* (emanations) which originate from him but are part of his true nature. Indeed five types of Vishnu's revealing of himself, which would be important in later Vaishnavism, begin to appear in Pāncarātra thought. They are his appearing in the form of the supreme deity, in the four emanations (*vyūhas*), in his incarnations, in his presence as the inner self in human beings, and in image form.

Whereas the Pāncarātras relate somewhat lightly to the Vedic tradition, the Vaikhānasa tradition was more Vedic and orthodox. Its stress was upon rituals and temple worship, processions and offerings, the importance of images and the centrality of attachment to and service of Vishnu. Although the *Vaikhānasasūtra* dates from around the third century CE, and there are indications that things were happening before the tenth century, it is difficult to pin down the life of Vaikhanasa communities in any detailed way. This situation of having access to the literature but not to the actuality of early Hindu traditions is a general problem. From the tenth century there were Vaikhānasa priests running temples in South India using the Sanskrit language, especially in the important temples of Tirupati and Kanchi. To this day Brahmin priests continue this tradition using Sanskrit solely.

Alvar movement

A strong devotional movement appeared in Tamilnadu between the seventh and ninth centuries. This was the Alvar movement, similar in sentiment to the Shaivite Nāyanmārs but focused on Vishnu. Founded on the writings and work of the Twelve Alvars they used the Tamil language, engaged with both men and women and reached out into all castes. The leading Alvars were sometimes taken to be 'further incarnations' of Vishnu in addition to the ten basic *avatāras*. Important Alvars included Nammalvar, from a low shudra caste, who dedicated his life to Vishnu in deep personal devotion. He composed verses aimed at deepening faith in Vishnu among the general populace. Another low-caste Alvar, Tiruppān, sang and played devotional verses aimed at helping ordinary people and against the Sanskrit ritual particularism of the Brahmins. Evan more unusual was Antāl, a female Alvar, who extolled devotional love for Vishnu. She became known as an incarnation of Shrī, the consort of Vishnu. At the other end of the social scale, King Kulacekara of Kerala abdicated his throne to immerse himself in serving Vishnu through writing poetry and devotional exercises.

The Alvars were a devotional movement of great fervour, attraction and persuasive influence who organised groups of people to tour, speak, dance, sing and debate in challenging ways. They were at least partly instrumental in deepening the demise of the Buddhist and Jain traditions in South India. Like the Nāyanmārs, with whom they were in some competition, their stress was upon personal experience of, in their case, Vishnu, ecstatic devotion to Vishnu, a sense of unworthiness requiring forgiveness, personal surrender to the deity, a desire to love others because of their love for Vishnu, and a sense that, under Vishnu, all people were equal. Their centre was at Srīrangam and it was there that the Srī Vaiṣṇava movement developed. It was to influence the Vishnu movement, rather like the Shaiva Siddhānta influenced the Shiva movement.

Rāmānuja

The preliminary leaders of the Srī Vaiṣṇavas were Nātamuni, who began to organise the Alvar poetry, and Yāmuna, who began to combine Vedanta philosophy with the ardent emotionalism of the Alvar heritage. The key figure was, however, Rāmānuja (trad. 1013–1137) who ranks, with Shankara, as one of the greatest Hindu philosophers. Rāmānuja was not only an eminent philosopher. He was also the head (*ācārya*) of the community and was deeply involved in the administrative leadership of the Shrirangam temple. Like Shankara he wrote famous commentaries on the Upanishads, the *Bhagavad Gītā* and the Vedantas sūtras, but he also defined the general organisation of the Srī Vaiṣṇavas.

Rāmānuja set out the daily rituals and services. These included the five daily acts and five sacraments of the tradition so as to draw attention to the outward side of worship, although his deeper concern was with inward devotion. Rāmānuja also outlined his stress upon *prapatti* (complete self-surrender to Vishnu) in three devotional works of great beauty. In addition he gave a new orientation to the administration of the Shrirangam temple. He reformed the conservative Vaikhānasa Brahmin-led leadership of the temple by adapting a more liberal and less exclusive pattern, giving ritual roles to members of the Shudra caste. Shudra servants were added to the Brahmin servants of the temple and Shudra ascetics were given a ritual place within the worship of the temple. His openness was shown in his daring proclamation of a secret text (*mantra*) from the temple roof to make it available to all. He was not able to ameliorate the lot of the Shūdras in wider society but he did give them a much higher status in religious life. He also emphasised the role of Shrī (Lakshmī) as 'queen of the world'. Hence the tradition is named the Srī Vaiṣṇavas wherein Shri was to be worshipped alongside her husband Vishnu.

Later groups dedicated to Vishnu

In the later development of the Srī Vaiṣṇava tradition it split into northern and southern schools. Each school had its own sets of leaders, harking back to Rāmānuja but they went in different directions. One difference of opinion was in regard to the grace of Vishnu and what surrender (*prapatti*) entailed. The northern school looked for some effort and works on the part of the believer. Vishnu's grace was not totally free. It required effort, striving and good *karma* on the part of the believer. The analogy is of a baby monkey who clings to its mother in the process of advancing in life. Vishnu's grace and one's own works were required. Colloquially, the southern school became known as the 'cat school': the cat picks up its kitten and carries it around, the kitten is totally dependent upon its mother. There is passive acceptance rather than active participation. Vishnu's grace is paramount and the believer is totally dependent on Vishnu. The northern school was more traditional, preferring Sanskrit to Tamil, preferring different *mantras* for different castes and supporting the notion that Shri, Vishnu's consort, could offer salvation equally with Vishnu. The southern school was less traditional, preferring Tamil to Sanskrit, preferring the same *mantra* for all castes and subordinating Shri to Vishnu.

Both schools of Srī Vaiṣṇavas have major temples, including the famous landmark temples of Tirupati in Andhra Pradesh and Shrirangam in Tamilnadu. They are visited by countless millions of devotees annually.

Krishna Tradition

As the history of Hindu religious communities developed, attention shifted towards the *avatāras* of Vishnu, and Rāma and Krishna emerge as major deities at the head of their own traditions. With the continued flowering of the devotional (*bhakti*) movement, especially in North India, allied to the increasing sense that Rāma and Krishna were divine as well as human, the stage was set for them to flourish. Madhva (c.1238–1317) followed the example of Rāmānuja in writing commentaries on Vedanta that established a new school of philosophy. Madhva's school became known as the Dvaita school of philosophy. Dvaita means duality or twoness. It indicates that *Brahman*, human beings and the world are not *advaita* (non-dual), as Shankara had suggested, nor were they *viśiṣṭādvaita* (partly non-dual) as Rāmānuja had suggested. They were completely dual and different.

Madhva settled at Udipi and became head of a temple dedicated to Krishna. He reformed its liturgy and converted an important court Brahmin to his Dvaita views. He wrote several important ritual works and devotional hymns. His faith was centred upon Krishna. Madhva appointed eight of his disciples as heads of monasteries in Udipi; each of these began a continuity of ordination that has lasted to the present day. Each of the eight heads served for two years as head of the prestigious Krishna monastery and this established a tradition that the two-yearly change of headship be publicly performed and praised. Although favouring Krishna, Madhva promoted religious harmony by venerating the other *avatāras* of Vishnu, together with Shiva and the five deities of the Smārta Brahmins. His movement still flourishes, especially in the south of India.

Nimbārka

Nimbārka (trad. 1125–62) also followed Rāmānuja's lead by setting up a new *Sampradāya* (tradition), which inaugurated a new Krishna movement, and by writing commentaries on Vedanta, which began a new school of philosophy. It seems likely that he lived longer than is traditionally assumed. His school of Vedanta was named dvaitadvaita and it claimed that *Brahman*, human beings and the world were both different and non-different from each other.

Little is known about the actual work of Nimbārka and the first twenty-eight preceptors of the tradition, but the twenty-ninth leader, Keshava Kashmiri Bhatta (b. 1479), was an important figure. He lived in Braj, a centre associated with Krishna's own life, and he revived the Nimbārka community and it began to spread more widely. He wrote devotional hymns, consolidated the ritual of the movement and strengthened the doctrine of the community. His successor Shrī Bhatta wrote in the language of the Braj area and furthered the theme of divine-human love between Krishna and Radhā that became paramount. The Nimbārka tradition developed twelve branches in twelve monasteries and it strengthened its lay leadership, which had been subject to the ascetic values of its leaders. Both Madhva and Nimbarka had been ascetics themselves. Household preceptors became more prominent and they were later called Gosvāmins. Their work and their wealth became important in the development of the Nimbārka tradition which remains especially strong in the Mathura–Braj area.

Vallabha

Vallabha (1479–1531) became the fourth Vaishnava leader to found a new movement and to introduce a new form of Vedanta philosophy. Vaishnava thinkers claim that Vallabha founded a new movement within a sect already founded by Vishnuswāmi in the fifteenth century that became known as the Vallabha Sampradāya. Unusually, he married and had two sons. He stressed the importance of being a householder rather than a renouncer. On pilgrimage around India in 1494 he had a vision of Krishna, and he was thought to have been taught directly by Krishna, whose mouthpiece he was. Philosophically Vallabha professed Śuddhādvaita, '*pure advaita*'.

The inference was that Shankara's *advaita* had not been pure non-dualism because of his stress upon illusion (*māyā*). For Vallabha the world was real and was *Brahman*. Humans and the material world had no independent being and were part of *Brahman* and one with *Brahman*. *Brahman* was equivalent to Krishna and at the heart of Vallabha's thought was a stress upon the absolute grace of Krishna. This grace was uncaused and pure (*puṣṭi*), and the way of puṣṭi was open to all people including women, outcastes, Muslims and also the 'fallen' who were considered to be outside the boundaries of salvation. Insofar as Vallabha's favourite texts were the *Bhāgavata Purāna* and the *Bhagavad Gītā*, elements of emotional attachment and affection (*prema*) could also have a part in the whole experience of devotion (*bhakti*). Eighty-four Sanskrit writings are ascribed to Vallabha, and his tradition continued this practice of voluminous writing both in Sanskrit and devotionally in Braj. In addition to traditional worship his tradition focused on service (*seva*) to Krishna. This included singing hymns (*kirtanas*), giving money to the temples of the movement, continual contemplation of Krishna and re-enacting the games (*līlā*) of Krishna.

The Vallabha Sampradāya remains strong, especially in the Braj and Gujarat areas. It is also present in America with the followers of Guru Maharaj Ji who traces his own ancestry back to one of the original followers of Vallabha.

Chaitanya movement

Krishna Chaitanya (1486–1533) lived in Bengal at the same time as Vallabha was alive. Although his movement is nominally linked to the Madhva tradition, Krishna Chaitanya is important in his own right. His movement was unique in its stress upon ecstatic love for Krishna, and its extreme emotionalism. Part of it is now known as the Hare Krishna Movement. Feelings and fervent love for Krishna lie at the heart of Chaitanya's message and work. He was not afraid to express his emotion in tears, sobbing language and expressive body movements. He only wrote one eight-verse work that is known to us.

Brought up in a traditional Bengali Vaishnava Brahmanical family, he remarried on the death of his first wife. At the age of twenty-two he was initiated into a mystical regime and returned to his home town in Bengal where he superintended singing processions in the streets, organised the regular singing of Kirtanas (devotional songs), and engaged in ecstatic dancing. Initiated again into renunciation, when he received the name Chaitanya, he spent many years in pilgrimage before retiring to Puri. From there he made a number of visits to Vrindaban and other Krishna places which he helped to identify and rehabilitate. The final part of his life was spent in Puri where he occupied himself in devotion to Lord Jaggarnath in the temple at Puri. Much of this closing period was spent in ecstasy involving the grace of Krishna inducing in his soul an experience of divine love (*prema*) through an intoxicating sense of aesthetic emotion (*rasa*).

After Chaitanya's death a group of his followers assembled around his companion Nityānanda in his home town in Bengal, while another group developed in Vrindaban around six of his disciples who became known as Goswāmins. Other smaller groups emerged elsewhere. The six Goswāmins were the main writers of the tradition and their writings include doctrinal and ritual material, as well as devotional verses in Bengali, and also Sanskrit biographies, drama and poetry.

Through Chaitanya other groups appeared. The Rādhāvallabhis stressed the eternal union of Rādhā and Krishna and this formed the basis of their devotion. The Bengali Vaishnava Sahajiyās were secretive and their voluminous literary output was not made available to others. This included many Tantras written in Bengali in an esoteric kind of language between the seventeenth and nineteenth centuries. They held the notion that Chaitanya had been born as Rādhā and Krishna in a single body and that, through their worship, they could realise the united presence of Rādhā and Krishna in their own being.

From the sixteenth century the main Chaitanya Movement, also known as Gaudīya Vaisnavism, has been a strong part of the Hindu tradition in India. It developed when the Muslims were at the height of their powers and it survived later persecution by Aurangzeb. Chaitanya and his early successors rediscovered the main Krishna sites and built temples in key places such as Vrindaban. The tradition invigorated nineteenth-century Indian renewal movements, and during that century it inaugurated new centres in many of the key cities. Kedernath Datta (1838–1914), a magistrate in British service, rediscovered and began to renew his own Chaitanya tradition. He established a printing press and wrote a hundred books. It was he who founded a branch of the movement named the International Society for Krishna Consciousness, popularly known as the Hare Krishnas. His successor, A. C. Bhaktivedanta Swami spread the Krishna message among English-speaking people. His visit to New York in 1965, at the age of seventy, stimulated the growth of the Hare Krishnas in the world.

Rāma Tradition

Another development, arising out of the 'sharing of *bhakti*' between Hindus and Muslims, is the rise of Rāma as a devotional deity 'without attributes' who could nevertheless be devoutly worshipped. Indeed the word 'Rāma' is a general name for God in various parts of North India.

Rāmānanda

The emergence of Rāma as a divine figure, and as the leading deity within a particular tradition, begins with Rāmānanda, whose dates are uncertain and whose historicity is not completely clear. By tradition he was born in 1299 and had been a successor to Rāmānuja. He subsequently formed a new tradition called the Rāmānandins who worshipped Rāma and Sītā as a combined deity. Three things stand out in his work. First, he was North Indian and it was from this time that devotional (*bhakti*) worship of Rāma became popular in North India. Secondly, he used Hindi rather than Sanskrit. It was from this time that Hindi became a favoured religious language in North India. Thirdly, he went beyond caste in his religious dealings. Tradition has it that his important followers included a Brahmin, a Rajput, a woman, a barber named Sen, a leatherworker named Raidās, a butcher named Dhana and a weaver named Kabīr. His stress upon *bhakti* (devotion), albeit directed towards Rāma, was in continuity with a *bhakti* tradition dating back to the Nāyanmārs and Alvars from the sixth century, in Tamil-speaking areas. It also continued with Basava and others from the tenth century in the Kannada-speaking areas, then with Jnaneśvar and the Vārkarī Movement from the thirteenth century in the Marathi-speaking areas, and with Rāmānanda in the Hindi-speaking areas.

The history of the movement named after Rāmānanda, namely the Rāmānandins, is mysterious and interesting. It probably arose in the fifteenth century and grew in the following two centuries. It counted among its membership women, members of all castes (including outcastes) and, possibly, Muslims too. Thereafter its membership became more and more restrictive until recently its membership has comprised mainly men. At the heart of the movement are a body of ascetic renouncers pledged to the service of Rāma. They are supported by a larger group of lay disciples who remain as householders and who are initiated by the ascetics who are their gurus. Among the Rāmānandin renouncers are two main groups. The 'devotionalist' Rāmānandins stress devotion to Rāma as the key to liberation and mainly stay in one place. The 'renouncer' Rāmānandins practice renunciation as the key to liberation but whilst one group remains sedentary another body wanders around. Within this wandering group there are 'perpetually wandering' total renouncers who travel continually. At the great twelve-yearly Khumba Mela in Allahabad, the large gathering of Rāmānandin ascetics vies with the Shaiva Dashanami ascetics in numbers and in public approbation.

The behaviour of the Rāmānandins (and Dashanamis) raises four fascinating issues. First, there is no complete separation between those sedentary devotees who stay in society and may recognise some caste differences and the ascetics who wander and do not emphasise caste differences. Second, Hindu traditions are not confined to those living in caste society; renouncers can belong to a tradition even though they have 'renounced' society. Third, not all renouncers are separate individualists but they have their own access to 'fellowship'. Finally, movements may change from being open, casteless and free to being restricted, or the other way round.

Tulsīdās

Among the other small Rāma traditions the name of Tulsīdās should be mentioned also. Tulsīdās (*c.*1543–1623) wrote the glorious *Rāmacharitamānas* (Lake of the Acts of Rāma) that reinterprets the Rāma story into Hindi in a fuller way than Kamban had reinterpreted the Rāma story into Tamil seven hundred years before. Tulsīdās unites a number of seemingly contradictory themes in his great work. First he picks up the question posed at the start of the original epic *Rāmāyana* (I.1.2–4):

> Who is there in this world today who is great and heroic, knows dharma and duty, speaks the truth and is firm in his vows? Who is endowed with good conduct, helpful to all creatures, learned, able, handsome, self-controlled, slow to anger, wise, free from jealousy and – when stimulated to wrath – can terrify the gods in battle?

The answer, of course, is the human Rāma whose exemplary life is so well portrayed in all its qualities by Tulsīdās. However, at a deeper level Rāma is also seen as an *avatāra* of Vishnu, later he is seen as Vishnu in all his fullness and, finally, he is seen to transcend Vishnu. More than this, Rāma is seen to be the ultimate devotional Lord who is the object of *bhakti* (devotion). At a deeper level still Rāma is seen to be *Brahman*, Absolute Reality. Tulsīdās offers deeper and deeper layers of the Rāma symbol until Rāma is seen as man and deity in all their fullness. Because of this Tulsīdās is revered by followers of Rāma in their different movements. He transcends them all with his more universal appeal.

Kabīr

Another important religious movement related to Rāma centres around the figure of Kabīr (1398–1518?). Kabīr takes his place amongst a group known as the Sants, who came from a variety of backgrounds including Muslims and lower castes. They worshipped the godhead directly, not through an intermediary deity such as Rāma. Yet their name for their godhead, who was *nirguna* (beyond attributes), remained Rāma (which has, in many parts of North India, become synonymous with God). Tulsīdās had ventured some way in this direction whilst maintaining devotion to the incarnate Rāma. Kabīr was born into a Muslim community living near Varanasi, and he was influenced by Sufi Islam, Vaishnava Hinduism, and the Gorakhnāth yogi tradition. He rejected the outward features of the Muslim and Hindu paths whether they be Muslim circumcision and their five pillars, or Hindu caste symbols and pilgrimage practices. Although his view of the deity pictured Rāma as *nirguna*, without attributes and without personal incarnate characteristics, nevertheless that deity could be known and indeed gloriously experienced in one's heart by love, by intense personal search and even by suffering. The goal for Kabīr was an intense union with the Supreme *Brahman* named Rāma via the path of love and through the grace of the attributeless godhead. This deep devotional approach was intense and personal – *bhakti* in all but name. A similar approach would also be adopted by Guru Nanak whose movement eventually became the Sikh tradition. Although there is a Kabīrpanthi movement, taking its name from Kabīr, the general Sant tradition remains widespread, especially in North India.

An important modern devotional movement in succession to Kabīr is the Swaminarayan tradition dating back to Sahānand Swāmī who was born in 1781. He is now worshipped as Swaminarayan in Gujarat which has remained central to the tradition. As a number of Gujaratis have migrated to East Africa, Britain and the United States, the Swaminarayans have played an important part in diaspora Hinduism. Unlike the Hare Krishnas, the Swaminarayans have not acted as an evangelising agency outside India but rather as a Hindu service agency for Hindus, and especially Gujaratis. Swaminarayan is seen as the fullest manifestation of the eternal Narayan (Vishnu) and as 'the first of the neo-Hindu saints' (Williams, 1984), but he is unique and has been 'deified' more than the medieval Sants and the neo-Hindu reformers.

Religious Traditions, Authority and Caste

Some general points are worth raising in relation to Hindu religious traditions. First, whilst India has been ruled mainly by non-Hindus, Hindu rulers have been important in helping, financing, or sustaining Hindu religious traditions. Argument has raged as to whether the highest caste of priests (brahmins) have been more or less important than the second caste of kings or rulers (Kshatriyas) in maintaining Hindu sects (*Sampradāyas*). The answer is that both have played their parts. Although there has been no Hindu 'state religion', and despite the functional background of the Brahmins, which has given them more regular contact with religious leadership, the support given by rulers to religious temples, festivals and ceremonies has been important. It remains so today even in an independent India where the original native states have disappeared. For example, the Maharajah of Banaras still plays an important part in the Rāmlīlā festival in that city.

Secondly, local families build up relationships with local temples and local religious traditions that are passed on down the generations. Change is important but it occurs against a background of continuity in religion. Thirdly, caste differences do matter. Small village deities, for example, are mainly served by non-Brahmin priests. However, *bhakti* religion is also important, and the lower castes have had their part to play in *bhakti* worship and propagation. Fourthly, although there may be some rivalry between Hindu traditions there has, in the main, been tolerance within the tradition as a whole, albeit punctuated occasionally by the protests of women and outcastes.

6

Social and Political life

The Hindu religious tradition has a strong involvement in social and political life in India. It would be equally true to say that social and political matters have influenced the Hindu religious tradition deeply. As well as being a religious tradition, the Hindu tradition has also functioned as a way of life. This chapter examines seven aspects of social and political life: the caste system; the role of householders; the role of renouncers; the role of women; the role of outcastes; the political background; and the implications of the rise of secularisation and modern capitalism.

The Caste System

It is clear that the caste system has had a deep effect upon Hindu life. Not only has it affected Hindus. It has also affected people of non-Hindu traditions, many of whom originated within a caste background and remained to some extent affected by it. The word for caste in its widest sense is *varna*, which means colour. The lower castes are darker in colour and the higher castes are lighter in colour. There is thus a darkening of colour in the caste system whereby the Brahmins are lighter-skinned at one end of the spectrum, and the Shūdras are darker-skinned at the other end of the spectrum. This also affects people who move into other religious traditions. For example, Christians who were formerly Brahmins, and Christians who were formerly Shūdras, differ in colour and have to adjust to their new situation. It is a fact of life in India that one can tell by looking at people roughly what their background is. Thus sadly, in riots such as those accompanying the partition of India, it was possible to tell what religion and also what caste people belonged to. There was nowhere to hide.

There have been a number of attempts to underplay, to question, and to lampoon the hierarchical inequality and even the existence of the caste system. As we will also see it differs, in some degree, from region to region. However, the concepts of *varna* and, more importantly, *jāti* lie at the heart of the caste system and they form an ideal core around which the complexity of detail and difference can then be erected.

The notion of the caste system first emerges in *Rig Veda* X.90.11–12, in a passage wherein the gods created the world and its contents by sacrificing the primeval Man (*puruśa*). The passage reads:

> When they divided the Man, into how many parts did they apportion him? What do they call his mouth, his two arms and thighs and feet? His mouth became the Brahmin, his arms were made into the Warrior, his thighs the People, and from his feet the Servants were born.

Thus the four *varnas* are the Brahmins who represent priesthood and learning, the Kshatriyas who represent the warriors and kings, who protect the people, the Vaishyas who represent the people who engage in agriculture, farming and trade, and the Shūdras who represent the servants who look after and serve the others. The Brahmins fulfil the function of the mouth, the Kshatriyas fulfil the function of the arms, the Vaishyas fulfil the function of the thighs, and the Shūdras fulfil the function of the feet. The model is clearly a hierarchy but it is a complementary hierarchy and unity, wherein the different elements sustain one another. It was later elaborated in the Sanskrit *Dharma Shashtra* literature, and worked out in practice in different settings.

In practice the key to the caste system are the sub-castes, or *jātis*. There are a great number of these in each *varna*, and in practice there is a hierarchy within each set so that only certain *jātis* can marry and eat with each other. Not all Brahmins, Kshatriyas, Vaishyas or Shūdras can marry or eat together. Those privileges are confined to a limited number of *jātis* within each *varna*. This system remains strong at the level of India's half-million villages although it is weakening somewhat in the towns and cities, although it still remains influential. Thus within a village setting members of a *jāti* tend to share clusters of houses, temples, eating arrangements, wells and so on. A Hindu inherits a *jāti*, is born into a *jāti*, marries within a *jāti* normally through an arranged marriage, has children within a *jāti*, and dies within a *jāti*.

To some extent *jātis* engage in specific occupations such as cooks, carpenters, nightwatchmen and so on, although the nature of the modern world, even in the villages, is modifying this practice. In any event there is a hierarchy of *jātis* and indeed of *varnas*. Everyone knows roughly how *jātis* are ranked within each area, with the Brahmins at the top and the untouchable Dalits, who are *avarna* (without caste) at the bottom. In North India the Brahmin, Kshatriya, Vaishya, Shudra and Dalit distinctions remain, together with the many *jātis* within each of them. In South India there is a tendency to separate out the Brahmins and the Dalits but to draw the other three middle castes more closely together, sometimes under the title of Shūdras.

Clearly there have been changes in the system over long centuries. Particular *jātis* have elevated themselves through economic means, through disputing status, through propaganda, through moving, through changing religion, and so on. But on the whole, over such a long period of time, the system has remained strong, especially in the villages. Even in the towns newspaper matchmaking columns tend to stress the *varna* and/or *jāti* background of the people seeking marriage partners.

The strength of the caste system has been enhanced by another principle emphasised by Dumont (1980) in his classical work entitled *Homo Hierarchicus: The Caste System and its Implications*. According to Dumont, in addition to the distinctions already outlined that fit *varnas* and *jātis* into hierarchies, another must be added. This distinction takes caste hierarchical divides beyond the kind of class distinctions found in eighteenth-century Britain or in the Ancien Regime in Europe, by stressing the opposition between purity and pollution. Caste difference, according to this classification, goes beyond class differences into this other realm of ritual purity and pollution. The Brahmins are the highest and purest *varna*, and the Dalits are the lowest, in that they are outside *varna* and are impure altogether. The other *varnas* rank in between. Pollution occurs in different ways. It occurs through bodily contact of one sort or another, with menstrual cycles, through birth and death, through emissions such as faeces, urine and saliva, and through contact with night-soil, dirty clothes, unswept rooms and so on. Thus marriage and sex have to function within the correct set of *jātis* in the correct *varna*. Polluting jobs such as laundering and sweeping are done by people of lower castes so that the blood of people of higher castes can remain 'pure'. Equally menstrual activity among older women makes them more 'impure' than men or pre-menstrual virgins, and therefore women are more polluting than men. They will thus often live semi-separately while menstruating, during which time they will also avoid going to the temple and therefore 'polluting' the gods. Furthermore, untouchable Dalits were prohibited from entering many temples before the post-Independence freedom-of-temple-entry legislation and even now they are kept out of some temples in many villages. Indeed in situations of menstruation, birth and death, many Hindus will absent themselves anyway. As cities grow and villages decline, things are changing. It is also true to say that Dumont's thesis suffers from exaggeration and other matters are important in discussing caste. Nevertheless, there is at least an element of truth in the notion that purity and pollution has relevance in any discussion of caste.

The Householder System

Within the totality of the caste system there are not only the four *varnas* that we have just examined, but also the four stages of life (*ashramas*). The first three of these stages centre upon this world and life within it. The last stage is that of renouncing the world (*sannyāsa*), abandoning the ordinary life of the householder in order to seek ultimate freedom and salvation. It involves leaving the household and living a life of renunciation. This raises the question of whether the Hindu tradition has the obligation of stressing this world and the life of the householder, or should it see this world and any concentration on it as a matter of secondary importance in a cosmology that involves rebirth?

Most of the sacraments of life are central to householder existence. The first three stages of life focus upon childhood and youth, upon marriage, work and having children, and upon semi-retirement. A child is conceived within the married householder stage, is eventually born into that situation and is named and nurtured in the household. After study, he or she will marry and, hopefully, conceive mainly male children. The attempt of Indira Gandhi's elder son to limit families by forceful methods, as happened in China, was a resounding failure. The four stages of life relate mainly to men. There are sixteen possible rituals in the life of a Hindu man lasting from pre-birth to death. Most of these rituals are less relevant to the renouncer, after renunciation, but they are very relevant to the householder. Most religious rituals assume a mainly householder focus in connection with temple and household worship in the settled, householder, stage.

Moreover, the *Dharmaśāstra* literature concentrates on the various demands of a householder's life. The householder state is eulogised as being the key to Hindu life. In one of his essays Louis Dumont (1980) argues that the dialogue between the renouncer and the householder is a key element in trying to understand the Hindu tradition, are they complementary or opposed?

The *Bhagavad Gītā* raises another perspective with its view that there are three ways of living and three kinds of spirituality. They are the way of knowledge, the way of devotion and the way of doing one's duty without thought of reward. The questions remain. What is one's duty? What is one's *dharma*? Is there a different *dharma* at each stage of life and do all the four stages have their own *dharma*? Is there a *dharma* of renunciation in the fourth stage of life that completes the other three *dharmas*? Or are the householder's position and the renouncer's position in opposition?

In practice Hindu households, especially at village level, are often 'joint' households. A family is usually extended beyond the nuclear mother, father and children living in one house. There will often be separate rooms in a large house, or a series of houses in a compound. A number of linked households may live in these separate rooms or houses. Kinship links hold households together. On marriage a bride moves into the house of her husband. She becomes the youngest wife and takes a full part, sometimes an overfull part, in the work and life of the family. The linked families are of linked *jātis* so that they can intermarry and eat together. They will share rituals, social gatherings and, perhaps, economic matters. They will bring up children together. They will share the same deity or deities at home and in the temple. They will share birth, initiation, marriage and death rituals. Hindu households are full of people and living alone is somewhat unusual. Living as a nuclear family can be even more unusual, particularly at village level. In the household the elderly are surrounded by others. They are cared for and respected. The partial exceptions to this milieu of domesticity are bachelors, childless widowers and, especially, widows, who are in the house but not fully in the household

The Renouncer System

The renouncer tradition appears to fly in the face of the householder tradition. Renouncing involves abandoning the comfort and conviviality of the household for a different ethos and a different ethic. It also involves a different goal, namely that of release from the round of rebirths (*moksha*). Sensuality (*kāma*), the work ethic (*artha*), and family society (*dharma*) are irrelevant to the renouncer. The sacred thread, marriage and family have less meaning. His (and occasionally her) lifestyle and ultimate aims seem to be an implicit threat to the *raison d'etre* of the householder. Renouncers seem to take more seriously the ultimate religious aim of the Hindu tradition that, as it were, gloriously supersedes the slow and reasonably amiable building up of merit within the ongoing round of rebirths. Renunciation can take many forms.

The first type of renunciation is at the fourth stage of life, once the worldly duties of a young person, a married person and a semi-retired person have been fulfilled. Undoubtedly, there is greater opportunity for men, less commonly for women, to consider the possibility of semi-retirement and then, mainly for men, there is the option of renunciation. The renouncer may then go away from home on a journey of pilgrimage or the renouncer may retire to an ashram or place of meditation, or he may stay near home to study or meditate and be looked after by his family.

A second form of renunciation may occur as a result of sorrow in life. A good example of this is the story of Ram Kumar Das (see pp. 12–13).

Adversity led him into a satisfying renounced life involving long meditation each day and giving help to other people.

Some of the religious traditions of India were founded by renouncers. These were people of spiritual vision who were willing to spend their lives as renouncers in order to reform or build up new or renewed traditions. A number of the founders of Shaiva and Vaishnava movements were renouncers. Shankara was a renouncer, and renunciation plays an important role in the Advaita Vedanta view of liberation. The way of knowledge was supreme according to Shankara's Advaita. Therefore the way of karmic involvement in the world, and even the way of devotion (*bhakti*), gave to the world and to human beings a sense of reality that was illusory. Ultimately there was no difference between *Brahman* and the *ātman* of humans and thus emphasis on involvement in the world through one's actions (*karma*), or even through one's devotion, was to miss the point. Knowledge and spirituality are the key and they involve a clear element of renunciation.

It is helpful to recollect that it was early on in the history of the Hindu tradition that renunciation arose as an option, as the Upanishads succeeded the earlier Vedic texts and gave rise to a fourth aim of life (*moksha*) and a fourth stage of life. There is evidence that, from that early period, four possibilities were open to young adults who had taken the sacred thread and finished their time of study. One option was to continue and to make study a vocation throughout life. This was not direct renunciation but it rejected the path of marriage and becoming a householder. The second choice was to become a householder, by far the favourite option. A third way was to disappear to live a solitary existence as a hermit. As the *Apastamba Dharmasūtra* (II.21.2) puts it: 'he should live as a silent sage with a single fire, but without house, shelter, or protection. Let him speak only when he is engaged in private Vedic meditation. Clothes made of materials from the wild are prescribed for him.' This option became much less common. Finally, a person might become a renouncer in the form of a peripatetic ascetic. An adjoining passage in the *Apastamba Dharmasūtra* reads: 'abandoning truth and falsehood, pleasure and pain, the Vedas, this world and the next, he should seek the *ātman*. When he gains insight, he attains bliss.'

It is helpful to remember that, at the period of the Upanishads, the Buddhist and Jain traditions were developing in India. Both Gautama Buddha and the Jain Mahavira renounced the world. The Buddha left his family in his search for enlightenment. The early Buddhist tradition saw individual wanderers gather during the monsoon season and this developed as the monastic movement where Buddhist monks could live together continuously. Monasteries appear much later in the Hindu tradition. Thus young

Hindus could continue in lifelong study, get married, become hermits or become wandering ascetics. The notion of the fourth stage of life was a way of placing the fourth renouncer choice into institutional form within the totality of the caste system.

Another way of renouncing, more common in recent times, is to become a charismatic Guru. Some renouncers effectively become Gurus who wander around, and they may wander for many years. Other Gurus settle in dwellings of their own and are visited by those attracted to them by their wisdom and saintliness. Examples include Ramakrishna, Ramana Maharshi and Sri Anandamayi Ma (see p. 13). Ramana Maharshi (1879–1950) was born in Tirukuli in the Madurai area. Following a religious experience in 1896, aged seventeen, he was attracted to the holy mountain of Arunachala about a hundred miles from Madras. He remained there until death. At first he lived in caves but then he allowed devotees to establish an ashram at the foot of the mountain. His search for self-knowledge through integration of personality in the 'cave of the heart', humbly and spiritually presented, was attractive to individual seekers and to large groups of visitors. Because of the appealing nature of their spirituality such renouncing gurus become spiritual 'celebrities', sometimes against their own inclinations, who are visited by growing numbers of admirers. They have considerable influence.

A final class of renouncer are those who follow a 'renouncer tradition'. An example in the Vaishnava fold is the Rāmānandins (see pp. 69–70). They have a sedentary householder section that is the most numerous. There are also renouncer sections within many different organisations. These include the regiments and divisions that participate in great pilgrimage festivals, such as the Kumbha Mela in Allahabad, according to their own banners and their own hierarchies. This renouncer section contains many different groups including wandering ascetics, militant ascetics, ascetics who smear themselves with ashes and more sedentary ascetics. They each have their own forms of initiation.

Within the Shaiva fold, the Dashanamis claim to have been founded by Shankara. Dashanami means 'ten names' and there are ten differently named sections of the Shaivite Dashanami ascetics. In some ways the Rāmānandins followed the organisational model of the Dashanamis. One group of Dashanamis, the Dandis, carry special sticks (*dandas*); they are male and include distinguished scholars. A second group, the Paramahamsas, do not carry sticks and allow women into their order. Whilst a third group, the Nagas, appear naked (as the name suggests) at great festivals and have organised regiments with several branches, some of whom are advocates of Hindu nationalism.

Another renouncer tradition, the Aghoris, was refounded by Kina Rāma in the eighteenth century. It dates back to the early Shiva groups such as the Kāpālikas who renounced the world through asceticism followed by anarchic behaviour. The Aghoris are said to drink alcohol and urine, to eat excrement, to smoke hash and to perform other very unusual acts. They do not follow the first three phases of householder life, in the pattern of renouncers who enter the fourth stage of life, and they also react against all the standards of householder life in their attempts to 'overcome' the worldly life of householders.

In response to the question 'is it more important to play a creative role in the world by being involved in it as a householder or to renounce the world to concentrate on oneself?', the Hindu tradition attempts to hold together these worldly and other-worldly aims and lifestyles. There are countless different types of renouncers. Renouncers range from some of the greatest saints on the face of the earth, an example to householders of the ultimate values of Hinduism, to those rebels against householder values who overturn the householder ethos in an exaggerated way. Some operate as individuals and some work in groups. Some wait until the fourth stage of life and others become renouncers earlier. Some become leaders of Hindu religious traditions and some prefer to live on their own in more or less solitary detachment. In very different ways they make the point that householder life is not the end of the journey. The ultimate aim lies beyond it. Even if householders live within the world, nevertheless their ultimate home, vision and destiny lies beyond the world.

The Role of Women

At times women have played a serious role in the Hindu tradition. Sri Anandamayi Ma earned profound respect as a modern woman guru-saint (see p. 13) and there are other such women in the contemporary world. The work of women within some of the devotional traditions has been insightful, including the Tamil Shudra saint Antāl, and the Rajput *bhakti* Princess Mīrābāī. In recent times India has had a woman Prime Minister, Indira Gandhi, whilst Sonia Gandhi is the influential widow of another Prime Minister. The important state of Uttar Pradesh has elected a female Dalit Chief Minister, Ms Mayawati.

Hindu goddesses have been very important from the caring Lakshmī to the threatening Kali. Long before a female theology was known in the Christian and other traditions, goddesses were present in the Hindu tradition. In modern times India has sometimes been symbolised as a Goddess – as *Tamilttāy* (Mother Tamil) and Bharat Mātā (Mother India). This modern sense reinterpreted a varied and deep sense of Devi, the Goddess, that had been built over many centuries in worship, in ritual, in literature and in Hindu perception. Before that the worship of grāmadevatās, village goddesses, probably dates back thousands of years to a time when the pre-Aryan tribes had a matriarchal society.

There lies a paradox in Hindu musings on femininity. At the religious level of deity the Goddess is very important, even though she is served mainly by male priests, but at the worldly level of the caste system women are subordinate to men.

Women deities may, at one level, be seen as consorts of deities. For example, Srī (or Lakshmī) is the gentle consort of Vishnu whilst Pārvatī is the gentle consort of Shiva. As such, the male and female deities may be worshipped jointly. On her own, Devi (the Goddess) may take the more ferocious form of Durga, who slays the demon buffalo, or the horrific-looking black Kali with her necklace of skulls. Nevertheless, the great mystic Ramakrishna, who was a priest at the temple of Kali in Calcutta, saw Kali as a goddess of love. Exclusive devotees of Devi are known as Śāktas and use the Tantras as their sacred texts. In the Śākta tradition, Devi, the great Goddess, becomes the active agent in the cosmos. Without her the male deity, whoever he may be, can do nothing. She is an actual divine person and a metaphysical principle or force. Thus, Devi can be seen in the Śākta community as the superior consort of a male deity who is separate from that male deity.

Returning to reality, in social terms women have been seen as inferior to men within the caste system and there is still a tendency for that to be the case. In the system of Hindu law known as the *Manusmriti*, divine sanction was given to the caste system. According to it, women are not within the orbit of the Veda which applies to men only. Women are not allowed to be initiated or to receive the sacred thread. They pollute through menstruation, they are dependent on men and their job is to bear children, especially sons. A woman's husband is her 'god'. He will remain so until death and, after his death, according to Śākta there is no possibility of remarriage. During the period of Muslim rule, the caste system became more rigid, and came to include the practice of satī, the burning to death of a widow on the funeral pyre of her husband.

The rise of the various *bhakti* devotional groups allowed women more opportunity to take part in worship and even to be active in the temple. There was more flexibility for women in the lower castes. However, whilst there might be greater freedom within the religious sphere, it was harder to achieve an equal freedom in everyday life. The female equality in the religious sphere was not available in everyday life.

The rise of neo-Hinduism and the Hindu reform movements of the nineteenth century allied with pressure from the British Raj, the rise of women's reform movements and a greater awareness of the wider world stimulated a desire for change. The British presence led to the rise of a larger middle class, with a more enlightened outlook. English language schools promoted wider ideas, although they were reserved mainly for men. There was a crisis of conscience, and to some extent there still is. The caste system varies according to region, according to severity, according to language, and according to politics. Yet, in spite of all its defects, it has buttressed a civilisation for something like four millennia. If it were to be reformed, what kind of reform should it be? How should it be administered, and by whom?

During the latter nineteenth and early twentieth century change came slowly. Women's education improved. For some women reformers, change was too slow, and women such as Pandita Ramabai (1858–1922) converted to Christianity in order to increase teacher training, medical education for women and help for widows. Others, such as Sarojini Naidu (1879–1926), remained within the Hindu fold and added to the call for more female education and began to point to the example of the Hindu goddesses. Foreigners such as Annie Besant, who had led the Theosophical Society in London, helped to found Banaras Hindu University and, like Sarojini Naidu, became leader of the Indian National Congress. Her spirited defence of Hinduism, women's rights and Hindu advancement in general was valuable and the example of women becoming leaders of the Indian National Congress was very helpful.

The work of Mahatma Gandhi was also helpful. Women were members of his ashrams and included women from religions other than Hinduism. Women joined in the civil disobedience movement alongside men to work for home rule and independence for India. They became involved in spinning cotton, in basic education, in non-violent protests and in other elements in Gandhi's campaign. This brought women together, across caste, and brought them into greater contact with men. Both British and Indians became aware that women were ready to be arrested, to picket, to face danger and to share comradeship in pursuit of a common aim.

A most striking example is the Brahmā Kumari movement which emerged in the late 1930s. Their development as a women's movement was facilitated by a millionaire diamond merchant named Dada Lekhraj. He lived in Hyderabad in Sind. He took the name of Brahmā Baba and his vivid spiritual experiences gave rise eventually to the Brahmā Kumaris Spiritual University led by women. Some young women refused sexual intercourse in marriage, others refused marriage and they met together in fellowship.

This led to persecution for they were in effect rejecting the caste system and Hindu *dharma*. They left Hyderabad and took refuge in Karachi where they spent the Second World War. At the end of the war they moved to Mount Abu in Rajasthan, which became their headquarters. They established centres around India and eventually in almost ninety countries of the world. They number almost a million. Their leadership is female, most of the leaders of their centres around the world are female and their spirituality has a female resonance. They are now better understood by the Hindu tradition which they had dramatically deserted.

However, for most women such a radical stance was neither an option nor a desire. The Independence of India brought further help to women. Theoretical equality was enshrined in the Constitution of 1950. Further reform of dowry arrangements, the right to divorce, better inheritance laws and improved marriage legislation brought some success, but further reform is needed. Although a law prohibiting dowries was passed in 1961 the situation is still unsatisfactory. Dowries remain central to many Hindu marriages and amounts are rising. The corollary is that the sense that sons are more desirable than daughters remains. To provide a large money dowry to marry off a daughter may be crippling for Hindu families who are already poor. Sons seem to represent wealth and daughters seem to represent money problems. Furthermore, the practice of requesting a dowry appears to be growing among lower castes as well as upper castes. Sons have traditionally been important as worship leaders, as workers and as persons who light the funeral pyres at the death of fathers. A daughter cannot fully perform these functions and she also needs to have a dowry spent on her. She may even be harmed or her family blackmailed if the dowry is not enough. The temptation is for women to take a pregnancy test and to abort if the foetus is female. There is evidence to show that this happens. Not all families think in this way but enough do to give cause for concern.

Progress has been made in bettering the rights of women. More women are educated and are able and ready to debate important issues. They question arranged marriages, domestic abuse and rape and oppose satī, which still happens very occasionally. Other issues include interfaith collaboration, climate change, employment protection and civil rights in general. New bodies are being set up, new journals are being published and new working parties are being formed to push these matters ahead.

Personal stories

For many women the opportunity of improved status still does not exist. A friend shared with me the story of his first wife, with whom he had contracted an arranged marriage when she was twelve and he was thirteen. She had moved into his linked household in the village from her own household and, as the youngest wife, she did most of the work – getting up first thing in the morning and going to bed last thing at night. She bore three children and died at the early age of twenty-two. Her temperament and demeanour had been beautiful but, as my friend sorrowfully said, she had never left the village and, to his knowledge, had only been in three buildings in her life – her own parents' home, his parents' home and their village temple. Such stories are common and there are a number of women who acquiesce gently and willingly in the life they are offered. Others do not.

The Role of Outcastes

Untouchability, and indeed the outcaste system of which it was a part, was legally abolished in 1950 amid strains of 'victory to Mahatma Gandhi!' In some ways improvements have been made and as we saw earlier a Chief Minister of Uttar Pradesh, Ms Mayawati, was not only a woman but also an outcaste. However the system remains and, in some ways, opposition to it is more militant than ever through the work of the Dalits. Mahatma Gandhi has been partly sidelined by the Dalit Movement as a lukewarm liberal who did not fully understand the severity of the oppression of the outcaste system. Untouchability remains a source of disagreement in the body politic of India today. While there is satisfaction over advances made there is also despair over setbacks.

Historically, outcastes were seen as *avarna* or outside caste. They arose out from marriages or liaisons between different castes, known as caste-mixing (*varna-śamkara*). This might happen through wedlock or through adultery. Some forms of *varna-śamkara* were worse than others: there was greater aversion to the son of a Shudra father and a Brahmin mother (*candālas*) than there was to the son of a Brahmin father and a Shudra mother. Marriage outside caste boundaries had social consequences: it affected normal family life and succession lineages. Ancestors were uncared for and there was no ritual pattern in which families could engage.

Present-day outcastes are the product of many centuries of development and change within the caste system involving distinctions of caste, ritual impurity and the evolution of lowly occupations.

In modern times neo-Hindu reformers, such as Ram Mohan Roy, Saraswati Dayananda and Mahatma Gandhi, worked on behalf of the outcastes. Especially important was Gandhi. When he was a boy his mother told him to keep away from some 'filthy outcaste' boys. Instinctively he felt this was wrong. He later renamed the outcastes Harijans (People of God). He spent much of his life fighting for Indian Independence and working for interfaith collaboration. He spent as much, or even more, of his life in working on behalf of the Harijans. He saw them as a valuable part of Hindu life whilst their contribution and service was important to the total community.

There have been profound legal reforms aimed at improving the outcaste condition. Outcastes were given the title of Scheduled Castes and were protected by the Untouchability Offences Act of 1955, which also gave them equal legal status to other Indians. The Indian government also created a system of 'quota places' within education and within government services. In practice other castes have protested at the privileges given freely to outcastes, arguing that other castes must fight for them through examinations. Outcastes can be subject to attack, rape and other forms of violence, including murder. The theoretical freedom they have with regard to entry to temple worship, educational possibilities, access to wells, ability to move and employment opportunities does not always come to fruition in practice.

Their reaction to these disappointments has taken a number of forms. First, there have been defections from the Hindu fold. The most explosive defection was led by B. R. Ambedkar (1891–1956) who led half a million followers into the Buddhist tradition in 1956. Ambedkar had studied at Columbia University in New York and at the London School of Economics. For a number of years he had intended to go further than Gandhi's moral gradualism by taking the radical step of switching religious affiliation. In the end he executed that intention. Other outcastes have also moved to non-Hindu traditions. Some 80% of Indian Christians are of outcaste origin. Even though, by becoming Christian, outcastes can lose their quota privileges, a number have continued to be Christians. Others have become Sikhs or have followed Ambedkar into the Buddhist tradition or have become Baha'is.

Another reaction is the Dalit Movement. The name Dalit means 'broken', the Dalits are the 'broken ones'. The taking of this name denotes a move away from Gandhi's compassionate term for outcastes as Harijans. It is a term of defiance, a term of honest self-definition and a term of hope. The term Dalit is being used increasingly for those outcastes who have strong feelings about their oppression within the caste system but do who not wish to leave the Hindu fold. Dalit members of parliament, Dalit journals such as the *Dalit Voice*, Dalit writers such as Neerav Patel and Sharankumar Limbale, and other Dalit voices have joined in the debate and the protest. The Dalit Movement is wide and varied according to state, region, language, and even *jāti* – for there are *jātis* even for Dalits. The movement has taken three main directions.

There are those who follow the Gandhi path but in a more militant way. They see themselves as in continuity with the caste system, yet they also oppose its depredations. They seek to improve their condition with a sense of dignity and they question the prevailing system, but they do not seek to completely overthrow it. They are Dalit reformers rather than revolutionaries.

Then there are the militant secular humanist Dalits. As the Dalit author Gangadhar Pantawane puts it:

> To me, Dalit is not a caste. He is a man exploited by the social and economic conditions of this country. He does not believe in God, Rebirth, Soul, Holy books teaching separatism, Fate and Heaven because they made him a slave. He does believe in humanism. Dalit is a symbol of change and revolution. (Clarke in Scott and Selvanayagam, 1996, p. 67)

This kind of statement and the movement that lies behind it implies a cultural counter-attack upon the dominant caste system. The attack is both social and religious. It involves a vision of a new world in which the Dalits can live unhaunted by dirt, disease, famine, humiliation, inequity, squalor and taunts. The answer lies beyond religion in a secular humanistic world of harmony and peace.

Finally, there are those who desire to reform and reuse their own Dalit religious forms in a Dalit way, rather than by replicating the religion of higher castes or becoming secular humanists. For example, the religion of the Tamil Paraiyars has a creative Dalit dynamic that unfolds its own worship. The Dalit goddess Ellaiyaman is a Paraiyar Dalit goddess not known elsewhere. She guards the boundaries of the Paraiyars and shields them from the incursions of others. A song sung to her reads as follows: 'O Mother Goddess Ellaiyaman, grant us the service of your true blessing, for you are the goddess who protects our religion' (Clarke, 1996, p. 72); and another states that 'you will protect us from the 4,408 diseases. You will protect the Harijans from the torture of the High caste' (Clarke, 1996, p. 74). In their songs and myths about Ellaiyaman the Paraiyars dismantle and reinterpret Hindu myths in a dynamic way in order to valorise their own religion and in order to manifest their own Dalit experience of Ellaiyaman. Thus, they remain wedded to a religious vision rather than a secular humanist vision: it is not an imitation of what other *jātis* have to say – it is their Dalit vision.

Elsewhere some Dalit communities have reversed the priorities of well-known sacred texts in order bring out their own points. Thus Vālmīki, the fabled author of the *Rāmāyana*, is revered by some Dalits, and the story of the *Rāmāyana* is reversed by others so that the hero Rāma becomes the villain whilst the villain Rāvana becomes the hero. However, the reinterpretations are kept within the field of the Hindu tradition rather than recast in a purely secular mould.

The Political Background, the Monarchy and Hindu Nationalism

This chapter has highlighted two basic features of the Hindu tradition. On the one hand the caste system, although it has changed over time, has provided the basic structure of Hindu society and is intimately connected with the Hindu religious tradition. This has been the case for about three and a half millennia and is unique in human history. On the other hand, in spite of this background of social stability, the Hindu tradition has never fully ruled the nation of India. The great rulers of India belonged to other religious traditions. Thus, the Hindu tradition has exercised social supremacy within India but not political supremacy.

There have been Hindu rulers at times in Indian history. They include the Magadha Empire (560–325 BCE), the Mauryan Empire (321–181 BCE), the Gupta Empire (320–650 CE) and the Vijayanagar Empire (1336–1565). However these empires were relatively small and were not pan-Indian. The Hindu religious tradition developed during their epochs, but it also survived during the Ashokan, Muslim and British epochs when states run by Hindu kings were under the political control of leaders from other religious traditions. At the end of the British era there were over five hundred native, mainly Hindu, states that continued the Hindu caste hegemony under the oversight of British agents. Thus the Hindu tradition exercised a major role in the social life of India, through the caste system, and a major influence on the religious life of India, while not exercising the levers of political power.

Priests and rulers

Part of the reason may lie in the relationship between the two higher *varnas*: the Brahmins and the Kshatriyas. The Brahmins, although 'priests', were higher in the caste hierarchy than the Kshatriyas, the 'rulers'. Not all Brahmins have been priests and not all Kshatriyas have been rulers. The complexity of the caste system, regional and linguistic differences and historical change have all militated against this rigidity.

Nevertheless, commentators on the Hindu tradition have remarked on the unusual nature of a system wherein priests are theoretically ranked higher than rulers and where, on the face of it, religion can be ranked higher than political power.

Brahmins have traditionally been seen as ritually more pure than Kshatriyas and more versed in religious knowledge. They are, in theory if not always in fact, the key scholars in the Hindu tradition. The Kshatriyas have traditionally been seen, again in theory if not always in practice, as the rulers who maintain society, uphold *dharma* and protect the householder system. They built and sponsored temples, protected their subjects and their deities and, to that extent, the Brahmins recognised a ruler's overlordship. However, the kingly role in ruling and guardianship duties involved more 'polluting tendencies' than were usual in a Brahmin's life. The Brahmins have had a dual role in society. Those who are active priests in temples have engaged in functions that involve being given gifts by worshippers and such temple priests are more involved with lower castes. Paradoxically Brahmins who are versed in promoting scholarship and in advancing religious learning but who do not act as serving priests are, in general, more widely admired because they have less contact with the public. Thus Brahmins who are not priests can be more akin to those renouncers engaged in lifelong learning and spirituality, rather than in the hurly-burly of householder life. To that extent they would receive greater respect than Kshatriyas.

However the complexity of the different roles of Brahmins and Kshatriyas is interpreted, the Hindu situation has been different from that of other cultures. Partly because of the general *varna* superiority of the Brahmins, the Kshatriyas have had less freedom, power and incentive to rule over the whole of India. They were affected by the differences between the mainly Aryan North India and the mainly Dravidian South India, by the differences between the twelve main language areas and by regional differences of culture. Thus, although the caste system was able to grow and develop throughout India, Hindu political rule over India did not materialise.

The Hindutva movement and Hindu nationalism

When India became independent, it became a secular state in which there was a Hindu majority. The Indian secular state aimed for different religious traditions to live in peace. Secularism did not entail the secularising of many functions of life so that they left the sphere of religion, as in many other parts of the world. It was not a quasi-religious creed. It was a balancing mechanism whereby different religious groups could live together in harmony. Thus India did not become a Hindu state but became a secular state that, in theory, protected different religious traditions. In recent times, with the rise of the Hindutva Movement, India has moved politically more towards becoming a Hindu state. This development implies, if it were to be successful, the rise of a Hindu state for the first time in the history of India.

The rise of the Hindutva movement

The first Hindu political movement was the Hindu Mahasabha, formed in 1915 within the Indian National Congress. It later became involved in direct political activity. The term 'Hindutva' was coined by V. D. Savarkar (1883–1966) who, in 1923, wrote a book entitled *Hindutva: Who is a Hindu?* Savarkar argued that Hindutva was basically tied up with Hindu/Indian 'culture' rather than Hindu 'religion' as such, although confusingly he saw India as a holy land. He thus began the process that equated Hindutva (Hinduness) with the Hindu religious tradition. The implication was that the Muslim and Christian invasions had oppressed the Hindus and compromised the Hinduness of the original Hindu state. At first Savarkar led the Hindu Mahasabha within the Indian National Congress but it was excluded from the Congress in 1937 for putting Hindu political ends before the wider cross-religious push for Indian independence. Savarkar had a strong influence on K. B. Hedgewar who left the Congress earlier to found the RSS (Rashtriya Swayamsevak Sangh) in 1925. Hedgewar built up the RSS using western-style organisational methods and borrowing partly from ascetic renouncer disciplines. M. S. Golwalkar added a strong ideological input, when he took over from Hedgewar, in a 1939 book entitled *We, or Our Nationhood Defined*. His stress was upon Hindutva as a Hindu 'nation' rather than a Hindu 'state'. Comprising a section of upper-caste, mainly Brahmin, men in Maharashtra and Karnataka, the RSS did not have the cross-caste, cross-religious and cross-regional appeal of the Indian National Congress, but it did have a potentially strong organisation and ideology.

Indian Independence both helped and hindered Hindu nationalism. On the one hand, although the partition of India was disliked by most Hindus, it decreased the number of Muslims in India, for many had gone to Pakistan. Moreover, Nehru's secular Congress Party was reasonably successful in founding an Indian secular state where all religious traditions could live together in peace. Even more important was the assassination of Mahatma Gandhi, the 'saint' of the independence movement, by a nationalist Hindu, Nathuram Godse. For ten years or so after Gandhi's death in 1948 things were calm. Yet the perception arose that other states in the sub-continent were guided by religious nationalism: Islam in Pakistan, the Buddhist tradition in Sri Lanka and in the Punjab there was the threat of Sikh nationalism. War with China in 1963 exposed India's military weakness against a 'quasi-religious' Marxist neighbour. After the independence of East Pakistan, which became secular Bangladesh, there was the disappointment of Bangladesh later reverting to the status of a Muslim state. The perception also arose that in secular India minor religious groups were gaining more advantage than the Hindu majority. Insofar as there was no Hindu religious leadership body or 'pope' who could lead the Hindu community, the Indian state took control with regard to Hindu reforms such as the Hindu Marriage and Divorce Act and the Hindu Endowments Act and the state was perceived as being unfair to Hindus. Educational advancement seemed more readily available to non-Hindus than to Hindus. Against this background Hindu nationalism regrouped and became much stronger.

The RSS revived the Vishva Hindu Parishad, founded in the 1960s, as a more activist body within Hindu nationalism. The Bharatiya Jana Sangh was also formed and began to draw closer to the RSS. With growing discontent within and beyond the Congress Party, due to Indira Gandhi's policies, the Janata Party united Socialists, Congress dissidents and the Jana Sangh Party. It then broke up and in 1980 the Jana Sangh became refounded as the Bharatiya Janata Party (BJP). It was the BJP that began to win political control of some states. By 1998 the BJP led a national government, albeit as the leader of a coalition of parties. Various reasons contributed to this dramatic development. The first was the decline of the Congress Party after Nehru with its inconsistent leadership and the ebbing of its reputation as the standard-bearer of independence. Second, there was the growing strength of the nationalist movement, and its ability to marshal greater cohesion and support. In addition there was the considerable influence of the media, especially television broadcasts of the *Mahābhārata* and the *Rāmāyana* that were viewed widely by mass audiences. These were seen as nationalist victories in ancient times that could be linked, allegorically, to modern Hindu nationalism. These weekly broadcasts over many months, seen by semi-literate as well as literate audiences, had their effect. Matters came to a head during the dramatic demolition in 1992 of the mosque in Ayodhya, allegedly built by the Mughal Emperor Babar in 1528 on the spot where the Lord Rāma had been born. Around 300,000 Hindu nationalists, led by the President of the BJP, descended on Ayodhya and demolished the mosque brick by brick with the threat to rebuild a Hindu temple on the site. This action must be seen against the growing disquiet, in some Hindu circles, at the loss of people from the Hindu tradition to the Christian, Buddhist, Sikh and Baha'i traditions, the rise of the Dalit Movement, attacks on the caste system and unrest among outcastes and women.

Hindu nationalism

However, India is a democracy. For Hindu nationalist parties to rule they require a majority in the Parliament of India, and in particular, in the Lok Sabha (the House of the People). This is not a realistic objective and therefore, in government, coalition and compromise are essential.

Furthermore, as we have tried to show, the Hindu tradition is complex. For example, Ayodhya is in Uttar Pradesh in North India where Hindi is spoken and Aryan Sanskrit is not uncommon. South India is mainly Dravidian and has many language and cultural differences from Aryan North India. Eighteen languages are recognised by the Indian Constitution. Overall, 42% of Indians speak Hindi (with Hindustani and Urdu), 16% speak Bengali, 7% Punjabi, 8% Telugu, 18% Dravidian languages. Other major languages include Marathi, Gujarati, Oriya and Assamese. India is vast, so regional differences in language, ethos and nature give Hindu nationalism more resonance in the north than in the south.

The responsibility of leading a national government, which demands compromise, also invites division within Hindu nationalism itself between the 'hard' nationalists who oppose compromise and the 'soft' nationalists who know that staying in power demands compromise. Thus, on thorny issues such as Kashmir and nuclear weapons there may be internal differences of opinion.

The rise of an elite middle class has placed more emphasis upon the accumulation of wealth. India accelerates as a leading power in the world, with nuclear families and a more pragmatic Hindu tradition. The fact that more Indians live abroad, often in the West, strengthens these trends as does the increasing interest of some Hindu groups in interfaith activity. This contrasts with the rejection of tolerant liberalism, suspicion of the West and the antipathy towards Christians and Muslims typical of much Hindu nationalism.

Economic liberalisation and globalisation

A final element in analysing the input of the Hindu tradition into the social and political arena relates to the Hindu approach to economic liberalism and globalisation in the early twenty-first century.

The situation in India has changed rapidly since the time of Gandhi and Nehru. Gandhi had galvanised the villages in the fight for independence and had championed the homely concerns of the village, such as basic education, the local cultivation of crops, local crafts and communal cooperation. He championed local virtues and the need for the lowest and the last to have access to the rudiments of life. Nehru had stressed the importance of science and technology and the need for expanding higher education, in order to promote a better life for his people. His instinct was to promote this betterment of life through a socialist approach which favoured the rise of towns and the increase of heavy industry. Contemporary India has advanced rapidly with industrial growth, capitalist economics, the growth of cities, the rise of rich and super-rich elites, the deregularisation of markets, and scientific advances. India is accelerating towards becoming a superpower and has modernised at a rapid pace.

With advances made in medicine and hygiene the population has grown rapidly. The Indian population is now well in excess of a billion of whom over 80% are nominally Hindu. Many people are migrating to cities from the villages to find work, more variety of life and more freedom from caste restrictions. Television and Indian Bollywood films highlight the attractions of cities.

However, unless relatives have accommodation in the cities for immigrants, there are not enough houses to accommodate everyone and poorer people may have to inhabit street pavement shanty homes with few facilities. There is not enough work for everyone and some may even scavenge the enormous garbage heaps for food and articles to sell.

In the cities *jātis* still combine, if they can, so that people from different areas of India will live in their own *jāti* areas within the city. However, Indian cities are more secular than Indian villages. Harvey Cox's book *The Secular City* (1965), although referring mainly to western cities, sounds wider truths about city life.

Middle-class families gravitate towards birth control and maintain nuclear families in which elderly relatives may be less effusively welcomed. People from other cultures and other religions share the life of cities. There is greater opportunity for marriage across castes or across faith boundaries.

Globalisation, with its tendency towards westernisation, is relevant in India. The glamour of being a Great Power, with a place in the higher echelons of the United Nations and having some of the richest people in the world as citizens, pulls the Indian elite towards a more capitalist, western world-view. By the same token the drawbacks of western capitalism are not unnoticed in India, with its mainly Hindu population.

To delve at more length into the ultimate implications of ultramodernity for India is beyond the scope of this book. It is interesting that a BJP-led government has been able to accommodate what appears to be mounting Indian involvement in international matters. India is engaging in world affairs on a basis not compromised by Hindutva concerns. A key problem facing India is how to modernise, paying full attention to her world influence, whilst, at the same time, taking seriously the Hindu tradition that is India's inheritance.

The irony is that if Hindu nationalists obtain political power in India, they can only keep it by downplaying Hindu nationalism. Hindu nationalism may probably fare better by strengthening the cultural appeal of Hindu nationalism rather than by emphasising its political appeal. Hindu nationalism in a resonant form is a new factor in Indian history, economic liberalism and globalisation.

7

Dharma and Ethics

The word *dharma* is a concept crucial to the Hindu tradition. It has a number of different meanings including duty, order, ethics, law, and right-eousness. In this chapter Hindu *dharma* is considered mainly as a vehicle of ethics and morality.

Universal Dharma

Universal *dharma* relates to all humanity and it includes ethical virtues such as compassion, generosity, gratitude, and non-violence. These virtues that are said to be common to all humans are known as *sadhārana* (common) or *sana-tana* (eternal) *dharma*. For example, the Law of Manu (X:63) argues that non-injury, truth, not stealing, purity and control of the senses summarise *dharma* for the four castes. Elsewhere Manu (VI:91–2) asserts that avoiding backbiting, hypocrisy, greed, infatuation, anger and discontent is approved *dharma* for all the stages of life. The problem is that there are different views as to what the actuality of universal *dharma* is. Radhakrishnan, for example, argues for a *sanatana dharma*, based upon Advaita Vedanta thought, that is said to be present in all religious traditions. It is a kind of perennial philoso-phy that is at the heart of every religious tradition not just at the heart of the Hindu tradition. Others concentrate upon a universal *dharma* within the Hindu tradition itself but there is no absolute consensus as to what it is. Nev-ertheless, in theory, the ethical virtues of compassion, generosity, gratitude, and non-violence are universally regarded by most Hindus.

Buddhist and Hindu Notions of Dharma

It is helpful to contrast the Hindu and Buddhist notions of *dharma*. The concept is important to both but in the Buddhist tradition *dharma* has a more deeply transcendent flavour. The Buddha rebelled against the caste system. He also rebelled against the notion of a transcendent *Brahman* that the Upanishads were introducing. Transcendence for the Buddhists included a transcendent goal, namely Nirvāna, that was beyond this world.

The Dharma was the transcendent teaching of the Buddha available through the Sangha. He did not invent it. He discovered or uncovered this cosmic truth and made it available to humankind. Although the word doctrine is used in the profession of faith for Buddhists *dharma* is a more transcendent category than the word doctrine implies. The Buddha 'turned the wheel of the Dharma'. Although it contains doctrine and teaching, it remains a transcendent symbol and a mediating focus. The Hindu view of *dharma* remained at a less transcendent and more worldly level.

The Hindu forerunner to *dharma* was present in the *Rig Veda*, in the form of *ṛta*, or cosmic law, which was promoted by the Vedic deity Varuna. Varuna through *ṛta* was the upholder of ritual and cosmic order and could be courted through sacrifice and prayer. However, Varuna declined in importance and was succeeded by other Hindu deities, *ṛta* lost its vitality and was succeeded by *dharma*. The view of *dharma* proceeded in a less transcendent and a more worldly direction. It became a key Hindu norm in a more grounded and more varied way.

Dharma in Hindu Life

At one level *dharma* became one of the four aims of Hindu life. It represented essentially the leading of a moral life. As well as being seen as one of the four aims of life, *dharma* could also be seen at a wider and more diffuse level: it worked at a worldly rather than a transcendent level and in different contexts. It could mean doing one's duty within life. The contexts of life varied, therefore *dharma* as doing one's duty varied according to *varna*, *jāti* and stage of life. Krishna found this out in the *Bhagavad Gītā* when Arjuna's *dharma*, his duty to fight as a Kshatriya, a warrior, conflicted with his desire not to kill his own kinsmen. *Dharma* could also mean a code of conduct within life influenced by regulations in regard to marriage, food, religion, and other matters. The working out of *dharma* in law gave rise to the extensive *Dharma Shāstra* literature that catered for most possibilities. One's *dharma* could even mean seeking liberation as a renouncer which, of course, contradicted the notion of *dharma* as being important in the life of a householder. *Dharmas* were different according to contexts and according to individuals.

Dharma and Karma

What then was the Hindu view about the differences of *dharma*, birth and station in life that gave rise to the disparities within the caste system? The main reason given by Hindus rests in the notion of *karma*. This word means works or actions. Thus, within the life of an individual there operate a lifelong series of actions of many different kinds, whether good or bad, that influence a person's future course and rebirth. One is reborn according to one's *karma*. Good *karma* enables the next rebirth to be a good one. Bad *karma* makes the next rebirth an unfavourable one. Thus the fatalistic view was that one is born into a higher caste because of past good *karma* and into a lower caste or outcaste situation because of past bad *karma*.

Arvind Sharma has offered interesting insights into the discussion about *dharma* and *karma* (1996). According to him the doctrine of *varnas* was present in the Hindu tradition before the doctrine of *karma*. This raises the possibility that the doctrine of *karma* arrived later to rationalise the Hindu division into higher and lower castes. This enables people to accept caste fatalistically as their lot when there is no direct need to do so. Sharma stresses free will in the present life, rather than dwelling upon *karma* in the past life. Good *karma* in the present life is important. It is, of course, more possible to take this view in middle-class, privileged and elite lives where there is greater freedom of life and thought, but it is part of the rethinking of Hindu views that is possible today.

Rāma and Dharma

The life of the Hindu deity Rāma illustrates the varieties of *dharma* in Hindu thought. Rāma himself, as a man, was a supreme example of *dharma*. He was a living example of what it means to live a life of *dharma*. The kingdom he set up after his return from exile and victory in battle was the ideal kingdom for Hindus. It was *Rāmarājya* (the kingdom of Rāma) based upon *dharma*. In the original *Rāmāyana* of Vālmīki two main meanings are brought out. *Dharma* is first living according to the rules of social life and, secondly, it represents the ethical norm of 'right living'. Both were important for Rāma. At different stages of his life Rāma used different notions of practical *dharma* according to social norms. Especially important for Rāma was *dharma* as an ethical norm. He must do what is 'right' at every crisis of his life. He was willing to undergo successive experiences of suffering in order to fulfil *dharma* as an ethical norm even though they might cause him deep pain. Rāma is unusual in this respect. In most cases within the Hindu tradition *dharma* as a social norm would outweigh *dharma* as a kind of transcendent ethical norm. Moreover, the notion of suffering as being the right way to live according to *dharma* would also be unusual within the Hindu tradition.

In the story of the *Rāmāyana* Rāma is a young prince who is designated to succeed his father, the king of Ayodhya. When the king abdicates he makes arrangements to pass his throne to Rāma. According to social *dharma* and according to *rājadharma* (the dharma of kings) it was necessary for Rāma to be inaugurated as king. He was ideal for the job. However, the old king's youngest wife Kaikeyi had been extremely helpful to her husband and in exchange the king had given her two wishes. Perverted by her maid, Kaikeyī requests that Rāma should be exiled to the forest for fourteen years and that her own son should succeed to the throne in his place. This is against social *dharma* and *rājadharma* but Rāma feels bound to obey his father's pledged word, in spite of his father's grief, because of the *dharma* of 'truth'. There-fore, Rāma obeys his father's word instead of succeeding to the kingship. As a result, he and his wife Sītā and his brother Lakshmana go into exile in the forest.

In the Dandaka forest, the ascetics living there ask Rāma to protect them against the demon king Rāvana who is persecuting them. However, Rāma is no longer living according to *rājadharma* or *Kshatriyadharma* (the *dharma* of a warrior) insofar as he himself is a married ascetic living in the forest. Rāma argues against his wife and brother who want him to refuse to give help to the ascetics. He claims that he must act as a king and protect the ascetics, even though he need not do so, and even though it might cause trouble. Indeed, this is precisely what happens. Rāvana, the king of the Rākshasas who is attacking the ascetics, kidnaps Rāma's wife Sītā and takes her to Lanka (which may or may not be Sri Lanka). This leads to a full-scale war between the forces of Rāma and the forces of Rāvana.

Both these decisions resulted in Rāma suffering. The next two decisions were unusual as well. Firstly, he shot the Vānara Vālin from behind a tree for offending *dharma*, although this action was itself against *dharma*. Then, against *dharma*, he welcomed Vibhīshana who came to him from his arch-enemy Rāvana's camp. Both actions make the point that *dharma* transcends race or nation. Vālin had offended against *dharma*, while Vibhīshana had followed *dharma*. *Dharma* thus becomes an ethical norm outranking caste or racial considerations.

After defeating Rāvana and winning back Sītā, Rāma grew suspicious about what, if anything, had happened in Lanka while Sītā had been impris-oned in Rāvana's palace. If Rāma was to set up the idyllic Rāmarājya on his return to the throne in Ayodhya, he must avoid all suspicion of misbehav-iour by Sītā. Rāma felt, according to *rājadharma*, that he had to make Sītā undertake a fire ordeal in order to prove her innocence. She did so success-fully and was vindicated.

Finally when Rāma was back in Ayodhya presiding over Rāmarājya, unfounded insinuations arose against Sītā and against Lakshmana, his faith-ful brother. Rāma again felt he had to banish them both for the sake of *rājadharma*. Therefore, when Rāma finally reigned over his idyllic kingdom of Ayodhya, he was broken-hearted over losing the two most important people in his life.

Rāma's story is an interesting one. It makes the point that there are different 'dharma-times' in individual lives. It also emphasises that although *dharma* in the social sense is important, it can sometimes be outweighed by the moral imperative of a truth that overrides *dharma*. Mahatma Gandhi admired the Rāma story and also saw *Rāmarājya* as his ideal for India. However, there is also a sting in the tail. The Women's Movement has pointed out that it is necessary to bring out Sītā's side of the story as a faithful and principled woman who is let down by Rāma by his ultimate insistence upon kingly and caste values.

Different kinds of Dharma

Much of what has been stated so far implies the relativity of *dharma*. It is possible to list any number of *dharmas*. There is an overall *dharma* that covers the natural world, the human world and the animal world and there is a *dharma* for each individual world. There is a *dharma* that focuses upon the ritual world of sacraments, festivals and worship and there is a *dharma* for each. There are *dharmas* for men and *dharmas* for women. There are *dharmas* for each stage of life, for each aim in life and for each set of *jātis* within the caste system. According to Gandhi and the *Rāmāyana*, there is also a *dharma* of 'truth' that can outweigh, in certain circumstances, general caste *dharma*. On the other hand, *Bhagavad Gītā* III:35 reads 'better one's own duty though ill done, than another's duty well-performed'. In other words it is better, say, to fight badly because its is one's *dharma* as a Kshatriya to fight than to do somebody else's job well. This takes the centre of gravity of *dharma* away from ethical norms back to caste norms.

Evolution of Dharma

What then is the way out of this dilemma? Are we to be satisfied with complete relativity in our understanding of *dharma*? After all, for virtually three and a half millennia the Hindu *dharma* has evolved and changed radically and yet remained recognisably 'Hindu'. Part of the answer is quite simply to admit that there is no one Hindu tradition that has remained relatively unchanged down the centuries. The earlier historical survey (see pp. 20–31) noted the rise and eventual demise of the Buddhist and Jain traditions in India and the Muslim and British rule of India. These developments, while politically crucial, occurred alongside Hindu religious and caste developments. Although affected by changes in political rulership, the Hindu religious and caste traditions developed according to their own momentum. The great Muslim commentator Al-Biruni (973–1048) commented that the Hindus considered the Muslims to be '*mleccha*, impure, and forbid having any connection with them, be it by intermarriage or any other kind of relationship, or by sitting, eating, and drinking with them, because thereby, they think, they would be polluted' (Embree, 1971, p. 19).

This is not to say that the Hindu tradition has not changed radically over the years. It changed and yet retained some semblance of continuity. The Hindu *dharma* evolved and changed from within. One essential reason for this was a general predisposition to tolerance. Although there have been occasions of inter-Hindu violence in general, Hindu traditions arose peacefully as a collection of traditions. They were bound together by an overarching notion of *dharma* and differed only in history and geography, economic and social backgrounds and cultural and racial norms. They shared certain elements, influenced one another and jointly form what may be called a Hindu culture within a Hindu *dharma* of India.

To put it another way the totality of the Hindu tradition is wider than the major religious traditions that appeared during the arduous course of its historical development. There is a sense in which the Hindu tradition has been an example of postmodernism, long before the term was coined in the West, because of the many differences and anomalies within it. We have looked at some of those differences and they are real. However, the Hindu story is not one of total difference and incongruity. The word *dharma*, although relative, still remains resonant.

The Hindu tradition has always been ready and able to add new elements to old ones, to absorb elements from other religious traditions and to abandon elements that seemed outdated (with the proviso that they could be revived if necessary). It has had an ongoing capacity for adaptation and renewal. Thus the Upanishads and later sacred texts adapted the Veda in different directions. To the original three aims of life was added *moksha* as a fourth aim. To the three stages of life was added renunciation as a fourth stage of life. The caste system proliferated. M. N. Srinivas (1952) distinguished between the Sanskritic all-India Hindu tradition and village Hindu traditions in local and regional areas, and Robert Redfield (1953) distinguished between the Hindu 'Great and Little Traditions'. There is some truth in these distinctions. There is also a sense in which the differences in caste, in language, in religion (high gods and low gods) and so on imply not so much dysfunction but gradual absorption and assimilation in the midst of difference. There are tensions within the Hindu tradition and they are perhaps greater now than ever. But the two greatest Hindu strengths have been the continuity of the extended family system and the *jāti* system, which have proved more important than *varna* in the caste system, on the one hand, and the capacity of the Hindu religious tradition to continue to add new elements on the other.

8

Scripture and Sacred Texts

The Hindu sacred texts are very numerous. It may be helpful to distinguish between the words 'scripture' and 'sacred text'. The Christian Bible incorporates the Jewish Bible as its Old Testament followed by the New Testament. However, at that point, the canon of the Bible was closed. Later writings, such as Milton's *Paradise Lost* or Bunyon's *Pilgrim's Progress*, although important, are not 'scripture' but important sacred texts. The scriptures of the Christians, Jews and Muslims are the Christian Bible, the Jewish Bible and the Qur'ān. Many later sacred texts have been important in these three traditions but are of less importance than the scriptures.

Eastern religious traditions have voluminous sets of sacred texts. As Kenneth Chen puts it, with regard to Buddhist sacred texts: 'make no mistake, their volume is colossal' (1968, p. 234). In addition to the Pāli Canon, or *Tripitaka*, which ranks as the scripture of the Theravāda Buddhists, and key Mahāyāna sūtras in different languages, which rank as scripture for Mahāyāna Buddhists, there is a vast accumulation of sacred texts in both traditions. The Jain situation is even more complex in that the two main communities have their own separate sacred texts and an extensive part of the Purvas has been lost. This makes it less easy to differentiate between scripture and sacred texts in the Jain tradition.

Hindu sacred texts are remarkable in their nature. The Veda, which is the nearest thing to 'revelation' in the Hindu tradition, is larger than any other scriptural revelation. It is written in the Sanskrit language, albeit Vedic Sanskrit is more ancient than later Sanskrit. It is not completely cut off from later Hindu sacred texts in the sense that some of those, although not 'revealed ' and not always written in Sanskrit, are more widely known and sometimes more widely venerated than the Veda. Its reputation as Veda and revelation is theoretical rather than actual. Although most of its gods are redundant, and although Vedic Sanskrit is known by a very small minority, it remains 'revelation', that which was 'heard' and brought down from the heavens. It is still learnt by heart and recited from memory by some scholars and Brahmins. However, this is an admired tour-de-force rather than one that is understood.

Hindu texts are unique in other ways. Summarising the main categories of Hindu sacred texts, both the 'revealed' texts (*shruti*) and the 'remembered' texts (*smriti*), and looking at the changing ideas and environments lying behind the texts allows a look at the different interpretations of those texts.

The Veda

The fountainhead of Hindu sacred texts is the Veda, that which was 'heard' (*shruti*) or revealed. The Veda in the narrowest sense is divided into four sections, namely the *Rig Veda*, *Yajur Veda*, *Sāma Veda*, and *Atharva Veda*. However, within the total Veda, there are also four sections, namely the four Vedas (hymns), Brahmanas (priestly rituals), Aranyakas (forest works) and Upanishads (philosophical texts). The Upanishads are also known as the Vedanta, as they come at the end (*anta*) of the Veda. The deepest and most important part of Hindu thought and philosophy is to be found in the Vedanta schools. They are taken partly from the Upanishads and are the foremost element in Hindu thought. There are diversities of nuance and thought within the total Veda, especially between the Vedas, Brahmanas and Aranyakas on the one hand and the Upanishads on the other hand. However, the four Vedas within the total Veda form, as it were, the main part of Hindu 'scripture'. It probably helps to see the Veda as a library of books rather than a single book. Few people are able to read the Veda now. In practice, more attention is paid to the Upanishads and to later sacred texts than to earlier parts of the Veda. Even so, and in spite of the fact that some elements within the Hindu fold ignore the Veda, it remains for most Hindus the fountainhead of scripture.

Later Sacred Texts

The second main group among Hindu sacred texts are the *smriti* or 'remembered' texts. In fact, the *smriti* texts are far too long to be remembered. There are Brahmins who can recite the Veda from memory but this is not possible with the *smriti* texts because they are too long and are not amenable to being memorised. The Vedas are said by orthodox Hindus to have no human author – they were heard and revealed – whereas the *smriti* texts were authored by human beings. In general, the Veda and especially the Upanishads relate to salvation (*moksha*), whilst the *smriti* texts refer to the more earthly (*dharma*) side of life.

The *smriti* texts can be viewed in two ways. They may be restricted to a series of law books covering the economic, personal, traditional and political elements of human living or they can be extended to cover *all* sacred texts that are authored by humans.

At the heart of *smriti*, in the sense of law books, lies the *Dharmaśāstra* (Book of Dharma) which runs to many volumes. It covers the four aims of life, the four *varnas*, the four stages of life, the *jātis*, the basic sacraments and the various rituals. It focuses upon householder life as householders are more involved in the social, practical and everyday sides of life than are renouncers. It may be asked what relevance the *Dharmaśāstra* has for Hindu religion as it centres upon the worldly element rather than on the transcendent element in life? The answer is that the 'worldly' segment of life is as important to Hindus as the transcendent segment of life that is stressed in the Upanishads. Both are part of the totality of the life of a Hindu. Being part of the Hindu tradition is to be part of a total way of life and not just being part of a Hindu 'religion'. Therefore the *smriti* writings, including the *Dharmaśāstra*, are 'sacred texts'.

Another feature of both the *shruti* and the early *smriti* sacred texts is that they were written in the Sanskrit language. Sanskrit is now less important as it is only spoken in some priestly and academic circles and is not a living language. Nevertheless it is, alongside English, the only countrywide language in India, and some of the later vernacular Indian literatures began as adaptations of Sanskrit.

There is some continuity between the Veda and the *smriti* (in the sense of the *Dharmaśāstras*) in the sense that the later Veda already contains some *Dharmasūtras*. A 'sūtra' is a thread, or brief statement, that can be amplified later. The link between the *Dharmasūtras* and the *Dharmaśāstras* is not strong, but it is there. The *Dharmasūtras* date mainly from before 200 BCE and the *Dharmaśāstras* from about 200 CE onwards. Commentaries on the *Dharmaśāstras* began around 700 CE and they often stray into interpretation rather than pure commentary. A fascinating postlude came when Warren Hastings was Governor of Bengal at the end of the eighteenth century. The new British administration in Bengal had already started to use the Qur'ān as a legal reference that could be applied to Indian Muslims. It was not easy to know what to do in the case of Hindus as they had no equivalent to the Qur'ān. The outcome was that Anglo-Indian courts began to use the *Dharmaśāstra*. This was extremely difficult because of their length and because few British had any knowledge of Sanskrit. One outcome was that leading British members of the East India Company began to learn Sanskrit. In 1794 Sir William Jones wrote on the Law of Manu (an important early part of the *Dharmaśāstras*). Others went further. In 1785 Charles Wilkins wrote his famous translation of the *Bhagavad Gītā*. Thomas Colebrooke discovered that the word '*dharma*' meant much more than 'law' and he wrote the first survey of the six Indian schools of philosophy, as well as *A Digest of Hindu Law* in 1797. Thus, the birth of influential British studies of the Hindu tradition began with the need to understand the *Dharmaśāstras*.

The *Mahābhārata* and the *Rāmāyana*

The second set of *smriti* texts are the two great Hindu epics: the *Mahābhārata* and the *Rāmāyana*. Like the *Dharmaśāstras* they cover many aspects of life, but they partly focus upon Hindu deities, especially upon the two *avatāras* of Vishnu, namely Krishna and Rāma. They are enormous. The *Mahābhārata* originally amounted to 100,000 verses, making it by far the largest epic the world has known. In the critical edition it still has 75,000 verses. The *Rāmāyana* is smaller but still has 20,000 verses. They are different from and yet have continuity with the Veda. Indeed the *Mahābhārata* is traditionally known as 'the fifth Veda', and the *Rāmāyana* traces Rāma's continuity with and succession to the great Vedic deity Indra. Even within the two epics, Krishna and Rāma are still at an early stage of their development. In the second to the sixth chapters of the *Rāmāyana*, Rāma is depicted as a great human king who is an outstanding upholder of *dharma* upon the earth. It is in the first and seventh chapters, added later, that he is identified with Vishnu. As far as the *Mahābhārata* is concerned, Krishna does not have a truly central role, but his significance is enhanced considerably by the insertion of the *Bhagavad Gītā* into the battle scene at the heart of the epic. At this point Krishna becomes not only the companion of Arjuna, a leader of the Pāndavas in the great Mahābhārata war, but also a supreme deity who shows his transcendent form to the startled Arjuna in an explosive vision.

Due to their great lengths the *Mahābhārata* and the *Rāmāyana* contain vast amounts of text that, whilst interesting, are not central to their main themes. For most people they are sacred stories that are not read. Until recently, most people were not literate. They heard translations from Sanskrit into spoken languages or in adaptations of key themes, presented on stage, at festivals or translated into carvings in temples. More recently, these epics have been adapted for television. The various episodes were carefully chosen and tended towards a nationalistic, Hindutva view of the two epics. However, interpretation is always necessary in producing anything, including sacred texts.

The *Bhagavad Gītā* and the *Harivamsha*

The main story of Krishna is not in the *Mahābhārata*, as Rāma's is in the *Rāmāyana*. The key texts are the *Bhagavad Gītā*, and the *Harivamsha*. The *Gītā* is an insertion into the *Mahābhārata* that deepens the meaning of

Krishna's own being. The *Harivamsha* was written later than the *Bhagavad Gītā* and centres upon Krishna alone. It opens up important facets of his later story.

In the eleventh chapter of the *Bhagavad Gītā*, Krishna is outwardly the charioteer of Arjuna, a Pāndava leader, as they wait for the great Mahābhārata battle to start. Krishna reveals himself to Arjuna in a supernal, overwhelming form as the supreme Lord. Arjuna is entranced by the vision and he offers his allegiance, devotion and repentance to Krishna whom he recognises as divine. In response to Arjuna's earlier qualms about fighting in the battle, wherein he would have to kill his own kinsmen on the opposing side, Krishna imparts various teachings to Arjuna. He tells him that his duty is to fulfil his role in society, which is that of being a warrior (Kshatriya), and that the self (*ātman*) is deeper than the body; therefore, if the body dies, the *ātman* does not. Thus, killing the body does not imply the killing of the *ātman*. He further tells Arjuna that one should do one's duty without thought of reward for its own sake. Thus, activity when done for the right reasons is not harmful but helpful. Involvement in the world for the right motives is good and proper. Krishna goes on to suggest that there are three kinds of spirituality that are proper: the way of knowledge associated with yoga and inwardness; the way of selfless action associated with disinterested service in the world; and the way of devotion (*bhakti*) to the godhead. He drops a bombshell by implying that, although all three ways are good, the way of devotion is basically preferable in that it is viable for all since the way of knowledge and the way of action are not necessarily available to all. This triggered a lively debate about whether the three ways were equal or not, and also what part ritual played. Importantly, Krishna claims that he is the divine godhead who is sometimes superior to *Brahman* but, at this point in time, there is no sense that he is either Vishnu or even an *avatāra* of Vishnu. It is no wonder that the *Bhagavad Gītā* has been a religious lighthouse for so many Hindu thinkers as it raised so many basic questions whilst offering so many possible ways forward.

The *Harivamsha* provided new insights into Krishna's life. In it we see him living in Vrindaban as a mischievous but divine child, as a cowherd and protector of cows, as the one who is loved by the cowgirls, as the miracle worker, as the one who raises up Mount Govardhana to preserve the village from violent rain, as the killer of his wicked uncle Kamsa and as the one who moves eventually from Vrindaban to Mathura and to Dvaraka, which would later become 'his' places. The way was opened, through the *Rāmāyana*, the *Mahābhārata* (especially the *Bhagavad Gītā*), and the *Harivamsha*, for Rāma and Krishna devotion to flourish.

The Purānas

The next main development in Hindu sacred texts occurred in the Purānas. There is an erudite and fascinating tradition of Purāna scholarship. However, as Freda Matchett puts it: 'in the last analysis the Purānas do not belong to the scholarly community and they will continue to be important even if the latter should neglect them completely' (Flood, 2005, p. 142).

Traditionally there are said to be eighteen Purānas, although in practice there are approaching eighty. The traditional list contains the following eighteen Purānas: *Brahmā Purāna*, *Padma Purāna*, *Vishnu Purāna*, *Shiva Purāna*, *Bhāgavata Purāna*, *Nārada Purāna*, *Mārkandeya Purāna*, *Agni Purāna*, *Bhaviśya Purāna*, *Brahmavaivarta Purāna*, *Linga Purāna*, *Varāha Purāna*, *Skanda Purāna*, *Vāmana Purāna*, *Kūrma Purāna*, *Matsya Purāna*, *Garuda Purāna*, and *Brahmānda Purāna*. They are summarised in the *Vishnu Purāna* 3.6.20–24. The dates of these Purānas range from *c.*250–350 CE for the *Mārkandeya*, *Matsya* and *Vayu Purānas*, to *c.*1550 CE for the *Brahmavaivarta Purāna*. It would be futile to attempt to summarise them all in a short work such as this or to go into detail about other Purānas not mentioned above. However, some general points about their importance as sacred texts can be made.

There is continuity between the *Harivamsha* and the Purānas in that Krishna's story as seen in the *Harivamsha* (and the *Bhagavad Gītā*) is filled out in the *Bhāgavata Purāna* and Krishna is portrayed even more as a supreme Lord who welcomes overt devotion in the form of *bhakti*. Likewise there is continuity between the *Mahābhārata* and the Purānas in that some of the Mahābhārata themes are pursued further and expanded. Greater stress is placed upon the various gods in the Purānas rather than upon the human leaders and their wars as in the *Mahābhārata*.

It is good to remember that the Purānas were told originally by bards and only later written down. Also text was added as the recitations and recording continued, so that the dating of the Purānas is difficult to fix. It is true to say that the Hindu Veda and the Hindu sacred texts generally became books rather than being written as books. Oral recitation was important in the beginning (with the partial exception of the *Dharmaśāstras*). The Purānas tell stories centred upon popular religion with gods and demons in conflict, with an emphasis on India (*Bharatvarsha*) and its holy rivers, cities, and places, its festivals and pilgrimages, its rituals and sacraments, its myths and legends and, above all, its concern with devotion. The sacrifices of the early Veda, the spirituality of the Upanishads, the desire for *moksha* (salvation) of the renouncers, the pursuit of *dharma* in the *Dharmaśāstras* and the stories of the two great Epics were not forgotten. They were even elaborated on. Life and death, the sacred and profane, the ascetic and the ordinary, the erotic and the chaste remain and are added to in the Purānas. However *bhakti*, devotional piety, grows in importance, whether as reflective devotion or exuberant devotion. This theme would be taken up with equal or even greater fervour in the vernacular devotional sacred texts. Some of the later Purānas were written in the vernacular rather than in Sanskrit and overlap with the vernacular literature that already existed in the Tamil and other vernaculars.

Bhakti devotional piety is part of the world-view of the Purānas. It centres upon different deities. Vishnu is featured in the *Vishnu Purāna*, Krishna in the *Bhāgavata Purāna*, Shiva in the *Shaiva Purāna* and the Goddess in the *Devi Māhātmya* section of the *Mārkandeya Purāna*. However some Purānas mention a number of deities. For example, the *Brahmā Purāna* praises Krishna, in his form as Jaggarnath at Puri, and also Suryā (the Sun) in his great temple at Konarak in Orissa. Mysteriously Brahmā as a deity in his own right never emerges as a great Hindu god. Equally the *Agni Purāna*, although named after a minor Vedic deity, contains mentions of the *avatāras* of Vishnu, of Krishna's childhood stories, of the Goddess, of the *Mahābhārata* and *Rāmāyana* and of innumerable other matters ranging from *dharma* to Varanasi, to spells, images, marriage, warfare, diplomacy, dancing and warfare! In spite of the compendium of subjects within the Purānas, the deepening stress upon *bhakti* is important. Although a number of deities and minor deities are mentioned, even in the titles of the different Purānas, two matters are especially striking. First, the main deities, Shiva, Vishnu, Krishna and the Goddess, assume greater importance – Rāma only receives serious mention in the *Adhyatma Rāmāyana*, a late insertion into the *Brahmanda Purāna* (Whaling, 1980, p. 111). Second, there is a growing sense that, whatever the name of the deity may be, there is an overarching Reality pervading space and time that is accessible to the *bhakti* of devotees. Alongside the encyclopaedic nature of the Purānas there is also the sense of a caring world of *bhakti* available to both the divine and the human.

Within the Purānas some of the basic themes of the Hindu tradition were either introduced or amplified. Let us give a few examples. The ten *avatāras* of Vishnu (see pp. 41–2) are outlined. Four of the Purānas are named after four *avatāras* of Vishnu, namely *Matsya Purāna* (fish), *Kūrma Purāna* (tortoise), *Varaha Purāna* (boar) and *Vāmana Purāna* (dwarf). Although unimportant in themselves, they make the point that at key times of danger to the world Vishnu became incarnate in their forms to save the world. The Buddha as an *avatāra* of Vishnu indicates that Buddhism had declined and elements of it were being integrated into the Hindu fold. Kalkin represents a kind of apocalyptic Vishnu who would eventually wind up the present world order.

Rāma and Krishna were human *avatāras* of Vishnu, although during the bulk of the Purāna period Krishna was more important than Rāma.

In the Purānas the Goddess became more important. In the *Devi Māhātmya* part of the *Mārkandeya Purāna* (ch. 81–93), as Devi, she is fierce and auspicious and she is connected with Vishnu in the creation of the universe. She is even seen as the essence of all the gods, the one in whom all the qualities of the gods are found. Also in the *Devī Māhātmya*, and in parts of other Purānas, the Goddess is portrayed as the one who kills the demon-lord Mahishāsura and his demon generals and saves the universe from destruction.

In the *Bhāgavata Purāna*, and in the *Vishnu Purāna* and the *Brahma-vaivartha Purāna*, Krishna's story and importance are taken forward from where they were in the *Harivamsha*. The *Harivamsha* had gone beyond the *Bhagavad Gītā*'s portrayal of Krishna as counsellor, politician and hero and had brought out details of Krishna's birth, life and death, and also the fact that he was an *avatāra* of Vishnu. *The Bhāgavata Purāna* goes much further. It stresses the līlā (the divine play) of the young Krishna in Vrindavan as a playful child and adolescent deity. He engages in pranks, he steals butter from his mother, he is unconventional and he is indifferent to regulation. As a youth his play sparkles even more and he brings out this aspect of the 'divine sport' in a unique way among Hindu gods. He is a beautiful youth who is at home with the cowherds and, as a lover of women, he explores the ecstasies of sexual love in a village setting. He remains the miracle worker who kills demons and defeats the serpent Kalīya. Later he kills his tyrant uncle and returns to Mathura as a faithful prince, before eventually moving on to Dwarakā. He marries Rukmini and other wives in respectable and formal fashion. He remains a deity and, finally, he dies. There is a certain dichotomy between the joyful līlā of the young Krishna and the formal dignity of the older Krishna.

Tantric Agamas

Another set of sacred texts, alongside the Purānas, are the Tantric Agamas. The Tantras comprise a vast volume of texts in Sanskrit that claim to supersede the Vedas or completely to reject them. They date from roughly the sixth to twelfth centuries. There are a few Jain Tantras, a great number of Buddhist Tantras, some Vishnu Tantras known as *Pāncharātras*, and many Tantric Agamas in the Shiva and Goddess traditions. There are approximately 28 Shaiva Agamas, 77 Shakta (Goddess) Agamas and many Vaishnava Pancharatra Agamas. The term Agama is often applied more specifically to the Shakta (Goddess) Agamas.

A reason for concentrating upon the Shakta Agamas is that some of their practices go beyond the bounds of normal custom and for this reason their followers have tended to receive a bad name. Part of the reason for this is that they tend to keep their practices and occasionally their writings secret. Some of the mystique concerning these texts and practices was removed by early western authors such as Sir John Woodroffe (1959) in his work *Shakti and Shakta: Essays and Addresses on the Shakta Tantrashastras*.

To summarise the thought lying behind the Agamas, the basic aim is to gain spiritual power (*siddhi*) and liberation in life (*jīvanmukti*) through realising one's own innate divinity. The body is regarded as a microcosm of the wider cosmos. Sacred formulae (*mantras*) are used in Shakti rituals whilst Shakti (the essence of female energy) is stressed. Shakti is often compared favourably with Shiva, the passive male consciousness, which, without Shakti, is weak and inert. There is thus a cosmic male-female polarity that is paralleled in human bodies. Indeed the Tantric texts often follow the procedure of a dialogue between Shakti and Shiva and they explore issues such as cosmology, initiation, *mandalas*, *mantras*, ritual and yoga. It is claimed that in Tantric ritual only a deity can worship a deity, therefore a worshipping participant (*sādhaka*) is purified and divinised by *mantras*. Thus *mantras* are sometimes regarded as identical with Tantric divinities. They themselves are manifestations of an absolute power regarded usually as Shakti but sometimes as Shiva.

Some Tantric Agama rituals involve sexual intercourse, free of caste restrictions, which aim to use sexual energy for spiritual ends and to receive power by breaking conventional taboos. Thus ritual use can be made of the so-called five Ms: wine (*madya*), meat (*mamsa*), fish (*matsya*), parched grain (*mudrā*) and sexual intercourse (*maithuna*). These rituals are unconventional, whether used literally by 'left-hand' followers or metaphorically by 'right-hand' followers, and orthodox Hindus view them accordingly. These practices are used in the context of cult, ritual and meditation. Underlying the whole usage is the sense that a particular practice can be overcome not so much by abstention but by over-involvement, a kind of spiritual therapy. Although Tantric texts date back only to the seventh century CE, elements of the Tantric Hindu tradition are very old and a tradition of ascetics living in cremation grounds dates back to the time of the Upanishads.

Other Tantric elements include Tantric yoga to awaken the power of kundalini which rises up the various centres (chakras) of the body to unite with Shiva at the crown of the head, filling the body with power and spiritual insight. The Agama texts are important because they set out procedures for the building of temples and the construction and installing of images.

They also stress the importance of *mantras* (dynamic sayings), and *yantras* (mystical drawings), together with the relevance of *asanas* (postures) and *mudrās* (gestures). These were important for human beings and also for the deities that, by the sixth century, were being installed in temples. The postures and gestures, especially the hand gestures, of the gods seen in temples were very powerful. In addition to the chanting of the Vedas and other Hindu texts by word of mouth, the seeing of the outwardly visible gods was important. Important too was the inward seeing of the invisible yet imaginably realisable messages of the gods through mystical drawings and through the Tantric innovations which inaugurated important spiritual advances.

Regional Bhakti Sacred Texts

The last great set of *smriti* texts focus upon devotional sacred works in regional languages. There is a certain continuity of sorts between these works and the *bhakti* devotional elements present in one or two of the Upanishads, evident in the Epics, and explicit in many of the Purānas. Although *bhakti* had been clearly apparent outside Sanskrit literature in the Tamil works of the Shaiva Nammalvars and Vaishnava Alvars, it was in the medieval and later medieval period that intense devotional *bhakti* in regional languages came to the fore. Thus the *Tevaram* and *Tiruvācakam* were well-known Tamil sacred works among the early Shaiva saints of South India, as the Tamil *Divyaprabandham* was well-known among the early Vaishava saints of South India.

The great vernacular *bhakti* texts deviated in two ways from the mainstream of Hindu sacred writings. They were in vernacular languages rather than Sanskrit. In the sixth and seventh centuries itinerant devotees among the Nammalvars and Alvars had travelled about South India, from shrine to shrine, singing the praises of their deity and praising his name in worship. Eventually a sizeable canon of devotional poetry arose that acquired the name of the Tamil Veda. Moreover, the saints who composed and recited these sets of Tamil hymns became objects of veneration. Secondly, a number of these hymns were composed by non-Brahmins and were admired by non-Brahmins. The loving, heartfelt and rapturous devotion, passed on through singing and recitation, tended to bypass the religious expertise of the Brahmins. It was therefore possible for lower *varnas*, who were excluded from engaging in worship and from having access to a deity in an orthodox temple, to have direct access to their deity in their own way through their own sacred writings. A third factor, which coincided with trends elsewhere in the world, was for local languages to become more popular at the expense of sacred languages. Thus, Latin in Europe, Arabic in Persia, Pāli and Sanskrit in the Buddhist world and Sanskrit in India lost ground to various local languages. This tendency was accentuated outside North India where Dravidian-type languages were the local languages rather than Sanskrit whilst, even in North India, Sanskrit would become modified into the more popular language of Hindi. A fourth psychological factor was that rapt, heart-warming, deeply emotional hymns and sacred writings in local languages were more accessible and amenable to ordinary non-Brahmins.

Thus it was that the Tamil devotional movement of the sixth to ninth centuries CE spread into other areas. Devotional literature in the vernacular appeared in the Kannada language regions in the tenth to twelfth centuries, in the Marathi language in the thirteenth and fourteenth centuries and through the Hindi regions from the fifteenth century onwards. It was not that Sanskrit disappeared, rather it declined whilst vernacular texts grew.

There is a sense in which *bhakti* movements, even though they focus upon different deities at different times, tend to be similar. Their essence is their hymns which bear the same basic message of loving devotion, albeit in different languages and to different objects of devotion. *Bhakti* stresses the love of deity for humans and deity as the giver of salvation to humans. That deity may be without attributes (*nirguna*) as with Kabīr or send forth *avatāras* as with Vishnu but the power of the deity is clear and all-embracing. It is through the grace of the deity that liberation is brought to followers. There is a relation of love between deity and believer based upon the submission of a person to deity and upon the grace of deity. According to *bhakti*, deity is personal and the human response to deity is personal.

Ritual, sacrifice and outward performance are not of consequence in their own right or for their own sake. Their outward show gets in the way of the devotional end. Over time there may be internal discussions about these matters as movements grow and have to adapt but in principle the stress on the grace and love of deity remains firm.

Bhakti Hinduism also questions undue caste domination, overbearing priests, the lowly status of women and caste restrictions on those outside the Brahmin caste. 'Deity has regard for all' is the implicit view. The power of Brahmins, of the Sanskrit language and of the Veda is questioned, as was the denial of remarriage to a widow and the outrage of satī. *Bhakti* Hindus are a reform movement within the Hindu fold but they stop short of absolute revolt. In order to accommodate emerging circumstances compromise may be necessary. The *bhakti* leaders and saints came from different castes – Kabīr from a weaver family, Namdev was a tailor, Tukaram was a Shūdra, whilst Rāmānuja and Nimbārka were Brahmins (who were relegated from their Brahmin *jātis* for their liberal stance).

Bhakti devotion is not a purely spiritual matter. For example, in temple worship the god is woken up through the music of a hymn, he is dressed and 'organised' personally for worship, he is asked for advice, called upon for help, beseeched for grace – and there is an exchange between temple *bhakti* and personal *bhakti*

Bhakti Hindus also have a strong sense of the anguish of separation from deity even as they have a strong desire for union with deity. And yet the union and oneness of the self (*ātman*) with the Absolute (*Brahman*) found in Advaita Vedanta philosophical mysticism is not ultimately feasible in *bhakti* Hindu traditions. In the other Vedanta *bhakti*-oriented schools a human being can reach the highest reaches of 'union' with *Brahman* but that 'union' is not absolute oneness. It is a love of the soul for deity and the love of deity for the soul that can reach the height of intensity but does not involve the annihilation of the self, the *ātman*, the soul. In *bhakti* spirituality devotees are not fused in deity in a total unity of oneness. They can serve deity (Rāmānandin sādhus take the name of 'Das' or servant), they can love deity, they can participate in deity but they cannot 'be' deity.

How then does *bhakti* differ within itself? The early vernacular devotees had exercised their Tamil *bhakti* in regard to Vishnu in the case of the Alvars, and in regard to Shiva in the case of the Nammalvars. Later movements gave less stress to Shiva or to the Goddess. Vishnu in his own right remained the focus of *bhakti* for Rāmānuja and for Madhva. Later *bhakti* came to be focused more on Krishna, and later still on Rāma. Although they are *avatāras* of Vishnu, *bhakti* traditions grew up that centred on them.

It is interesting to compare the kind of *bhakti* that developed in the Krishna and Rāma traditions. As far as Krishna is concerned more attention was paid among some groups to his love, as a cowherd, for the cowgirl Rādhā (who was not his wife) and that became a human paradigm for divine love. This theme had appeared in the *Bhāgavata Purāna* and was carried further in Jayadeva's twelfth-century *Gītā Govinda* ('Song of the Cowherd'). Thus romantic love became paramount and of all the *bhakti* ways to salvation, impassioned adoration of Krishna became the most powerful. His *līlā* (play), its spontaneity and freedom, became a model of the *līlā* that followers could exercise in regard to Krishna. The Varkari group in Maharashtra viewed their deity Vithoba as being a manifestation of Krishna, especially in his love for Rādhā. In 1591 Keshav Dās wrote the *Rasika Priya* in Hindi in which, as Archer puts it (1957, p. 92), Krishna is 'deemed to know love from every angle and thus to sanctify all modes of passionate behaviour. He is love itself'. In Krishna, *bhakti* and the love for Krishna as a divine romantic lover and also as a divine child receive much attention.

Rāma *bhakti*, by contrast, advanced more slowly and along more sedate lines. The *Rāmāyana* had already introduced the notion that Rāma was an *avatāra* of Vishnu. The *Adhyātma Rāmāyana*, part of the medieval *Mārkandeya Purāna*, enhances the sense that Rāma has a strong *bhakti* element in his nature. As Sugrīva puts it in this work: 'O Rāma, I don't want victory over enemies nor wives and happiness and so on; I just want always devotion to You which releases from bondage' (IV.1.79; Whaling, 1980, p. 185). There are four devotional attitudes towards Rāma reflected in the *Adhyātma Rāmāyana*. The *mādhurya* attitude, the feeling of a lover for his beloved, as symbolised in the love of the *gopis* for Krishna, appears only occasionally. Rāma *bhakti* is moral and chaste and relatively restrained as opposed to the effusiveness of some Krishna *bhakti*. The *vātsalya* attitude, the feeling of parental or fraternal affection for a son or brother, is surprisingly rare in the *Adhyātma Rāmāyana*. More important is the *sākhya* attitude, the love that a friend feels for a friend. Rāma is not so much the lover or the parent of the believer but he is a divine friend. Still more important is the devotional attitude of *dāsya* (service). It is no accident that, on initiation, Rāmānandin sādhus take the name of 'Das' (servant). Family, friends and the world desired to serve Rāma, and as Sugrīva puts it: 'we are all the servants of Rāma'. An additional aspect of devotion to Rāma is that of surrender. Occasionally devotees are described as those who are 'surrendered'. Allied to this notion of the surrender of devotees is Rāma's grace in meeting them. Sometimes Rāma's grace is a response to the devotion of his people, sometimes it triggers devotion in his people. Just as we find four attitudes of devotion, so also do we find four goals of devotion. The usual goal is 'heaven', going to the same world as Rāma, namely *sālokya*, then there are *sāmīpya* (going into the presence of Rāma), *sārūpya* (becoming the same form as Rāma), and *sāyujya* (attaining union with Rāma). The *Adhyātma Rāmāyana* tips over into an Advaita Vedanta strain to the effect that through *sāyujya* (union with Rāma), one is absorbed into Rāma, one is one with Rāma and one no longer exists. The devotional attitude found most frequently in much Krishna *bhakti* is muted in Rāma *bhakti*, namely the *mādhurya* attitude of a lover towards a lover. The attitudes more exalted in Rāma *bhakti* are more muted in Krishna *bhakti*. Tulsīdās would take Rāma *bhakti* deeper than in the *Adhyātma Rāmāyana* so that the various aspects of Rāma's lordship would be integrated within his nature as devotional lord in the *Rāmcaritmanas*, a work of genius. As Tulsīdās writes: 'Fie on the pleasures, actions, dharmas wherein there is no love for Rāma's feet! Yoga is useless, and knowledge is ignorance, wherein Rāma's love is not supreme' (II.291.1).

The fifteenth-century Sant poets – Kabīr, Dadu and Guru Nanak – worship a deity who has no qualities (*nirguna*) and can yet be approached through *bhakti*. They are influenced by Islam. The name that Kabīr especially gives to this 'absolute beyond qualities' remains Rāma, which becomes a general name for godhead in North India, separate from the particular Lord Rāma of the Rāma tradition. Kabīr combines the devotionalism of the Vaishnava tradition with the yoga of the Nātha tradition, and the three main collections of his *bhakti* literature are found in the Eastern (Bījak), Rajasthani (Kabīr Granthāvali) and Punjabi (Adi Granth) poetry. For the Sant movement the Absolute is beyond rational thought and language, and yet the *bhakti* repetition of the name and sound of the godhead, perceived in meditation, liberates one from illusion (*māyā*) and from rebirth (*samsāra*).

Further Reading

There is an extraordinary length and breadth of Hindu scripture. There is a wider literature that, so to speak, lies on the fringes of sacred texts. This would include the great literature of Kālidāsa in the fifth century and of Bhavabhuti in the seventh–eighth century. Indeed, Sir William Jones's translation of Kālidāsa's *Shakuntala* in 1789, followed by comments from Goethe in 1819, was a landmark in the early western attraction to India and the Hindu tradition. Important, as 'auxiliary scriptures', were the *Brahmasūtras* (or *Vedantasūtras*) of Bādarāyana which summarised the teachings of the Upanishads in a series of short aphorisms and were drawn on by the great Vedanta philosophers from Shankara onwards.

Lastly, 'scripture' in all religions can be seen under three main headings: the original written version; the interpretations of that version given down the ages; and then there is the question of what the scripture means for people now. There is a sense in which, in spite of their seemingly enormous differences, scriptures interpret, or reinterpret one another. Thus it is possible to trace some continuity, albeit sometimes indistinct, between these writings.

Modern Interpretations of Sacred Texts: Great Thinkers

The modern age has seen the rise of a number of great thinkers who have reinterpreted their own religion in the light of the modern world including: Ram Mohan Roy, Ramakrishna, Vivekananda, Dayananda Saraswati, Tilak, Gandhi, Radhakrishnan and Sri Aurobindo.

The clear-cut differences in the thought of modern Hindu thinkers have, nevertheless, enabled them to debate along the different branches of the great banyan tree that is the Hindu tradition. A different kind of postmodernism already exists in India. The Jain proverb of the blind men who touch different parts of an elephant, assuming that each touches the whole elephant, whereas all of them touch only part of the elephant, applies to the Hindu tradition as well.

Ram Mohan Roy (1772–1833)

Sometimes called the 'morning star of the Indian Renaissance', Roy was a great man who combined interests in Islam, Unitarian Christianity, social betterment, education, science and Hindu reform. He was able to retire early and apply himself to the reform of the Hindu tradition, especially in the areas of caste and the plight of widows. He founded the Brahmo Samaj as a medium of reform and he was especially interested in the Upanishads. Roy's interest was not in the early Vedas or in the sectarian deities of the Purānas, Tantras or vernacular *Bhakti*. His concern was to appropriate what he saw to be the implied monotheism of the Upanishads as being relevant to the abolition of dated Hindu practices, such as satī, and as helpful to a general updating of Hindu theory and practice.

Ramakrishna (1834–86)

Ramakrishna was more confident in the spiritual power and depth of the Hindu tradition. His own deep spiritual experience incorporated elements of Sufi Islam and Christ as well as devotional, Tantric and Advaita Hinduism. Hinduism was seen as a corrective to the materialism and spiritual shallowness of the West. He queried the need for conversion of other persuasions but promised them hospitality alongside the Hindu tradition within the total religious spectrum. As one who served in a Kali temple in Calcutta, he owed a debt to Kali and the Tantric textual tradition and also to the Upanishads and some Bhakti texts, although he knew neither English or Sanskrit. Like Ram Mohan Roy, he was also interested in some Sufi and Christian texts as relevant to a greater Hindu inclusivism, although his ultimate interest was in the samādhi of spiritual experience

Swami Vivekananda (1863–1902)

Vivekananda was a follower of Ramakrishna and founded the Ramakrishna Mission in honour of his mentor. Whereas Ramakrishna had used image worship in his spirituality, Vivekananda's main interest was in Vedanta as found in the Upanishads, especially Advaita Vedanta. According to Vivekananda, Vedanta contained different levels of truth and a spiritual hierarchy that made it possible for the Hindu tradition to encompass other religious traditions while retaining Vedanta as the fountainhead of all traditions. Following him the Hindu tradition became dynamic outside India and other guru figures followed him in extolling Vedanta and the insights it could bring. Through the Ramakrishna Mission's organising power Vivekananda promoted social work, Vedanta thought, and Hindu values at a more global level. The Hindu tradition, centred upon Vedanta, now became a proselytising force. Vedanta thought and scriptures became known around the world.

Dayananda Saraswati (1824–83)

Saraswati took a different direction. He founded the Arya Samaj in 1875 in order to reform the Hindu tradition in India and to proselytise in India, including reconverting people who had left the Hindu fold. Dayananda Saraswati gave priority to the original *Rig Veda* as his key scripture. Ironically, he first studied the *Rig Veda* through Max Muller's seminal translation of that work in the latter's ground-breaking *Sacred Books of the East* published in Oxford. Dayananda Saraswati misconstrued the *Rig Veda* by supposing that it promoted monotheism and anticipated modern science. He opposed the worship of images and exaggerated rituals, and he advocated the original *homa* fire offering of the *Rig Veda* as an appropriate worship of the one God. His aim was to go back to the pristine Aryan practices of long ago when there were only four *varnas* and not multitudes of *jātis*. He supposed that the four *varnas* were based on merit and not on birth. Although missing out the later layers of sacred texts as being superfluous, Dayananda Saraswati was an unusual and important Hindu reformer.

B. G. Tilak (1856–1920)

Like Gandhi Tilak opposed the British occupation of India and like Gandhi he wrote on the *Bhagavad Gītā*. However, he was more militant than Gandhi and his long commentary on the *Bhagavad Gītā* was written while he was in prison. For him the *Bhagavad Gītā* was partly a call to seek independence for India, if necessary through violence. This could involve killing the British. As Tilak put it, when killing the body of a British policeman or soldier, one was not killing their real self, their *ātman*, one was only killing their body. Their *ātman* could be born again. Gandhi, as we shall see, agreed that the *Bhagavad Gītā* was the key scripture, but he interpreted it very differently from Tilak. Tilak also promoted the reputation of the long-dead ruler Shivaji, who had fought for Maratha independence against the Mughals. Tilak reinstated the worship of the Hindu deity Ganesha in Maharashtra and this is the largest public event in the state of Maharashtra today.

Mahatma Gandhi (1869–1948)

Gandhi stressed non-violence (*ahimsa*), holding fast to the Truth (*Satyagraha*) which, for Gandhi, was almost equivalent to God. His key sacred text was the *Bhagavad Gītā* to which the Christian Sermon on the Mount came second in importance. Another key text for Gandhi was the *Rāmāyana* and his ideal was for an independent India to become Rāmarājya, the kingdom of Rāma on earth. For him the *Bhagavad Gītā* was a symbolic presentation of the warfare within the self between good and evil, rather than referring to an actual battle. Although a Hindu text, the *Bhagavad Gītā* was relevant at a wider, interfaith level and Gandhi engaged at an early stage in what would now be called interfaith activity.

Sarvepalli Radhakrishnan (1888–1975)

Radhakrishnan was a thinker rather than an activist. He was a great teacher and philosopher and his political interests culminated in service as President of India. The key to his thought lies in Vedanta and the Upanishads, although he wrote on Indian philosophy in general. His many writings reinterpret some of the classical Hindu doctrines in the light of the modern world. He stresses the role of philosophy but takes a Hindu view of how it works. For him philosophy is entwined with religion; it uses intuition as well as intellect and it recognises mystery as well as reason. Radhakrishnan reinterpreted Hindu ideas for our time (see pp. 146-9).

Sri Aurobindo (1872–1950)

Aurobindo carried Radhakrishnan's concern for reinterpretation of Hindu thought further. His sources included a wide variety of Hindu texts. He had a high regard for the *Bhagavad Gītā*. He also paid almost unique attention to the *Rig Veda* and gave due attention to the Upanishads as well. Aurobindo also used the Tantras of his native Bengal with their references to the Goddess. Thus his Hindu textual sources were wide. Like Radhakrishnan he applied them in a Hindu way and like Radhakrishnan he reinterpreted them in the light of the contemporary world. It is Aurobindo who has most persuasively articulated a Hindu vision of future human unity. He appropriated the theory of creative evolution, and he emphasised what he called 'integral yoga' which melded bodily yoga, mental yoga, heart yoga and spiritual yoga. His is the most significant attempt to bring together, in a viable whole, the insights of the different kinds of Hindu scripture.

9

Hindu Aesthetics

The Hindu tradition has arguably the richest aesthetic tradition among all the world's religious traditions. From early tribal and Indus Valley times to the present day, the Hindu tradition has experimented with and developed a variety of aesthetic forms ranging from tribal and village arts, architecture, sculpture, temples, images and painting (whether realistic or more abstract), to the performing arts of theatre, song and dance.

It has been suggested that for most people at most times aesthetic representations have been more important and immediate than theology, ideas and scriptures. Throughout most of historical time the majority have relied upon artefacts of one kind or another, rather than words, for living their religious life. Moreover, until recently, most art has been religious art.

Tribal and Village Art

The number of people living in the tribal areas of India is not known exactly but numbered around sixty-eight million in the 1991 Census. The tribal and also the village religions have received little attention partly because of the small and ephemeral nature of their artefacts. In the case of the tribal communities it is also true to say that, in the main, they are not Hindu. However, they and the village religions have fed into the mainstream Hindu tradition.

The main tribal communities are neither Aryan nor Dravidian in background. They represent older groups. Either through oppression or choice, they live in the most out-of-the-way and detached parts of India, for example in the hilly forest areas of Central India, where they live by fishing, hunting and gathering. Economically, culturally and linguistically they are different from the mainstream and yet their contact with the surrounding farmers and town dwellers has been relevant to Hindu art and religion.

Tribal cults appear to have been linked to natural forces such as trees, certain animals and climatic factors such as the monsoon. There is some evidence of the absorption of tribal elements into later Hindu traditions.

For example, although there is little trace of animal deities in Vedic religion, they are fairly common in later religion. Thus the early descents of Vishnu include the fish, tortoise, boar, and man-lion *avatāras* (incarnations) whose origins may have been in tribal groups. These groups appear to have provided a reservoir of religious and aesthetic notions that 'orthodox' Hindus could use. These seemingly excluded groups have thus gradually contributed to Hindu culture often in important ways. Some tribal communities in various parts of India paint decorations on the walls or floors of their houses. This painting is often done by women. In Gujarat walls are covered in white paint interspersed with vegetable and flower designs. Tribal Saoras in Orissa paint pictograms in their homes to serve as shrines. Warli tribes in Maharashtra create important chowk paintings for family marriages. In other places wall or floor paintings are created in times of crisis, to help with fertility, to protect huts from malign forces and to demarcate homes for deities. The motives for tribal art are usually fertility, health, prosperity, protection and purification.

Tribal groups often have simple shrines. They may also have a priest, who has no special status. The tribal image may be as simple as a large coloured stone, a group of wooden posts or terracotta pots. However, the tribal gods are deities in the sense that they are a focus for prayer but not always for worship. In some tribal areas the shrine may be a platform covered by a thatched roof held up by four supporting posts, and grass is placed on top of the roof for special ceremonies. Clay figures of animals ranging from horses to elephants are sometimes left behind after being offered in ritual to the god. In other areas special dolmens or standing stones are raised to serve as memorials for those who are dead.

Fieldwork has brought this tribal art to wider notice. The problem is, of course, that tribal art is often ephemeral. It is not made to last for ever. It is made for a particular purpose. Contemporary Indian painters, such as Jamini Roy in Bengal and Jyoti Sati in Karnataka, are using tribal themes in their paintings today.

Village art shares some of the characteristics of tribal art. However, it is not so marginal. India still remains a land of villages even if globalisation and the inexorable rise of cities are making strong inroads into village life. The flight from villages to cities has been somewhat slower in India than in many other parts of the world. It has been claimed that 70% of Indians still identify with a village rural community, but it would be naïve to underestimate the importance of the shift away from villages.

In Hindu villages there are a variety of gods. There is often greater emphasis upon the Goddess than in the wider Hindu tradition. In the villages there is sometimes overlap between worship of the orthodox 'high god', served by the Brahmin priest, and the worship of other gods and goddesses. There will normally be one or two temples served by a Brahmin priest, and a far greater number of shrines of local gods and goddesses and these are usually much better frequented. Especially in South India, most villagers are devotees of village deities rather than of major Hindu gods. Female deities, known as grāmadevatās, are especially important. Sometimes village goddesses have shrines in simple buildings. At other times they have an image in the open air that may be as simple as a pile of stones marked by a flag. In village India a variety of gods may be worshipped ranging from a major deity, to a goddess, to a ghost, to a tree spirit.

As far as art is concerned, there is the tendency for village art, like tribal art, to be ephemeral. Potters are important. In addition to making terracotta figurines of various kinds, in South India potters sometimes take up ritual responsibilities of bestowing form and power into their creation. When passed on to a patron, life is breathed into the image they have created. Occasionally potters worship their tools and celebrate the power of their deities to help them change matter into sacred form.

The ritual of wall and floor painting, mainly by women, is also common in village India. A variety of patterns, symbols and designs are used that are deemed to be auspicious. One motive for painting them is to protect the home from harm. However, another motive is to revere and celebrate the gods who are the protectors of the home. Due to wear, floor and wall paintings often need to be repainted and this is often done seasonally at the time of major festivals and also at rites of passage such as birth, puberty, marriage and death. Hindu village folk art exists side by side with Brahmanical temple art. It offers the lower *jātis*, and the women who are often worship leaders, alternative means of communicating with the divine. From the medieval *bhakti* groups, who used regional languages and appealed to a wider range of castes, music was incorporated into village life in the form of *bhajans* (hymns) that could be sung in local languages. However, hymns cannot be seen and village visual art is mainly ephemeral. More significant were architecture and sculpture and these arts were influenced by the tribal and village art that reflect part of 'wider Hinduism'.

The Sacred Architecture of Temples

The most obvious example of Hindu sacred architecture is to be found in temples. The theory of temples is found in the *Shilpashastras*, dealing with sculpture, and the *Vastushastras*, dealing with architecture. Brahmins were more concerned with the *Vastushastras*, covering the theory and the rituals necessary for building a temple. The Kshatriyas and Vaishyas (craftsmen) were more concerned with the active running of the temples to be found in the *Shilpashastras*. Brahmins shared ideas with the architects whose exact plans were crucial for temple building and at the end of the building work Brahmins led the ritual solemnisation of the temple.

In Vedic times sacrifice itself was the key event, not so much the place where sacrifice was offered. As the religious focus switched from sacrifice to worship and to entering the presence of deity, more attention needed to be paid to the building where the worship was being held. The temple building had to be correct, ritually, for both the humans who visited it and for the god or gods who inhabited it. The temple became a kind of microcosm of the universe with the deity at the centre.

At the centre of the temple there was an image of the deity in an appropriate sanctum. He was surrounded by various followers who served him in one way or another, organised in order of rank. His consort came first, then his mount, then other helping deities, then eight deity guards, then the planetary deities, then folk deities, and finally his sacred plants. The geographical setting was important too. Preferably it would be near potent water, such as the Ganges at Varanasi or the Sangam of sacred rivers at Allahabad. A second alternative would be next to a sacred tank of water.

Over two thousand years temples have evolved from little more than shrines, in places like Mathura, to enormous structures like Madurai and Rameshvaram. Increasingly they became free-standing structures in their own grounds. A less common alternative was for temples to be built into rock formations, such as those at Ellora and Ajanta in the Western Ghats, at Badami in the Deccan and at Mahabalipuram in South India. One development was the differentiation in style between North Indian and South Indian temples. Some of North India's great temples at Varanasi, Mathura and Somnath were sacked during the Muslim invasions, whilst those in South India were safer and bigger temples were built with impunity. Stylistically northern temples had a taller tower (*shikhāra*) than those in the South whereas, in the South, the temple gateway (*gopura*) was elevated and often strikingly colourful, especially in Tamil Nadu at places such as Shrirangam, Madurai and Tiruvannamali.

In temples offerings are made to the presiding deity of flowers, food, fruit, incense and money by the devotees who visit. Their motives range from simple gratitude and love, desire for a good life, gaining advantage over others or just pacifying the deity. In return for his or her offerings and attendance at the temple the devotee has the opportunity to 'see' the deity through *darshana*, and to receive a present from the deity in the form of *prasāda*. *Prasāda* is sometimes the return of the devotee's own gifts, blessed by the deity. *Darshana* is a very special experience of seeing and being seen by the deity. Insofar as it is the basic reason for entering the temple, the shape of the temple is geared towards channelling the worshipper from the entrance towards the image of the deity.

While in the temple the visitor may visit other parts of the temple complex. Tiny temples have a simple design that may be only an entrance door leading to the shrine where the deity is placed. Above the shrine a tower may indicate to the outside world that it is a temple.

In large temples there is an abundance of rooms and items. Inside the gateway of the temple there are sculptured figures of guardian deities, and often of Ganesha, the 'Lord of Openings'. Inside the courtyard there are smaller buildings leading up to the main sanctum of the deity. In the *mandapa* space surrounding the central shrine, hymns (*bhajans*) to the god may be sung, stories told and teaching given. On the walls of the *mandapas*, paintings and sculptures illustrate basic episodes from sacred texts, such as the Epics and Purānas. After the *mandapa* space there is a vestible chamber leading up to the sanctuary in which there is often a statue of the mount of the presiding deity gazing devotedly into the sanctum of its lord. Many Hindu temples are filled with aesthetic features and figures. These are designed to protect the building and to instruct devotees. They are also there for ornamentation. The lower sections of the walls often have flower designs and niches containing subsidiary gods. Above there are friezes that feature the chief deity accompanied, on either side, by attendant deities and guardians. These friezes may include musicians, animals and heavenly maidens. The corniches above the friezes may depict narrative scenes from the Epics and Purānas. Temple doors represent a passage from the ordinary world to the divine world, from the secular to the spiritual arena, and they are decorated accordingly. Windows and doors are enhanced by symbolic features.

One element that sometimes surprises is the maithuna images in Hindu temples. These are couples engaged in various forms of sexual activity. They were present in the Kailasa temple at Ellora as early as the sixth century. From the tenth century, in temples such as those at Bhubaneshvar and Khajuraho, these images became more aesthetic, erotic and sophisticated. They came to illustrate most sexual couplings known to humans and include some that are little known as well. The background to this development is complicated. The pre-Aryan tribal background with its greater sexual freedom, the growing influence of Tantric ideas, literary works such as the Kāma Sūtra, the mystical and sacral input of yoga and the notion that loving maithuna embraces could symbolise *moksha* all combined to give multiple meanings to the maithuna images in Hindu temples. Kāma, after all, was the first aim of life, and the maithuna images recognised the sensual part of life. Yet these images could also conjure up, metaphorically, the sense of union between humans and deity transferred to the spiritual realm. In other words, Hindu aesthetics could comprehend the different realms of life that make up the whole. One footnote to this theme is the fact that human female figures, in the form of *surasandaris* (women of celestial beauty), are also depicted on temple walls without the sexual connotations of the maithuna images.

Images of Hindu Deities

Countless images of the Hindu gods have been made down the ages. There are many images of each of the main deities that explore different elements of their characters and traits. They are multifaceted in their complexity. They demonstrate the sheer variety of the Hindu tradition and the many-sidedness of Hindu insights into life. By contrast with other religious traditions, which concentrate on the benevolent aspects of their deities and saints, the Hindu gods are portrayed in different moods and guises. They are capable of malevolence as well as graciousness. They are portrayed in abstract terms as well as through vivid pictures. They can be fierce as well as beautiful. Because of this they offer endless aesthetic scope.

Shiva

Shiva is a more complex god than Vishnu. He can be an example or he can depart from normally accepted boundaries of behaviour. He can be fierce or gracious. He is the ascetic figure but he can yet be worshipped in the form of the male *lingam*. He is the lone wanderer who also has a wife and two children.

Shiva's most familiar symbol is that of the *lingam*. He is commonly symbolised as an upright stone phallic symbol. This penis representation is not offensive in India. It is recognised and venerated by young and old, by men and women. It symbolises Shiva's power, his energy and his inherent capacity for growth. An early Shiva *lingam*, at Gudimallam in Andhra Pradesh, has Shiva in human form standing in the shaft of the *lingam* itself, thus combining the human and symbolic Shivas. Later Shiva *lingams* were often set inside *yonis* (symbols of female sexual organs). However, the *yonis* were fashioned so that they arose out of the *lingam* rather than surrounding it in sexual fashion. The Lingāyats of Karnatika carried a *lingam* in a box around their necks. They did not keep stone pillar *lingams*, nor could the *lingam* in their boxes be seen, yet they still used the *lingam* as a precious symbol of Shiva. Yet another sculptural variation appears when Shiva appears in

Shiva Nataraja: Shiva dances in a ring of fire that symbolically destroys ignorance, represented by a demon dwarf, and raises his hand in mercy to all. He brings together power and mercy, awe and serenity.

human form in an opening within a *lingam*, while above and below him appear Vishnu and Brahmā, disputing who is the greatest, until Shiva shows himself in human form in the *lingam* as the greatest deity of them all.

Another well-known representation of Shiva in human form is Shiva as Nataraja, the Lord of the Dance. There are many of these circular symbols of Shiva, the most famous being at Chidambaram in Tamil Nadu. The Nataraja portrays Shiva dancing vividly within a ring of fire. The dance is fierce and yet controlled. The dance is frenzied, yet Shiva is serene. He is surrounded by the fire that symbolically destroys ignorance whilst he plays on a drum, a symbol of creation. Within the famous wheel circle of the Nataraja, Shiva crushes a demon dwarf, who represents ignorance, and he raises his hand in a merciful caring gesture while pointing to his foot, a place where the devotee can find help. The Nataraja is a symbol of the round of life and death. It is also a symbol of Shiva reconciling these seeming opposites in a portrayal that combines both his power and his mercy. In it we see both the awe and the serenity of Shiva.

A third portrayal of Shiva is as the patron of asce*tics*. In the *Dakṣinamūrti* (image facing South) he appears as a teacher who is a yogi ascetic. He is a young, long-haired teacher whose image (*mūrti*) is facing south (dakṣina) in the way that Shiva faces south from his mountain stronghold in the Himalayas. He sits in front of a sacred tree, using his hands as a teacher and preaching to ascetics and to others who will listen, in the tradition of the Buddha. In such indirect ways the Buddha was absorbed into Hindu thought and imagery.

A fierce portrayal of Shiva shows him in less appealing form as Bhairava. Bhairava is seen, somewhat dramatically, as a different kind of ascetic who has a long stick, wild matted hair and an erect penis. He wears a garland of skulls and bears a horrific skull in his hand. He had beheaded a Brahmin and in penance had to travel round endlessly with a dog until he finally found redemption in Varanasi. The Bhairava Tantras were named after him, and the Aghori ascetics of Varanasi still continue the tradition of the Shaivite Kāpālikas. They use ashes from cremation grounds and generally frowned on left-handed Tantric practices. At the other extreme the Sanskrit alphabet 'can also be considered as an alphabetic form of the god Bhairava' (Padoux, 2005, p. 487). Such are the complexities within Shiva.

A fifth portrayal of Shiva connects him with his family. His wife is the goddess Pārvatī. A Maharashtra glass painting shows Pārvatī sitting with Shiva. She is young and attractive and they are fond of one another. Shiva is sitting on his mount, Nandi the bull. Pārvatī has the elephant-headed deity Ganesha on her lap. The goddess Gangā is on Shiva's head and from Gangā flows the water that forms the river Ganges. A number of South Indian sculptures also show Shiva and Pārvatī sitting in comfort with their child Skanda between them. There are also aesthetic representations of Shiva and Pārvatī combined in the same image. Shiva is on the right and Parvati on the left but they are joined in one person. Shiva carries his favourite implements, a trident and a drum whilst his river, the Ganges, flows from his hair. Pārvatī carries a rosary. Two of Shiva's favourite places are featured in symbols of him. They are Varanasi, the city on the Ganges never forsaken by Shiva, and Mount Kailash, which is his home in the Himalayas.

The combinations of these images represent an extraordinary selection of the modes of Shiva's nature. Hindus bring to their aesthetic viewing not just mental ideas, that tend to separate, but also gifts of the senses and an emotive power of feelings that tend to connect and unite.

Vishnu

Vishnu represents an aesthetic contrast to Shiva. Shiva combines contrasting gifts of beauty, power, danger, asceticism, mercy and unusualness. Vishnu symbolises order, security, harmony, well-being and continuity. He is the preserver of order, the kingly figure, the deity of love, the incarnating lord and the god of salvation.

The image of Vishnu that is most common shows him with four arms and standing upright. He wears a crown on his head to mark his kingly aspect. In his four arms he carries two weapons, namely a club (*gada*) and a discus (*cakra*), and also a conch shell (*śankha*) and a lotus. These four symbols, especially the discus and conch shell, also appear as decorative symbols on the utensils and vessels used in Vishnu rituals. Stones sacred to Vishnu, called *śālagrāmas*, have the shape of the cakra (discus) already present in the ammonite fossils they are made from. Sometimes Vishnu images have one arm vacant, in which case the two spare hands are used in order to portray well-known hand gestures (mudrās) also associated with the Buddha, namely the no-fear (*abhaya*) gesture and the giving-of-a-gift (*varadā*) gesture. Vishnu is thus seen to be a granter of boons and the one who casts out fear. Since the twelfth century, Vishnu has been worshipped as Varadarajaswami, the giver of gifts, at Kanchipuram in Tamil Nadu. The image has him extending his palm outwards to grant the wishes of those who want their wishes fulfilled. At the world-famous temple at Tirupati in Andhra Pradesh, where Vishnu is known as Venkateshvara, he holds out his palm in the same *varada* gesture. At Pandharpur temple in Maharashtra, made famous by Jnaneśvara, Vishnu as Vithoba holds out one of his hands to devotees.

Vishnu wears a kingly crown, and in his four arms he carries two
weapons (a club and a discus), and also a conch shell and a lotus flower.

The spouse of Vishnu is Lakshmī. She has a cult of her own as the goddess
of prosperity and wealth. As the consort of Vishnu, she is often shown seated
on Vishnu's lap and they are known in this image as Lakshmī-Nārāyana,
Nārāyana being another name for Vishnu. In Nepal they are sometimes
joined together in a single figure, one part of the image being male and the
other female. This is similar to the Shiva-Pārvatī icon in which they too are
joined together in one image.

Another representation of Vishnu portrays him, in painting and iconography, as involved in the creation of the world at the beginning of each cycle.
He is seen lying in a trance in the interim between the end of one era and
the beginning of another. He is asleep on top of the coils of the cobra Śeṣa,
whose hood fans above Vishnu in a canopy of protection. In the prelude to
creation, from the navel of the recumbent Vishnu a lotus blossom rises up
carrying Brahmā. It is Brahmā who creates the new world cycle, with auxiliary help from Vishnu.

More prolific aesthetic symbols are thrown up when we consider the ten
avatāras (incarnations) of Vishnu. The motif of almost all of the *avatāras* is
that Vishnu came, in different forms, to help the world at its times of need.

Fish (Matsya)
The *Avatāra* is depicted in a striking ninth-century Central Indian sculpture as a stone fish carrying a shrine that it had saved from a tremendous flood at the dawn of creation. According to the myth, Vishnu, in the form of a fish, saved primal humans and also the sacred Vedas from the great flood.

Tortoise (Kurma)
The second *Avatāra* involves a creation myth centred upon the Tortoise as the stable base upon which the world was made. This is shown in paintings from Maharashtra and elsewhere. The cosmic ocean was churned by using the mountain Mandara as a churning pole, firmly placed on the Tortoise *Avatāra*, and by the gods using the snake Vasuki as a churning rope. Some versions of the story depict poison being thrown up along with heavenly nectar in the successful process of creation. At this point Shiva enters the Vishnu story to swallow the poison and save the human race but in the process he has his throat discoloured so that he becomes the blue-throated deity.

Boar (Varāha)
The third *Avatāra* also has a creation theme. When the earth was totally flooded, Varāha brought the earth back from the bottom of the ocean where it had been kept by a sea-demon. In the images of the story the earth is personified as the goddess Bhu. Varāha has the body of a human but the head of a boar. He is often shown defeating the sea-demon while carrying up the world balanced on his tusks. He also holds in his hands the four Vishnu attributes of club, conch shell, lotus and wheel. From the fourth to eighth centuries the Varāha *Avatāra* was popular in rock caves and temples in South India.

Man-Lion (Narasimha)
The story tells of the killing of the Shiva king, Hiranyakapishu, who was given the gift of immortality in return for penances done. However, immortality was given with three provisos: he could not be killed except by someone who was neither man nor beast; when it was neither night nor day; and when he was neither inside nor outside his palace. The Man-Lion *Avatāra* managed to do this and he murdered the king as is shown in paintings from the Deccan. The story is unusual in that it is cruel and is anti-Shaivite.

Dwarf (Vāmana)
The fifth *Avatāra* is also the first human one. He is often depicted as a Brahmin Dwarf, holding a water-pot and an umbrella. Vishnu appears as Vāmana to counter the threat to the world by King Bali. He asks the king

for land that he could cover in three small steps. When this is granted he becomes a giant who covers the whole world in three steps as shown in sculptures from east India. It is a classical Hindu, indeed common, story of the little man defeating the big one.

Rāma with the Axe (Paraśurāma)

The sixth *Avatāra* is another more obviously martial incarnation. Like the Man-Lion *Avatāra* story, it emerges from an era of dispute. This time the conflicting parties are the Brahmin and Kshatriya castes. In return for the murder of his Brahmin father, Paraśurāma kills the members of the guilty Kshatriya family. Moreover, according to the myth, this killing of the family would continue over twenty generations. There is no strong cult of Paraśurāma today, and the depictions of the story tend to be rather gory ones portraying the death of the Kshatriya leader and his entourage.

Buddha

The ninth *Avatāra* of Vishnu was the Buddha. This was unusual in that the Buddha was a human being who lived in historical time and he was the founder of another religious tradition. However, it marked the start of a process whereby attempts would be made to incorporate Christ and figures from other religious traditions into the Hindu fold.

Kalkin

The tenth *Avatāra* of Vishnu is still to come. He has no following in any cult. He is the final *avatāra* who will usher in the end of this world cycle known as *kali yuga*. After an interim period, the first age (*kṛta yuga*) of a new world cycle will begin and at the end of that cycle Kalkin will repeat his role. He is mainly depicted as a horse-headed human wielding a sword and crown. Occasionally he is depicted as a horse itself.

Rāma

Throughout this book Rāma and Krishna have been dealt with as separate deities, with great followings in many parts of India, and in the case of Rāma a reputation that is known throughout South East Asia. They are strictly speaking the seventh and eighth *avatāras* of Vishnu. On the one hand, they enhance the general virtues of Vishnu but, on the other, there is evidence that they derive from historical figures and they bring out the *bhakti* devotional glory that is their hallmark. In so doing they, so to speak, transcend Vishnu and become cherished deities in their own right. Indeed the name of Rāma is now used in much of North India as a general word for God.

There is a sense in which (in Kamban's Tamil version, Buddharāja's Telugu version, Tulsīdās's Hindi version and other versions of the *Rāmāyana*) the original sense of Vishnu as the kingly figure who preserves and promotes the established order of things is filled out. In another sense the divine/human qualities of Rāma and Krishna, as evidenced in their literature and iconography, go far beyond the elements of divinity found in Vishnu and his other *avatāras* and propel them into uniqueness.

In the great popular acting of Rāmlīla festivals, the story of Rāma is illustrated aesthetically in open-air drama. The story is represented in painting and sculpture in a myriad of different ways. The original story of the Epic *Rāmāyana* is depicted in great temples, in paintings, in images and in decorated manuscripts. The later stories of the divine Rāma are added so that his divinity and his kingly human *dharma* are enhanced.

Favourite portrayals, in sculpture and in painting, are of Rāma, his wife Sītā and his faithful brother Lakshmana in the forest after Rāma's tragic banishment. Their adventures in the forest are portrayed aesthetically. Particular elements in Rāma's tussle with the demon king Rāvana are brought out. They include the abduction of Sītā from the forest to Lanka by Rāvana. The role of Hanumān, the monkey god, is crucial in rescuing Sītā. Representations of Rāma, Sītā, Lakshmana and Hanumān together are common. The bear Jambavān and the vulture Jatāyu are important, too. The epic battle between Rāma and Rāvana, and Rāma's victory, are highlighted in various reliefs. Sītā's ordeal to prove her innocence after the victory is a favourite theme. The triumphant return of Rāma to Ayodhya, his becoming king of Ayodhya, and his presiding over Rāmarājya are given aesthetic portrayal as well. Rāma is the ideal king and an exemplary figure. Many presentations of him attempt to signal this. There are attempts to bring it out in iconography. He is unusual among Hindu deities in that he has a religious sense of 'grief', a kind of empathy combined with admiration and awe, in that he does what is right even though it may not be prudent. The story of the *Rāmāyana* is carved on the walls of a modern temple in Varanasi, so that one sees Rāma's story, in marble, imprinted on the walls.

Krishna

Krishna is the subject of a number of different stories and therefore of a number of different aesthetic representations. Although there are many sculptures of Krishna, the main examples come from the extensive tradition of painting that has been induced by Krishna. The paintings are inspired by the *Bhagavad Gītā*, *Harivamsha*, *Bhāgavata Purāna*, *Gītā Govinda* and many later *bhakti* writings associated with Vallabha, Chaitanya and others.

Sometimes Krishna is shown as the god-child at Vrindāban on the river Jumna. He is the frolicsome divine child, who is mischievous and steals the butter when his foster-mother is not looking, in a Basohli Punjab painting from 1790.

He is also the cowherd-god who disports erotically with the cowgirls (*gopis*) in Vrindāban. He steals their clothes in one Kangra Punjab painting of 1790 and he charms them with his enticing flute in another Kangra Punjab painting. These scenes are allegories of the love of the soul for god and the love of god for the soul.

Then the dark-blue skinned Krishna is entranced by Rādhā and she is entranced by him in scenes that lead to intense love, then separation, then love again – as seen in a number of Punjab paintings. This intensity of love is now particular rather than general. It portrays the sheer fervour of love between Krishna and devotees exemplified in the depth of emotion for Krishna shown by Vallabha and Chaitanya, and also the present-day Hare Krishnas.

In a Punjab painting in New Delhi Museum and also in sculptures at Varanasi, Krishna is shown helping the cowgirls to stop worshipping the Vedic god Indra. Indra is incensed at Krishna's actions and sends violent rain on the cowgirls, at which point Krishna lifts up Mount Govardhana and holds it like an umbrella over the cowgirls.

Krishna also performed other miracles. These include his fight with the great snake Kalīya, which he defeats by dancing on the head of the cobra king. When defeated, Kalīya accepts an invitation to become a devotee of Krishna, showing Krishna's power and grace, seen in symbols in Varanasi and Calcutta.

Krishna is also featured in paintings and representations of the *Bhagavad Gītā* as the one who reveals himself as god, who teaches Arjuna and persuades him to fight in the great battle at the centre of the *Mahābhārata*. Although the *Bhagavad Gītā* is very popular, this important saga in Krishna's life is present more in popular art than in classical paintings.

In the latter part of his life Krishna married Rukmini who becomes his queen and, having defeated his wicked uncle Kamsa, he ruled over Dwārakā, which is now a key centre of Krishna devotion. The Dwārakā temple on the west coast of India is a key place for Krishna worship. It is also one of the four places of pilgrimage (*dhamas*) that are the four-cornered boundaries of sacred India, the others being Badrināth in the north, Purī in the east and Rāmeshvaram in the south. Scenes from the eve of Krishna's final encounter with Kamsa and of him saving Rukmini and marrying her are shown in a Kangra Punjab painting (1790) and a Milaspur Punjab painting (1795).

A final parable of Krishna's divine love occurs when a poor Brahmin named Sudama goes to Krishna when he is the king ruling in pomp at the court in Dwaraka. Sudama is in rags but Krishna welcomes him, washes his feet and hails him as a Brahmin. It duplicates in a different way Krishna's dances with the cowgirls and makes the point that there can be some continuity between the seemingly different episodes in Krishna's life. It is found in a Kangra Punjab painting from 1785.

Devi

Finally we consider aesthetic representations of Devi. The stories of the Goddess and the very different symbols that depict Devi range from her being very fierce to her being benign. In one sense she is symbolised not so much in artefacts but in the very soil of India itself. She is concerned with the fertility of the earth. The great rivers of India, especially the Ganges, are sometimes worshipped as symbols of her as the fertile mother goddess who replenishes and purifies the earth. Great cities are named after her, including Calcutta that was originally Kalighat derived from her name as the goddess Kali. In the struggle for independence from the British Empire she became a symbol for Bharat Mātā, Mother India. Especially in Devi temples at the village level she may be associated with blood-offerings taken from animals, with alcohol-offerings and with fertility. These accord less with Brahmin and with sophisticated concerns than with the proclivities of more humble people, especially women, for whom fertility, the earth, blood, birth and regeneration are more immediate issues. At another level, within more 'orthodox' Hindu traditions, goddesses such as Pārvatī, Saraswatī and Sītā are seen as the consorts of male deities. There is also the tradition of the Mother Goddess as Mahādevī, the Great Goddess, who combines various aspects of wider goddess traditions. Since the time of the sixth-century *Devī Māhātmya*, which was incorporated as a text in the *Mārkaneya Purāna*, the idea of the Great Goddess has grown.

One interesting development in Devi iconography is the combination of a number of goddesses into an integral figure. Examples of these are the Nine Durgas, the Eight Great Lakshmīs and the Sixty-four Yoginīs. Outstanding among this type of sculpture is the Seven Mothers (*Saptamatrikās*). In the famous sixth-century cave of Elephanta these Seven Mothers are seated together, flanked at either end by two minor male deities. However, they project fear rather than love

The animal on which Devi rides is usually a lion or tiger and less often an elephant. Her weapons are usually a sword, chopper and trident. Sometimes she has many weapons, especially in the case of Durga.

Many forms of Devi portray her as Śakti (action). This is especially the case in the Tantra texts. In the Tantra texts Devi tends to act alone. She is sometimes connected with orthodox (right-hand) Tantra rituals, and on other occasions she is connected with unorthodox (left-hand) Tantra rituals. In the latter case she is frightening, she is ultimate *śakti* (power) and she carries various bloodthirsty weapons in her numerous arms. There is a sense, too, in which Devi is seen to be active in nature on the earth, compared with Shiva who, in part of his being, prefers inactive aloneness in his fastness in the Himalayan mountains. The Shakta Tantra texts symbolise this part of Devi's nature, as do various sculptures.

In her particular forms Devi appears firstly as Durga. She is portrayed famously as the goddess who overcomes and kills the great demon Mahiṣa, who takes the form of a buffalo. In the classic aesthetic symbol of this incident, the many-armed Durga remains calm as she kills Mahiṣa and restores the cosmic equilibrium that had been lost by spearing Mahiṣa with her trident. The Durga Pūjā festival centred in Bengal celebrates this event. The brightly-coloured, enormous clay figures of Durga killing Mahiṣa are worshipped in shrines in the Bengal area and then thrown into the water after the festival.

A more benign face of Devi is seen in Annāpurnā. She is the goddess of plenty and of food. She is peaceful, fertile and kind. She does not have weapons. She is sometimes symbolised as a full and fertile pot. More often she is seated with a ladle across her knees, surrounded by full vessels of food and milk. She has a connection with Shiva and is therefore popular in the city of Shiva, Varanasi. At the Varanasi autumn festival of Annakuta (Mountain of Food) at the Annāpurnā temple, large amounts of rice and other foods are prepared to be given away to needy folk in the form of *prasāda*. Clay images are made also of Annāpurnā giving food to Shiva as a down-at-heel ascetic who finds final peace in Varanasi in his form as Bhairava.

Kali

Kali, the Black Goddess, is well known. On the one hand she is terrifying; on the other, to Ramakrishna at his Kalighat temple in Calcutta, she was the Mother to be loved with deep devotion. Some images of her show Kali as gaunt in countenance, with sagging breasts and a huge and horrifying tongue covered in blood; she wears a skirt of severed arms and a necklace of skulls. Another image of Kali shows her dancing on the body of Shiva with a view to tapping his transcendent power. She is the goddess who is proactive and engaged, while he is the god who is inactive and needs to be aroused.

Saraswatī and Lakshmī

Saraswatī is worshipped and honoured throughout India as an intelligent and benign goddess. As well as being the spouse of Brahmā and occasionally pictured with him, she is admired in her own right. She has become associated with speech, poetry, music and learning and is appreciated by scholars and everyone interested in the arts and aesthetics. She is sometimes pictured holding a musical instrument called the *vina*, and she is also pictured seated on a lotus. Lakshmī too, although associated with Vishnu, is appreciated in her own right and is also pictured seated on a lotus being purified by elephants. Most temples contain an image of Lakshmī. She is revered through *pūjā* at the autumn festival of Dīwalī, as the patron saint of business. Ledgers are closed and opened again, new businesses are undertaken, financial reward is sought and lamps are lit in honour of Lakshmī. She is widely appreciated as a fine goddess, as is Saraswati.

Manasa

More popular in North India is Manasa. She is portrayed with a canopy of snakes above her head. She is called upon to control snakes and to protect people from them. There are festivals to her in Bengal and Bihar in the autumn when her help is needed. There are elegant bronzes of her in those areas. She is portrayed as human with a full stomach, a slim waist and an ample bosom. She holds out her right hand to indicate her wish to grant vows whilst, in her left hand, she holds a small child figure with a snake (nāga) headdress. Women pray to her for the gift of children. Wandering poets carry interesting painted scrolls and hold them up to tell her story. The scrolls are reproduced in paintings.

Political Patronage

To begin with there were no great temples or images, partly because Kshatriya kings paid more attention to hiring poets to enhance their power. It was not until the sixth and seventh centuries that temples were inscribed by kings, and deity and temples came together. By the tenth century kings began to increase their power by identifying themselves with temples and with deity. The Islamic invasions increased the incentive for kings to build and support great temples and to support the Brahmins who were essential to their management. The temple became the centre of social and spiritual life as well as enhancing the king's power. Temples organised *pūjā*, generated community spirit and provided work for sculptors, painters and musicians. Thus temples, supported by kings and led by Brahmins, became intellectual, charitable and spiritual powerhouses during the medieval era. Although focused on serving the deity, the temple served the people and enhanced the credibility of the monarch. This led to the building of many of the great medieval temples.

Hindu kings remain, but their power is less than it was. Educational institutions, famous Gurus, Bhakti groups, universities and new movements such as the Hare Krishnas build their own temples. In some new temples, alongside images of Hindu deities, images of Christ, Guru Nanak, and other figures from the wider religious field may be found. More modern architectural designs are developing and the state shows more interest in Hindu aesthetics, some of it unwelcome.

10

Hindu Spirituality

Professor Ewert Cousins, in the opening paragraph of an article on 'Spirituality in Today's World' in *Religion in Today's World* (Whaling, 1987, p. 306) wrote:

> Spirituality refers to the experiential dimension of religion in contrast with formal beliefs, external practices, and institutions; it deals with the inner depth of the person that is open to the transcendent; in traditions that affirm the divine, it is concerned with the relation of the person to the divine, the experience of the divine, and the journey of the person to a more intimate relationship with the divine.

This is a good insight into spirituality in global terms. It may well be that the Hindu tradition has penetrated further into the breadth and depth of spirituality in its own history and experience. With the possible exception of the Buddhist tradition it has explored spirituality in a unique way. In modern times Hindu gurus have brought Hindu spirituality to the wider world. Through their influence upon young people, through the InterFaith Movement, through outstanding saints and through the media, Hindu spiritual leaders have appealed to a global audience. This appeal is not only to young westerners seeking for a spiritual fix with few strings attached or to people exploring Ayurvedic medicine and healing possibilities but also to thoughtful persons desiring a deeper spirituality.

Classical Hindu Yoga

Patañjali succinctly put it in *Yogasūtra* I.2: 'yoga is the removal of fluctuations of consciousness'. For Patañjali the counterflow of the usual tendencies of the mind can be achieved through the 'eight limbs of yoga', through steady practice and increasing inwardness.

The eight limbs of yoga begin with *yama* (self-restraint) through abstention from acquisitiveness, falsehood, incontinence, theft and violence. This is the negative not-doing of what is unhelpful to others and oneself. It is basic morality.

The second limb is *niyama* (restraint) in a very positive sense through observing austerity, contentment, purity, self-study and devotion to the lord. They are the opposite of the unhelpful elements mentioned in *yama*. They deal with basic morality in an active sense.

The third limb relates to *asana* (right posture) which enables one to be relaxed, fit and alert. Some yoga practitioners have taken this to extraordinary extremes of bizarre postures that miss the point, and yet right posture and bodily position are important.

The fourth limb relates to *prānayama*, breathing disciplines that regulate the breath and allow one to remain alert and relaxed. The stress upon helpful posture and correct breathing are part of *Hatha yoga* which is more to do with physical culture than with deep spirituality.

Pratyahara which advocates an inward turning of the senses away from external impressions in order to obey the mind is the fifth limb. This goes beyond *Hatha yoga* and is the beginning of a deeper concentration upon the inward world that does not abandon the outward world but puts it in its proper place.

Dhārana, the sixth limb, refers to a deep inner concentration whereby consciousness becomes fixed upon a single spot or object. It is a more specific form of concentration and is the first of the final three 'inner limbs' of yoga.

The seventh limb of yoga, and the second inner limb of yoga, is *dhyāna*. Dhyāna refers to a very real state of inner contemplation and of meditative depth in which there is an uninterrupted process of attention between the observer and the observed. However, observer and observed still remain separate.

The final limb of yoga is reached when *samādhi* occurs. It is a sense of deep stillness and silence in which the observer becomes the observed and in which the mind, as it were, becomes the object. It is a state of pure seeing with no mediator between the seer and the seen. It is an experiential seeing not reliant on traditional knowledge or inference. For those who experience it, it is no longer the mind taking impressions about an object from the senses and imposing itself on them. In samādhi the mind is the arena that reflects and becomes the object.

In classical yoga as outlined by Patañjali, the steps do not have to take place in order. Indeed not all the steps may be necessary. The aim is to bring about a quiet mind through which the 'object' can reveal itself, revealing its own nature and being enabled to colour the mind with its own flavour.

The eight limbs of *Patañjali yoga* are an ideal progression towards this goal and are a very great help but they are not sacrosanct in every detail. They are on a different spiritual wavelength from Ewert Cousins' quotation about 'experience of the divine' (Whaling, 1987, p. 306) as they go beyond the devotee having deep access to the divine, into a mysticism of oneness that transcends the I–Thou relationship. Although the second limb mentions 'devotion to the lord' and though the first and second limbs stress the need for a firm moral life, Patañjali's yoga goes beyond the *bhakti* way of devotion and the way of living morally in the world. There is also a sense in which it goes beyond the *jñāna* way of knowledge in its more intellectual sense. It is a form of experiential mysticism. As such it is more congenial to renouncers and to spiritual gurus who have this experience and are able to pass on its fruits to others.

The Outward Self

It is helpful in understanding Hinduism to appreciate that Hindu India sees the self, or the person in the sense of the ego, as basically a kind of 'outward self' that is not the real self. There is a difference of world-view, at this point, between Hindu India and the West. For Hindus, the self, in the sense of the ego (outward self), is not the self that we really are. It is the self that we parade in the world. It is the 'I', 'me' and 'myself' that separates us from others, that lives for itself and that sees the world of nature, humanity and the spirit in the light of its own interests. The real self is our *ātman* which we need to become attuned to. This is different from the western notion of the autonomous self that looks out upon, evaluates and judges the outside world. In Hindu India today there is a dialogue between these different sets of values and there remains a sense of need for the ego to go beyond itself and proceed to the *ātman* stage. This is an ever-present element in discussion. The wider topic of religion remains a lively part of everyday discussion There is a greater willingness among people of different religious traditions in India to talk about religion and to discuss it responsibly. In other words, a more inherent 'sense of spirituality' remains within Hindu India.

The Main 'Ways' of Spirituality

Three main modes of spirituality are prominently mentioned within the Hindu tradition. At a deeper level, as set out in the *Bhagavad Gītā*, the three 'ways' of spirituality – active engagement in the world without thought of reward (*karma yoga*), the way of devotion (*bhakti yoga*), and the way of inward spirituality (*jñāna yoga*) – have dominated Hindu spiritual practices. *Jñāna yoga* may include both spirituality of knowledge and spirituality of inwardness, in the *raja yoga* Patañjali sense, which may be seen as separate. There is, perhaps, a fourth, namely ritualistic spirituality. This includes the everyday use of home and temple rituals, the ongoing engagement in worship of different kinds in family worship rooms and in temples, the ongoing celebration of sacraments and periodic participation in festivals and pilgrimages. These sets of outward rituals have their place within Hindu spirituality. Indeed for many ordinary people within all religious traditions the progression of rituals lies at the heart of their religious faithfulness. It has done so for Hindus from the time of the Vedic sacrifices until now. However, the three (or four) ways are not necessarily completely separate. When examining them individually, it helps to see how they have been lived out by representative modern Hindus.

Karma yoga

The *Bhagavad Gītā* advances the case for doing one's duty in the world, not for reward but for its own sake. This is Arjuna's role in the Mahābhārata battle where he is a Kshatriya warrior whose duty it is to fight, even though he will almost certainly kill his own kinsfolk in the course of the battle. Pity for them is outweighed by the fact that Arjuna, in good faith, will not kill their real self, their *ātman*, but only their outward self. However, this presupposes a caste system in which one has to act according to one's caste duty rather than according to one's universal obligation to all human beings. Arjuna's duty as a warrior overrides any moral obligation not to kill others. However, in the case of Rāma, the obligation to do what was morally right often ranked higher than his caste duty to act as a king.

When I lived in Varanasi, the Brahmin Pundit who taught me Hindi came every weekday by cycle rickshaw six miles across Varanasi. He arrived at seven in the morning. Insofar as the cycle rickshaw would take a long time to get across Varanasi this means that he must have got up at something like five o'clock in the morning to do *pūjā*, have a quick breakfast and reach me. He loved to teach. He was happy to do it for a small fee. He basically taught without thought of reward. It was his role in life.

Bhakti yoga

The second way of Hindu spirituality is that of devotion (*bhakti*). It is the way of love. We have looked at the way of *bhakti* as seen in the *Bhagavad Gītā*, in which it is portrayed as the key avenue of spirituality. Compared with Patañjali's yoga, *bhakti* does not require absorption into the Absolute. It is exercised in regard to divinity. It can be lavished upon different deities ranging from Shiva, Vishnu, Devi, Rāma and Krishna to minor gods. It can vary in the depth and nature of the love offered to a particular deity.

However, it is a deep personal piety offered to a deity who can respond. From the indescribable depths of *bhakti* found in Vallabha, Chaitanya and the Hare Kṛishnas to the calmer devotion found in more philosophical *bhakti*; from the many vernacular outpourings of *bhakti* to the Sanskrit outpourings of a great devotional leader such as Rāmānuja, the spiritual feelings of the heart are portrayed. We have looked at many aspects of Hindu devotion, often in the vernacular during the medieval period, and it is obviously different in provenance from the way of unselfish service done without thought of reward. In Sanskrit and in many vernacular languages, many deities are approached with joy, love and even rapture. *Bhakti yoga* is a way of spirituality that is different from the experiential mysticism of Patañjali's yoga which transcends life in the world. It is also different from the unselfish action-based *karma yoga* exemplified by people such as Mahatma Gandhi, which is very firmly fixed in the world.

Ramakrishna

An unusual and outstanding example of *bhakti yoga*, the way of devotion, was Ramakrishna (see p. 29). Like Gandhi, he was a staunch Hindu who went outside the bounds of the Hindu tradition. Throughout his life he went into periods of ecstasy or trance (samādhi). These times of extraordinary devotion were offered to Hindu deities and also to deities of other religious traditions. He spoke neither English nor Sanskrit, and he communicated through his own native language of Bengali. However, his thoughts and sayings on *bhakti* and religion became known through a book with the title *The Gospel of Ramakrishna*.

In 1855, Ramakrishna became priest of the temple dedicated to the goddess Kali at Dakshineshwar near Calcutta. In the temple there were three sets of shrines dedicated to different Hindu deities. The main shrine with its nine pinnacles was dedicated to the goddess Kali, the second great shrine was dedicated to Krishna, and twelve Shiva *lingams* were dedicated in the third shrine. This was perhaps a premonition of Ramakrishna's extraordinarily wide religious experience. At first he was engulfed with emotional fervour towards Kali herself. However, as time went on he took instruction into other religious ways. They came to include Advaita Vedanta, the Rāma tradition and Tantra within the Hindu fold. He also enquired into the Christian and Muslim traditions. Moreover, he was initiated – by a Hindu Sufi – into Islam for a while. At the times when he took instruction and even initiation into different types of religion, he entered into a deep experience of their devotional modes of spirituality and he eventually had deep *bhakti* experiences of the tradition concerned. Those who witnessed

Ramakrishna's spiritual experiences, which sometimes involved bodily emotions, felt that they were in the presence of one who had entered into higher states of consciousness. These episodes added to Ramakrishna's aura of saintliness. A striking photograph picture of Ramakrishna in samādhi, an experience of ecstatic bliss, adorns the walls of Ramakrishna Missions around the world. Although Vivekananda used Ramakrishna's name to promote Advaita Vedanta as a world philosophy, it was not so much philosophy or active service in the world or Patañjali-type spirituality that summarised the genius of the priest of Kali. It was an extremely deep emotional way of bhakti that he portrayed.

Jnāna yoga

The third way of Hindu spirituality is that of knowledge (*jnāna*). It has its textual base mainly in the Upanishads and it shares some of the experiential base found in Patañjali's yoga.

Shankara's Advaita Vedanta argued that although *Brahman* (Ultimate Reality) appears to be different from the *ātman* (self) of humans, in fact it is identical with *ātman*. There is a non-twoism, a non-duality, between *Brahman* and *ātman* that chimes in with the central *tat tvam asi* ('that art Thou', *Brahman* is You) and *aham Brahman asmi* ('I am Brahman') statements in the Upanishads. Central to Shankara's Advaita Vedanta is the notion that ultimately *Brahman* and *ātman* are one. Ultimately we are not in relationship with *Brahman*, we are *Brahman*. Shankara used the notion of the two levels of truth to argue that at the lower level of truth there is a personal deity, but that at the higher level of truth *Brahman* alone exists and the world is not real. It is an illusion (*māyā*) fostered by ignorance (*avidyā*). Thus, at the lower level of truth personal allegiance to deity is valid and *bhakti* is valid. When one reaches the higher level of truth the illusion and ignorance vanish, and one becomes one with *Brahman*. One has ultimate knowledge (*jnāna*). The spirituality of *jnāna* involves oneness with *Brahman*. Realisation of this gives salvation (*moksha*) and true knowledge and it enables one to become *jīvanmukti* (liberated in life). An allied route to salvation while still alive is Patañjali's yoga which is experientially similar but intellectually diverse. The way of knowledge (*jnāna*) is therefore different from the way of *bhakti*. It is also different from the way of doing one's duty in the world without thought of reward.

Ramana Maharshi

A supreme modern example of the way of knowledge (*jnāna*) was Ramana Maharshi (see pp. 33–4). Ramana came from a Brahmin family and had his early schooling in Madurai. Two events changed his life from that of an ordinary young boy into that of a great sage (*Maharshi*), into that of *jīvanmukti* and knower of *Brahman* (Brahmavidya). As he put it, the characteristics of a guru are: 'Steady abidance in the Self, looking at all with an equal eye, unshakeable courage at all times, in all places and circumstances' (Osbourne, 1964, p. 49). He became a great guru himself but not through long training. The first event that changed him was a relative telling him about Arunachala, where he would live for the rest of his life. The second, when he was seventeen, was a sudden fear of death. Instead of seeking medical help he lay down and stilled his body. He came to realise that death was a matter not to do with the body, it was to do with the *ātman*, the Self, which was beyond death. As he put it: 'Fear of death had vanished once and for all. Absorption in the Self continued unbroken from that time on' (Osbourne, 1971, p. 10). After that extraordinary experience his life changed radically and realisation of the Self continued with him for the rest of his life. The answer to the basic human question of life and death came to him not through studying Advaita Vedanta or the Upanishads. The experience came first. Textual study and verification of the experience came later. For a while, during his early stay at Arunachala, Ramana was 'out of this world', absorbed in the Self, silent and fasting. He had come to realisation without analysis. Although textual and philosophical debates were helpful they were also endless and it was more helpful to turn the mind inward rather than to endlessly dispute things outwardly.

Ramana Maharshi is generally recognised as an outstanding guru. He stayed for the rest of his life at Arunachala, the 'Fire-Hill', at Tiruvannamalai in Tamil Nadu. He was not the first great saint to stay there but he became the most famous. Paul Brunton (1934) was one of the first westerners to make a search for Hindu holy men, which he then wrote about in *A Search in Secret India*. For Brunton, Ramana Maharshi's calmness, simplicity, silence, obvious saintliness and contagious bliss were outstanding among all the saints that he met.

Ramana's 'realisation framework' was basically that of Advaita Vedanta. Accordingly reality is one and non-dual. It is that which is. It is as it is. It transcends words and description. According to him the basic categories of God, human beings and the universe are not different from *Brahman/ātman*. The problem, for him, lies with the ego that we think of as real but is not in fact. The aim is to discover the Self, the *ātman*, the reality, beyond the ego. Thus 'phenomena are real when experienced as the Self and illusory when seen apart from the self' (Osbourne, 1971, p. 10). This way of knowledge, *jnāna yoga*, is a different way from those of *karma yoga* (working in the world without thought of reward) and *bhakti yoga* (the way of devotion). We see it clearly in Ramana. His spirituality and way of spirituality is clear-cut. His spiritual example is crystal clear.

For many Hindus, spirituality is less clear-cut. They embrace two or even three elements in their spirituality. They may combine them equally or combine them in a way where one is more important than the others. This is part of the kaleidoscope that is the Hindu tradition. In fact Ramana allows that some people, those who are not temperamentally suited for *jnāna yoga*, may follow *bhakti yoga* or *karma yoga*. The *Bhagavad Gītā* makes a case for all three ways of spirituality and appears to favour the way of *bhakti*. Yet it leaves open the question as to whether the three ways are equal. An underlying question is whether all three ways of spirituality relate to the same level of life and the same aims of life. If a Hindu's aim is for *moksha* (ultimate release from the round of rebirths) then the way of knowledge will be the main aim. If the aim is for a better rebirth, then *karma yoga* may be more apposite. In the case of *bhakti* yoga the aims of ultimate release and a better rebirth are both possible. Some times the conundrum of living life is enough in itself without completely clear-cut aims

Hindu Spirituality and Nature

The word 'spirituality' has wider meanings in the contemporary world and relates to life in spheres wider than that of religion in a narrow sense. One of those meanings relates to nature.

The Hindu tradition has an interest in nature even though the three ways of spirituality do not directly touch upon the topic. The *Rāmāyana* story takes Rāma and his entourage into exile in the forest where they, and others living there, can enjoy a simple but idyllic kind of existence. In a compound where I lived in Varanasi, which had a school for girls within its walls, a cobra would be found occasionally that was clearly potentially dangerous in such an environment. If a Hindu nightwatchman caught the snake he would not kill it; he would take it to a non-Hindu nightwatchman to be despatched. Indians have been, and to some extent still are, close to nature in spite of the spread of cities. Ecological spirituality is natural to Indians and especially to Hindus. The Ganges and many other rivers are held to be sacred. The Himalayas and other mountain ranges are revered. In many parts of India the cow is a protected animal. The land of India is seen as Bharat Mātā, Mother India. Hindu gods have their own animals that are their mounts. Four of Vishnu's *avatāras* take animal or fish form. The god Ganesha has an elephant head and the deity Hanuman is the monkey god. There are something like eleven words in Sanskrit for 'elephant'. The historic

Hindu closeness to nature involves an awareness of nature and an implicit spirituality with regard to nature that is pragmatically present.

The spiritual investigation of nature has been of interest within the Hindu tradition. We have touched upon two of the six Indian philosophical systems so far, namely Vedanta and Yoga. Three others are not directly apposite to this book, namely Vaiśeṣika, Nyāya and Mīmāmsā. The sixth and earliest system, that of Sāmkhya, is relevant. It is not directly part of Hindu scripture and it was attacked by Shankara, whose thought implied that *Brahman* was real and the world was false. The Samkhya system is associated with the Yoga system and together they form a kind of spiritual philosophy that indicates a way to transcendence by way of nature. This insight was expressed in different ways. Arjuna in his vision of Krishna in the *Bhagavad Gītā* (XI.7) sees 'the whole universe, with its manifold divisions gathered together in one, in the body of the god of gods'. This notion of nature as the body of deity was taken up by Rāmānuja who refers to the Vedas, the *smriti* literature, the *Dharmaśāstras* and the Purānas in his analysis. According to Rāmānuja, in his commentary on the *Bhagavad Gītā* (VII.12), 'all spiritual and non-spiritual beings, whether effects or causes, constitute god's body and depend on god who is their soul'. The *Bhāgavata Purāna* (XI.1.23ff) posits a view of creation according to which the body of god is connected with the material universe. Thus god's bones feed into the structure of mountains and god's arteries into the flow of rivers. Within Rāmānuja's Vaisnava tradition there are five levels of God's presence: his presence as *Brahman*, his presence in his four *vyuhas* as channels of meditation, his presence through his *avatāras*, his inner presence in the hearts of followers, and his presence in image form. God could be present to humans in different ways. He could also be involved in nature in different ways. Even as Hindus move from villages into cities, they take with them this sense of nature as being in some way illumined by transcendence.

Sri Aurobindo

The life of Sri Aurobindo (see p. 33) presents a final Hindu example of spirituality which draws together the five elements of spirituality that have been mentioned. Aurobindo had interests in nature, in activism in the world, in *bhakti*, in knowledge, and in spiritual experience. He included nature in his comprehensive system of creative evolution. When in prison in Calcutta he had a vivid vision of Krishna that changed his life in a *bhakti* fashion. He imaginatively reinterpreted the Indian intellectual tradition in a way at least as insightful as the reinterpretation made by Radhakrishnan. In his work in setting up and leading the Aurobindo Ashram he used an integral (*pūrna*) system of yoga that combined the ways of work, love and thought but placed them within his own life experience. In combining *karma yoga*, *bhakti yoga* and *jnāna yoga* in an experiential ashram setting he entered a deeper spiritual inwardness. He also used a wide range of Hindu sacred writings ranging from the Veda itself through the Upanishads, the *Bhagavad Gītā* and the Tantras in order to set his thought and experience into an integral Hindu spirituality. Towards the end of his life, through the town of Auroville, he set up a physical expression of his spiritual vision.

11

Hindu Concepts and Philosophy and the Modern World

We have considered various Hindu concepts and elements using the model outlined in the Introduction based on eight interdependent elements: Hindu religious traditions, rituals, ethics/*dharma*, social and political involvement, sacred texts, aesthetics and spirituality. In summary, they suggest that the world has no beginning or end and that it has gone through vast periods of time moving from a golden age to an iron age, at which point the process is wound up and begins its eternal round again. Absolute Reality is *Brahman*. The *ātman* is the real inner self of human beings which is deeper than the outward ego (jiva) we present to the world. Human life consists of a round of rebirths (*samsāra*) and one is reborn according to one's deeds (*karma*). Salvation from the round of rebirths is through release (*moksha*). There are a number of personal deities, the main ones being Shiva, Vishnu and Devi (the Goddess), together with Rāma and Krishna who are seen both as *avatāras* (incarnations) of Vishnu and as gods in their own right. The main ways to salvation and the main modes of spirituality are by means of devotion to a personal deity (*bhakti*), inward spiritual knowledge of *Brahman* (*jnāna*) and doing one's duty in the world without thought of reward (*karma*).

It is important to remember that Hindu philosophy and Hindu religion are held together in a way little known in the present-day West. Western universities, in the main, deal with philosophy as something that is separate from religion. In most Indian universities religion is taught as part of philosophy. At the heart of this tendency to incorporate philosophy with religion is the coming together in Hindu thought of what westerners would separate as philosophy and theology. This is especially evident in Vedanta philosophy – the jewel in the Hindu philosophical crown – in which 'philosophy' and 'theology' are combined. This final chapter summarises the approaches to Vedanta found in Shankara, Rāmānuja and Madhva and then looks at the work of Professor Sarvepalli Radhakrishnan. Radhakrishnan was a Vedantist who had his own modern interpretation of Vedanta and who raised relevant questions about the Hindu tradition in the modern world. We will use him as a fulcrum to consider how Indian Hinduism relates to the Hindu tradition in the wider world, how the Hindu tradition relates to other religious traditions, how it relates to modern science and how it relates to the problems thrown up by modern globalisation.

The Great Vedanta Philosophers

The three greatest Vedanta philosophers were Shankara, Rāmānuja and Madhva (see pp. 25–6, 64–6). All of them wrote commentaries on the Upanishads, the *Bhagavad Gītā* and the Vedanta Sūtras. They were great philosophers but not 'pure' philosophers in the western sense. They were philosophers who were also critical interpreters of scripture. They differed about the relationships between *Brahman*, human beings and the world. They lived in different eras and spoke to different needs. And yet, together, they introduced a philosophical system that has been of untold importance from the ninth century until the present day. It ranks as one of the outstanding religious philosophies produced by humankind.

Shankara lived at a time when the Buddhist tradition was declining in South India and the Hindu tradition was growing in importance. The Buddhists did not accept the concepts of *Brahman* (Absolute Reality) or *ātman* (Self), but they did employ the notion of two levels of truth, higher truth and lower truth. Shankara adapted this two-truth theory to Hindu thought and practice. For him there was a non-duality or non-twoness (Advaita) between Absolute Reality (*Brahman*) and the Self (*ātman*). At the lower level of truth, *Brahman*, humans and the world appear to be different. There appears to be a duality or separateness between them. Shankara applied the famous analogy of a person who saw a rope lying on the ground but falsely thought that it was a snake. In the same way, he argued, we impose false impressions upon the Self and imagine that it is our body or our senses. At the level of ordinary life and empirical reality, the world and human beings and a personal godhead are real. However, at the higher level of truth and of Absolute Reality, the world and the human ego are unreal. Because of *māyā* (illusion) and *avidyā* (ignorance) they appear to be real. Only *Brahman* is real. *Brahman* is *ātman* and *ātman* is *Brahman*. However, Shankara was not solely a philosopher. For him philosophy was a means to achieve release (*moksha*) and not an end in itself.

Rāmānuja lived three centuries later than Shankara. The Buddhists were even fewer in India. Rāmānuja was the leader of the Shri Vaishnavas who had a strong devotional (*bhakti*) impulse centred upon Vishnu. He agreed with Shankara that *Brahman* was non-dual. However he disagreed with Shankara's monism. For him there was a qualified non-dualism (Vishistādvaita) whereby the godhead is independent and real, but selves are also real and at the same time dependent upon the godhead. Moreover, the world is also real but it too is dependent upon the godhead. For Rāmānuja the world was the 'body of God'. For him the deity was Vishnu who was *Brahman* with qualities (*saguna Brahman*). Thus humans and the world are separate from but dependent upon Vishnu. However, the human dependence upon Vishnu operates through *bhakti* (devotion) which may see Vishnu as master, lover or friend of the devotee. Rāmānuja had more affinity than Shankara for *the Bhagavad Gītā* and its three ways of action, knowledge and devotion. All were important but *bhakti* was most important. Through submission to Vishnu by *prapatti* (surrender) one can have access to divine transcendence and to divine grace. Vishnu as *Brahman* is then the inner controller of self and the world. Thus, it is not only knowledge (*jnāna*) of *Brahman* that is involved in liberation, as Shankara had suggested. It is Vishnu's grace and the devotee's response that are relevant. Even after death one is not absorbed into *Brahman*, after liberation one returns to the presence of Vishnu but remains distinct from Vishnu/*Brahman*.

Madhva in the thirteenth century remained within the *bhakti* mould. He joined a Vaishnava order when aged sixteen, learnt about Vedanta and wrote thirty-five works including his famous commentaries. He finally settled in Udipi where he built his important temple to Krishna. He went further than Rāmānuja in separating *Brahman*, *ātman* and the world. For him there was a complete difference between *Brahman*, *ātman* and the world. However he went even further than that. He suggested that there were five basic differences built into the heart of things. They were the differences between Vishnu and human beings, between Vishnu and the world, between human beings and the world, between human beings and other human beings and between different objects in the world. His position was that of Dvaita Vedanta, the Vedanta of radical duality. He totally rejected attempts to suggest that the world was an illusion or an emanation from *Brahman*. The worlds of matter and humans depend upon Vishnu but are separate from Vishnu. They will remain separate for ever. Thus, whereas for Shankara the Upanishadic phrase *tat tvam asi* ('you are *Brahman*') signified the non-duality between *ātman* and *Brahman*, and for Rāmānuja it signified that *ātman* and *Brahman* were separate and yet closely related, for Madhva it meant that *ātman* and *Brahman* were totally separate (although the self was made in the divine image). With his love for Krishna and the *Bhāgavata Purāna*,

Madhva points further in the direction of fervent *bhakti* to be seen later.

At the beginning of the twentieth century many Hindus and outside commentators viewed Shankara's Advaita Vedanta as being the key philosophical and spiritual glory of the Hindu tradition. More recently it has been recognised that various *bhakti* movements of different kinds have been more important than formerly admitted, whether emanating from Rāmānuja, Madhva or other sources. It is probably true to say that *bhakti* has not only become stronger but is also recognised as stronger in recent times. However, in terms of intellectual impact, the neo-Advaita Vedanta popularised by Swami Vivekananda and by Radhakrishnan has been more important in the overall Hindu context.

Radhakrishnan and Twentieth-Century Advaita Vedanta

Radhakrishnan was born in 1888 at Tirutani in South India and died in 1975. A critical study of Hindu ideas fuelled in him an interest in philosophy in general and in Indian religion in particular, provoking a lifelong journey of exploration. In 1936 he was installed to the Spalding Chair of Eastern Religions and Ethics at Oxford. This was the first time an Indian had been appointed to an Oxford Chair. The beauty of style and clarity of thought of his many writings made him a key figure in a variety of fields and his worldwide eminence made him influential on a wider scale.

He had a broad view of philosophy and a conviction that religion and philosophy were integral rather than separate studies. He was Indian in that he regarded intuition as being a way of knowledge and not just an alternative to it. He was an idealist with a predilection towards Shankara's Advaita Vedanta, although he was by no means uncritical of it. He viewed Ultimate Reality (*Brahman*) as 'the Beyond who cannot be comprehended by our concepts or recognised by our understanding ... He can only be described negatively, or through seemingly contradictory descriptions' (Radhakrishnan, 1939, p. 298). He had a deep interest in the dynamics of the global religious situation and felt that it could be an element in building a new world culture. As far as Indian religion was concerned he saw its dialogue with other world religions as being crucial for future global developments. Radhakrishnan represented a kind of 'counterattack from the East' that could speak on equal terms with other cultures and religions. His approach was both pacifist and wider than Hindu thought but yet grounded in Hindu thought. He recognised the importance of maintaining Hindu continuity with the past when reinterpreting it in the light of modern needs.

Radhakrishnan was aware that the Hindu tradition, as we have seen all along, was more akin to a league of religions than to a single tradition with a defined creed. It was a way of life as well as a religion. In the Hindu house there were various rooms available to different kinds of persons from different backgrounds and with different needs. Under the Hindu umbrella, so to speak, there was shelter for many varieties of thought, practice, ritual, spirituality and approaches to the divine. Enclosed within the Hindu tree were many branches. Radhakrishnan could not intellectually defend all the rooms in the Hindu house, all those sheltered under the Hindu umbrella and all the branches of the Hindu tree. He could not foresee the growing force of Hindu nationalism. The semi-despair of the Dalits and women he could not fully envision. The spread of Hindus abroad was still in its relative infancy. India's rapid rise in population and wealth lay ahead. Radhakrishnan, through his vision, intellect, and political position had an early insight into India's problems of modernity and the Hindu tradition's problems with modernity.

Radhakrishnan was a not uncritical supporter and advocate of Vedanta Hinduism. He wrote:

> Religion, however, has been the master passion of the Hindu mind, a lamp unto its feet and a light unto its path, the presupposition and basis of its civilisation, the driving force of its culture, and the expression – in spite of its tragic failures, inconsistencies and degradations – of its life in God. (Radhakrishnan, 1939, pp. 20ff)

He defended Advaita Vedanta against its critics in India and in the West. He reinterpreted *māyā* to mean that the world is not 'illusion' at the worldly level and thus ethical action is relevant in the world. He argued that the metaphysical identity between *Brahman* and *ātman* refers to the real self (*ātman*), not to the outward active ego (jiva) that lives ethically in the world. He argued that *avidyā* (ignorance) is not just an intellectual matter but a whole attitude to life that mistakes the relative for the absolute and causes bondage. Morality is essential until *avidyā* is removed. Thus moral living is vital at the ordinary level of life. He argued that asceticism is not the denial of the body but self-sacrifice that frees one from attachment to the body. In reply to the accusation that Advaita has no place for social responsibility and civil society he pointed to Shankara's own civic achievements in society. These were based on the notion that there should be emphasis not on retirement from the world but on renunciation of the self (ego) in the world.

Radhakrishnan stressed what he saw to be the basic strengths of the Hindu tradition. He emphasised the comprehensiveness of the Hindu tradition as a vast, complex but unified system within which there was room for all. He suggested that the Hindu tradition is universal in character with its stress upon inward realisation and spiritual experience. It is 'a movement, not a position; a process, not a result; a growing tradition, not a fixed revelation' (Radhakrishnan, 1927, p. 129). He also posited that the Hindu tradition is tolerant. As the *Rig Veda* puts it: 'Truth is One, the sages call it many' (I:164:46). His sense was that the Hindu tradition does not rely on history, historical founders, or historical facts but on eternal truths. This led him to discount the historicity of Krishna as being of secondary importance. Lastly, his position was that the Hindu tradition stresses intuition (*anubhava*). Thus 'intellect is subordinated to intuition, dogma to experience, outer expression to inner realisation' (Radhakrishnan, 1927, p. 13). These five strengths were what he saw to be at the heart of the Hindu tradition.

Radhakrishnan reinterpreted some Hindu concepts in the light of modern knowledge. What was important to him was not sticking to past forms of Hindu thought for their own sake but seeking their meaning and relevance for his own time. Thus, he reinterprets the view of maya as illusion. He writes 'when the Hindu thinkers ask us to free ourselves from maya, they are asking us to shake off our bondage to the unreal values which dominate us. They do not ask us to treat life as an illusion or be indifferent to the world's welfare' (Radhakrishnan, 1939, p. 47). He also reinterprets the notion of *karma* to make it more positive and balanced. As he puts it: 'life is like a game of bridge. The cards in the game are given to us. We do not select them. They are traced to past *karma* but we are free to make any call as we think fit and lead any suit' (Radhakrishnan, 1947, p. 279). Therefore human beings are not the playthings of fate, rather they can actively mould the future instead of passively suffering for the past. In *Religion and Society* (1947) he condemned the traditional caste system which he recognised still to exist in spite of variations. He urged India to change it and reinterpret it less rigidly. He was able to put some of these reforming thoughts into practice when in politics. In terms of political thought he acknowledged his strong commitment to democracy for which he felt the Hindu tradition supplied a strong spiritual basis.

History is part of the total cosmic process beginning and ending in *Brahman*, but it has its own reality. Thus, for Radhakrishnan time is not all, though the temporal world is the stage on which spiritual values are enacted. *Avatāras* are divine interventions in history, but they are also a sign of the divine potentialities in human beings. The process of history for Radhakrishnan is not the classical cyclical view that history goes on for ever in deteriorating *yugas* that repeat themselves. He has an evolutionary view of history. Within that viewpoint individuals are liberated in life and become *jīvanmuktas* but, in turn, they work to ameliorate the burden of the world. In the fullness of time a new community will emerge that will be a new fellowship of beings, a new earth life for all.

Indians and others have raised queries about Radhakrishnan is work from different viewpoints. However B. G. Gokhale, with some justification, argues that Radhakrishnan, Gandhi and Aurobindo have picked up 'where ancient India left off and work out the spiritual view of history as developed by ancient Indian thinkers ... into a consistent, logical and imperative philosophy of history' (1960, p. 465). Radhakrishnan's reinterpretation helped to put India onto the plateau of virtual religious and political equality that it enjoys today. Radhakrishnan reinterpreted Advaita Vedanta and opened it up to include wider visions and new vistas of Hindu thought that are in turn being reinterpreted.

Diaspora

The Hindu tradition retains the majority of its people in India. When Gandhi applied to his caste elders in Mumbai to go to England, they refused to allow him to leave the sacred shores of India. He went anyway. When the Maharajah of Jaipur was invited to the coronation of King Edward VII in 1902, he travelled to Britain in a cleansed, refurbished, consecrated, food-stocked vessel that he anchored offshore and retreated to every evening. Ganges water and Indian soil on the ship were dual reminders of the sacred shores of India and of the unsacred shores of Britain. Radhakrishnan, when he lived in England, was one of relatively few Indians in Britain at the time and he made a good impact. There was only one Hindu kingdom in the world, Nepal, until the rise of a new non-Hindu rulership. Hindus are scattered around the world in relatively small numbers.

The Hindu tradition began to expand into South East Asia at the beginning of the Common Era, although now only Bali remains significantly Hindu and Thailand has historical Hindu links. Through the British Empire, Hindus emigrated to Fiji, where the Hindu tradition is still strong, to Trinidad, to South Africa, to Malaya, to Mauritius and to Burma. In the twentieth century the lure of work on the railways and in small businesses took Gujarati and Punjabi Hindus to East Africa. These expatriates generally lacked Brahmins who could organise rituals for them but they kept contact with India and a succession of relatives joined them. Visiting gurus and other religious leaders came from India to help and visit and they were able to set up social, educational, cultural and religious institutions. Temples were built, societies were founded and festivals held. There are thriving Hindu communities in some of the main cities of Britain. Elsewhere, for example in the United States and Australia, Hindus are more likely to follow the professions in education, law and health care. A plethora of Indian Societies, Hindu Cultural Centres and temples have appeared to accommodate these Hindu immigrants. Lay persons, including women, are often crucial in organising and leading Hindu societies in most parts of diaspora Hinduism. They may even take a leadership part in *pūjā* when there is no priest available. As diaspora Hindus live away from the sacred shores of holy India they innovate and adapt.

However, aside from occasional interreligious marriage unions, Hindu emigrants have generally speaking maintained the institution of caste marriages although they have left the shores of Mother India.

The Hindu tradition in India can learn from Hindu traditions abroad. These will grow and will no longer be seen as coming from those who have betrayed the Hindu tradition by leaving India.

Hindus abroad represent a proselytising opportunity for the Hindu tradition. When Swami Vivekananda spoke inspiringly at the World Parliament of Religions at Chicago in 1893 and when he founded the Ramakrishna Mission he was saying to the world that the Hindu tradition was no longer confined to Hindus. As Radhakrishnan said, it had a message for the world. Already Dayananda Saraswati (1824–83) and his Arya Samaj had promoted a Vedic Hinduism that allowed a ritual whereby Hindus who had converted to another tradition could be readmitted into the Hindu fold. The chants of the Hare Krishna Movement have become familiar outside India in the last forty years as a means by which non-Hindus can, so to speak, become Hindus 'by faith'.

Finally, Hindu newspapers and Hindu organisations are being founded to bring together Hindus around the world. *Hinduism Today*, published in Hawaii, keeps Hindus in contact with what is happening around the Hindu world. The two best-known world organisations are the Vishva Hindu Parishad led by Maharana Bhagwat Singh, and the Virat Hindu Samaj led by Dr Karan Singh. In his keynote address at the 1984 conference of the Virat Hindu Samaj, Karan Singh made a moving appeal to Hindu youth around the world:

> Living outside India you retain your Hindu identity and yet must become citizens of the world ... We are members of the human race, and you must discover within yourself the core of spiritual power with which you can show a new light to humanity. (Pamphlet printed in Delhi, 1984)

Bibliography

Alston, A. J. (1980) *The Devotional Poems of Mirabai*, Delhi: Motilal Banarsidass

Archer, W. G. (1957) *The Loves of Krishna in Indian Painting and Poetry*, London: Allen and Unwin

Assayag, J. and Fuller, C. J. (2005) *Globalising India*, London: Anthem

Babb Lawrence, L. A. (1987) *Redemptive Encounters*, Delhi: Oxford University Press

Baird, R. D. (ed.) (2001) *Religion in Modern India*, Delhi: Manohar

Basham, A. L. (1959) *The Wonder that was India*, New York: Grove Press

Basham, A. L. (1989) *The Origins and Development of Classical Hinduism*, Boston: Beacon

Bazaz, P. N. (1975) *The Role of the Bhagavad Gītā in Indian History*, New Delhi: Sterling

Bharati, A. (1975) *The Tantric Tradition*, London: Rider

Brockington, J. (1984) *Righteous Rama: The Evolution of an Epic*, Oxford: Oxford University Press

Brockington, J. (1996) *The Sacred Thread: Hinduism in its Continuity and Diversity*, Edinburgh: Edinburgh University Press

Brockington, J. (1998) *The Sanskrit Epics*, Leiden: E J Brill

Brunton, P. (1934) *A Search in Secret India*, London: Rider & Co

Bruteau, B. (1971) *Worthy is the World: The Hindu Philosophy of Sri Aurbindo*, Rutherford: Fairleigh Dickenson University Press

Bryant, E. (2001) *The Quest for the Origins of Vedic Culture*, New York: Oxford University Press

Burghart, R. (ed.) (1987) *Hinduism in Great Britain*, London: Tavistock

Burghart, R. (1996) *The Conditions of Listening: Essays on Religion, History and Politics in South Asia*, Fuller, C. J. and Spencer, J. (eds) (1996) Delhi: Oxford University Press

Carman, J. T. (1974) *The Theology of Ramanuja: An Essay in Inter-Religious Understanding*, Newhaven and London: Yale University Press

Cassirer, E. (1955) *The Philosophy of Symbolic Forms,* Vol. 1, *Mythical Thought*, Oxford: Oxford University Press

Chatterjee, P. (1989) *Caste and Subaltern Consciousness*, Calcutta: Centre for Studies in Social Sciences

Chaudhuri, N. (1979) *Hinduism: A Religion to Live by*, Oxford: Oxford University Press

Chen, A. (1995) 'Buddhism', in Sharma, A. (ed.) (1995) *Our Religions*, New York: Harper Collins, 1995, pp. 93–4

Chen, K. (1968) *Buddhism: The Light of Asia*, Woodburn: Barton

Clarke, S. (1996) 'Re-Viewing the Religion of the Paraiyars' in Scott, D. and Selvanayagam, I. (eds) (1996) *Re-Visioning India's Religious Traditions*, Bangalore: ISPCK, pp. 65–85

Copley, A. and Paxton, G. (eds) (1997) *Gandhi and the Contemporary World*, Chennai: Indo-British Historical Society

Cousins, E. (1989) 'Preface' in Sivaraman, K. (ed.) (1989) *Hindu Spirituality: Vedas through Vedanta*, New York: Crossroads, p. ix

Cox, H. (1965) *The Secular City*, London: SCM

Dandekar, R. N. (1979) *Insights into Hinduism*, Delhi: Ajanta Publications

Das, G. (2002) *India Unbound: From Independence to the Global Information Age*, New Delhi: Penguin

Das, Veena (1982) *Structure and Cognition: Aspects of Hindu Caste and Ritual*, Delhi: Oxford University Press

Deshpande, Satish (2003) *Contemporary India: A Sociological View*, New Delhi: Viking Penguin

Dhavamony, M. (1982) *Classical Hinduism*, Rome: Universita Gregoriana Editrice

Dimmit, C. and van Buitenen, J. A. B. (eds), (1978) *Classical Hindu Mythology: A Reader in the Sanskrit Puranas*, Philadelphia: Temple University Press

Dumont, L. (1980) *Homo Hierarchicus: The Caste System and its Implications*, translated from French by Mark Sainsbury, Chicago: Chicago University Press

Eck, D. (1983) *Banaras: City of Light*, London: Routledge and Kegan Paul

Eck, D. (1985) *Darshan: Seeing the Divine Image in India*, Chambersburg, PA: Anima

Elgood, H. (1999) *Hinduism and the Religious Arts*, London: Cassell

Eliade, M. (1969) *Patanjali and Yoga*, New York: Funk and Wagnalls

Embree, A. T. (ed.) (1971) *Alberuni's India*, New York: W.W.Norton

Embree, A. T. (ed.) (1988) *Sources of Indian Tradition*, Vol. 1, New York: Columbia University Press

Fenton, J. Y. (1988) *Translating Religious Traditions: Asian Indians in America*, New York: Praeger

Feuerstein, G. (1982) *The Philosophy of Classical Yoga*, Manchester: Manchester University Press

Feuerstein, G., Kak, S. and Frawley, D. (1995) *In Search of the Cradle of Civilisation*, Wheaton, Ill: Quest Books

Flood, G. (1996) *An Introduction to Hinduism*, Cambridge: Cambridge University Press

Flood, G. (ed.) (2005) *The Blackwell Companion to Hinduism*, Oxford: Blackwell

Fuller, C. J. (1992) *The Camphor Flame: Popular Hinduism and Society in India*, Princeton: Princeton University Press

Fuller, C. J. (2003) *The Renewal of the Priesthood: Modernity and Traditionalism in a South Indian Temple*, Princeton, Princeton University Press

Gandhi, M. K. (1993) *Autobiography: the Story of my Experiments with Truth*, Boston: Beacon

Gokhale, B. G. (1960) *Making of the Indian Nation*, London: Asia Publishing House

Golwalkar, M. S. (1947) *We, or Our Nationhood Defined*, Nagpur: Bharat Prakashan

Halbfass, W. (1991) *Tradition and Reflection: Explorations in Indian Thought*, Albany: State University of New York

Hawley, J. S. (1984) *Surdas: Poet, Singer, Saint*, Seattle: University of Washington Press

Hawley, J. S. (1988) *Songs of the Saints of India*, New York: Oxford University Press

Hawley, J. S. (ed.) (1994) *Sati, the Blessing and the Curse: The Burning of Wives in India*, Oxford and New York: Oxford University Press

Hawley, J. S. and Wulff, D. M. (Eds), (1996) *Devi: Goddesses of India*, Berkeley: University of California Press

Hiltebeitel, A. (1987) 'Hinduism' in Eliade, M. (ed.) (1987) *Encylopaedia of Religion*, Vol. 6, London and New York: Macmillan, pp. 633–60

Hiriyanna, M. (1958) *Outlines of Indian Philosophy*, London: Allen and Unwin

Hopkins, T. J. (1971) *The Hindu Religious Tradition*, Encino, CA: Dickenson

Humphrey, M. (1914) *Travels in the Mogul Empire 1656–68*, Oxford: Oxford University Press

Jordens, J. T. F. (1978) *Dayananda Sarasvati: His Life and Ideas*, Delhi: Oxford University Press

Joshi, B. R. (ed.) (1984) *Untouchable Voices of the Dalit Liberation Movement*, London: Zed Books

Juergensmeyer, M, (1982) *Religion as Social Vision: The Movement against Untouchability*, Berkeley: University of California Press

Kane, P. V. (1973–90) *History of Dharmashashtra*, 5 vols, 2nd ed., Poona: Bhandarkar Oriental Institute

King, R. (1999) *Indian Philosophy; An Introduction to Hindu and Buddhist Thought*, Edinburgh: Edinburgh University Press

Kinsley, D. R. (1979) *The Divine Player (A Study of Krishna Lila)*, Delhi: Motilal Banarsidass

Klostermaier, K. (1994) *A Survey of Hinduism*, Albany: State University of New York Press

Klostermaier, K. (1998a) *Hinduism: A Short Introduction*, Oxford: One World

Klostermaier, K. (1998b) *A Concise Encyclopaedia of Hinduism*, Oxford: One World

Klostermaier, K. (2000) *Hinduism: A Short History*, Oxford: One World

Knott, K. (2000) *Hinduism: A Very Short Introduction*, Oxford: Oxford University Press

Kramrisch, S. (1954) *The Art of India: Traditions of Indian Sculpture, Painting and Architecture*, London: Phaidon

Kramrisch, S. (1977) *The Hindu Temple*, 2 vols, Delhi: Motilal Banarsidass

Kripal, J. J. (1995) *Kali's Child: The Mystical and the Erotic in the Life and Teachings of Ramakrishna*, Chicago and London: University of Chicago Press

Krishna, D. (1996) *The Problematic and Conceptual Structure of Classical Indian Thought about Man, Society and Polity*, Delhi: Oxford University Press

Leslie, J. (ed.) (1991) *Roles and Rituals for Hindu Women*, London: Pinter Press

Lipner, J. L. (1994) *Hindus: Their Religious Beliefs and Practices*, London: Routledge

Lodrick, D. O. (1981) *Sacred Cows, Sacred Places*, Berkeley, Los Angeles and London: University of California Press

Ludden, D. (ed.) (1996) *Making India Hindu: Religion, Community, and the Politics of Democracy in India*, Delhi: Oxford University Press

Madan, T. N. (ed.) (1991) *Religion in India*, Oxford and Delhi: Oxford University Press

Majumdar, R. C. (ed.) (1952) *The Vedic Age*, London: Allen and Unwin

Marshall, P. J. (1970) *The British Discovery of India in the Eighteenth Century*, Cambridge: Cambridge University Press

Martin, N. M. (2002) *Mirabai: Woman Saint of India*, New York: Oxford University Press

Matchett, F. (2005) 'The Purānas' in Flood (ed.) (2005) *The Blackwell Companion to Hinduism*, Oxford: Blackwell, pp. 129–43

Mayer, S. (1960) *Caste and Kinship in Central India: A Village and its Region*, London: Routledge and Kegan Paul

Mehta, J. L. (1984) 'The Hindu Tradition: The Vedic Root' in Whaling, F. (ed.) (1984) *The World's Religious Traditions: Current Perspectives in Religious Studies*, Edinburgh: T & T Clark, pp. 33–54

Michaels, A. (1996) in Michaels *et al.* (eds.) *Wild Goddesses in India and Nepal*, Berne: Peter Long

Michaels, A. (2004) *Hinduism Past and Present*, Princeton and Oxford: Princeton University Press

Michell, G. (1988) *The Hindu Temple: An Introduction to its Meaning and Forms*, Chicago and London: Chicago University Press

Minor, R. N. (ed.) (1986) *Modern Interpreters of the Bhagavadgita*, Albany: State University of New York Press

Minor, R. N. (1987) *Radhakrishnan: A Religious Biography*, Albany: State University of New York Press

Mookerjee, A. (1988) *Kali: The Feminine Force*, London: Thames and Hudson

Nandy, A. (1998) *Creating a Nationality*, Delhi: Oxford University Press

Naravane, V. S. (1964) *Modern Indian Thought*, Bombay: Asia Publisihing House

Narayan, R. K. (1990) *Gods, Demons and Others*, London: Mandarin

O'Flaherty, W. D. (1973) *Asceticism and Eroticism in the Mythology of Śiva*, London: Oxford University Press

O'Flaherty, W. D. (1975) *Hindu Myths*, Harmondsworth: Penguin

O'Flaherty, W. D. (1981) *Siva: The Erotic Ascetic*, Oxford: Oxford University Press

O'Flaherty, W. D. (ed.) (1988) *Textual Sources for the Study of Hinduism*, Manchester: Manchester University Press:

O'Flaherty, W. D. (ed.) (1991) *The Laws of Manu*, Harmondsworth: Penguin

Olivelle, P. (1998) *The Early Upanishads: Annotated Text and Translation*, New York: Oxford University Press

Openshaw, J. (2002) *Seeking Bauls of Bengal*, Cambridge: Cambridge University Press

Osbourne, A. (ed.) (1969) *The Collected Works of Ramana Maharshi*, London: Rider

Osbourne, A. (ed.) (1971) *The teachings of Ramana Maharshi,* London: Rider

Padoux, A. (ed.) (2005) 'Mantra' in Flood, G. (ed.) (2005) *The Blackwell Companion to Hinduism*, Oxford: Blackwell, pp. 478–92

Panikkar, K. M. (1962) *The Determining Periods of Indian History*, Bombay: Bharatiya Vidya Bhavan

Panikkar, R. (1964) *The Unknown Christ of Hinduism*, London: Dartman, Longman and Todd

Panikkar, R. (1978) *The Intra-Religious Dialogue*, New York: Paulist

Panikkar, R. (1979) *The Vedic Experience*, London: Dartman, Longman and Todd

Parekh, B. (1997) *Gandhi*, Oxford: Oxford University Press

Parpola, A. (1994) *Deciphering the Indus Script*, Cambridge: Cambridge University Press

Radhakrishnan, S. (1923,1927) *Indian Philosophy*, 2 vols, New York: Macmillan

Radhakrishnan, S. (1927) *The Hindu View of Life*, London: Allen and Unwin

Radhakrishnan, S. (1932) *An Idealist View of Life*, New York: Macmillan

Radhakrishnan, S. (1939) *Eastern Religions and Western Thought*, Oxford: Oxford University Press

Radhakrishnan, S. (1947) *Religion and Society*, London: Allen and Unwin

Radhakrishnan, S. (1967) *Religion in a Changing World*, London: Allen and Unwin

Radhakrishnan, S. and Moore, C. A. (1967) *A Sourcebook in Indian Philosophy*, Princeton: Princeton University Press

Rajagopal, A. (2001) *Politics After Television: Religious Nationalism and the Reshaping of the Indian Public*, Cambridge: Cambridge University Press

Rambachan, A. (1992) *The Hindu Vision*, Delhi: Motilal Banarsidass

Rawson, P. (1973) *Tantra: The Indian Cult of Ecstasy*, London: Thames and Hudson

Redfield, R. (1953) *The Primitive World and its Transformations*, Ithaca: Cornell University Press

Renou, L. (ed.) (1962) *Hinduism*, New York: Braziller

Richards, G. (1985) *A Sourcebook of Modern Hinduism*, London: Curzon

Samartha, S. J. (1974) *The Hindu Response to the Unbound Christ*, Madras: Christian Literature Society

Savarkar, V. D. (1969) *Hindutva: Who is a Hindu?*, Bombay: Savarkar Sadan

Scott, D. and Selvanayagam, I. (1996) *Re-Visioning India's Religious Traditions*, Bangalore: ISPCK

Sen, K. M. (1961) *Hinduism*, Harmondsworth: Penguin

Sharma, A. (1993) 'Hinduism' in Sharma, A. (ed.) (1993) *Our Religions*, New York and Francisco: Harper Collins, pp. 1–68

Sharma, A. (1996) *Hinduism for our Times*, Oxford and Delhi: Oxford University Press

Sharma, A. (1998) *The Concept of Universal Religion in Modern Hindu Thought*, London: Macmillam

Sharma, A. (ed.) (2003) *The Study of Hinduism*, University of South Carolina: University of South Carolina Press

Sharpe, E. (1975) *Comparative Religion: A History*, London: Duckworth

Shinn, L. (1987) *The Dark Lord: Cult Images and the Hare Krishnas in America*, Philadelphia: Westminster

Singer, M. (1972) *When a Great Tradition Modernises: An Anthropological Approach to Indian Civilisation*, London: Pall Mall Press

Sivaraman, K. (ed.) (1989) *Hindu Spirituality: Vedas through Vedanta*, New York: Crossroad

Smart, N. (1964) *Doctrine and Argument in Indian Philosophy*, London: Allen and Unwin

Smart, N. and Konstantine, S. (1991) *Christian Systematic Theology in a World Context*, London: Marshall Pickering

Smith, D. (2003) *Hinduism and Modernity*, Oxford: Blackwell

Smith, J. Z. (1998) 'Religion, Religions, Religious' in Taylor, M. C. (ed.) (1998) *Critical Terms for Religious Studies*, Chicago: University of Chicago Press, pp. 269–84

Smith, W. C. (1964) *The Meaning and End of Religion*, New York: New American Library, Mentor

Smith, W. C. and Burbidge, J. (eds) (1997) *Modern Culture from a Comparative Perspective*, Albany: State University of New York

Sontheimer, G. D. and Kulke, H. (eds) (1991) *Hinduism Reconsidered*, Delhi: Manohar

Sreenivasa Rao, G. S. S. (1994) *S. Radhakrishnan: A World Philosopher*, Madras: CLS

Srinivas, M. N. (1952) *Religion and Society among the Coorgs of South India*, Oxford: Clarendon

Srinivas, M. N. (1996a) *Village, Caste, Gender and Method: Essays in Social Anthropology*, Delhi: Oxford University Press

Srinivas, M. N. (1996b) *Cohesive Role of Sanskritization and Other Essays*, New Delhi: Penguin

Stevenson, I. (1974) *Twenty Cases Suggestive of Reincarnation*, Charlottesville: University of Carolina Press

Surya Kanta (1981) *A Practical Vedic Dictionary*, Delhi: Oxford University Press

Taylor, M. C. (ed.) (1998) *Critical Terms for Religious Studies*, Chicago: University of Chicago Press, pp. 269–84

Thapar, R. (1994) *Interpreting Early India*, Oxford and Delhi: Oxford University Press

Thomas, P. M. (1987) *Twentieth-Century Indian Interpretations of Bhagavad Gītā: Tilak, Gandhi, and Aurobindo*, Bangalore: CISRS

Tinker, H. (1977) *The Banyan Tree: Overseas Emigrants from India, Pakistan and Bangla Desh*, Oxford: Oxford University Press

Tripathi, G. C. (1978) *Cult of Jagannath and the Regional Tradition of Orissa*, New Delhi: Manohar

Tully, M. (1992) *No Full Stops in India*, Harmondsworth: Penguin

Vanaik, A. (1997) *The Furies of Indian Communalism: Religion, Modernity, and Secularization*, London: Verso

Vaudeville, C. (1993) *A Weaver Named Kabir*, New Delhi: Oxford University Press

Veer, P. van der (1994) *Religious Nationalism: Hindus and Muslims in India*, Berkeley: University of California Press

Vertovec, S. (2000) *The Hindu Diaspora: Comparative Patterns*, London and New York: Routledge

Weightman, S. (1997) 'Hinduism' in Hinnells, J. (ed.) (1997) *A New Handbook of Living Religions*, Oxford: Blackwell

Werner. K. (ed.) (1993) *Studies in Bhakti and Devotional Mysticism*, Richmond UK: Curzon

Whaling, F. (1980) *The Rise of the Religious Significance of Rama*, Delhi: Motilal Banarsidass

Whaling, F. (1984) 'The Study of Religion in a Global Context', in Whaling, F. (ed.) (1984) *Contemporary Approaches to the Study of Religion*, Vol. 1, Berlin, New York, Amsterdam: Mouton, pp. 391–451

Whaling, F. (1984) *The World's Religious Traditions: Current Perspectives in Religious Studies*, Edinburgh: T & T Clark

Whaling, F. (1987) 'The Hindu Tradition in Today's World', in Whaling, F. (ed.) (1987) *Religion in Today's World*, Edinburgh: T & T Clark, pp. 126–71

Williams, R. B. (1984) *The New Face of Hinduism: the Swaminarayan Religion*, Cambridge: Cambridge University Press

Williams, R. B. (ed.) (1992) *A Sacred Thread: Modern Transmissions of Hindu Transmissions in India and Abroad*, Chambersburg, PA: Anima

Woodroffe, J. (1959) *Shakti and Shakta: Essays and Addresses on the Shakta Tantrashastra*, Madras: Ganesh, 5th ed., rev.

Worthington, V. (1989) *A History of Yoga*, London: Arkana

Wulff, D. M. (1984) *Drama as a Mode of Religious Realisation*, Chico-California:

Scholars Press

Zaehner, R. C. (1962) *Hinduism*, London: Oxford University Press

Zaehner, R. C. (1966) *Hindu Scriptures*, London: Oxford University Press

Zaehner, R. C. (1973) *The Bhagavad Gītā*, New York: Oxford University Press

Zimmer, H. (1955) *The Art of Indian Asia*, New York: Pantheon

Glossary

abhaya – no fear, as in the no-fear hand gesture

advaita – non-duality, as in Advaita (non-dual)Vedanta

Agamas (Āgamas) – sacred texts associated with Shiva ā ā

Agni– fire, name of Vedic deity

ahimsa (ahimsā)– non-violence

Alvars (Alvārs) – Tamil poet saints

ananda (ānanda)– joy or bliss

Ananta – infinite; cosmic serpent on which Vishnu rests at end of the ages

anubhava – intuition, experience

Aranyakas – forest texts that are part of the *Rig Veda*

arathi (āratī) – lamp or light

artha – wealth or making a living, one of the four aims of life

Aryan – Aryan race

asanas (āsanas) – postures

Ashoka (Aśoka) – early Indian ruler who promoted Buddhism

ashramas (āśramas) – stages of life

ātman – the real self of human beings

avarna – outside caste, outcaste

avatāras – incarnations mainly of Vishnu

avidyā – ignorance

Banaras – Hindu holy city of Varanasi on the River Ganges

Bauls – unorthodox semi-Hindu group

Bhagavad Gītā – very important text, part of *Mahābhārata*

Bhāgavata Purāna – important *Purāna* focusing on Krishna

bhajans – hymns usually devotional in nature

bhakti – loving devotion, bhakti yoga, the way of loving devotion

Bharat (Bhārat) – India

Brahmā – personal deity, part of trinity of Brahmā, Vishnu and Shiva

Brahman – Absolute Reality

Brahmanas (Brāhmanas) – second set of sacred texts in the *Rig Veda*

Brahmin – the highest Hindu caste, priest

chowkidar – night watchman

cít – consciousness

Dalits – 'broken ones', name given to themselves by ex-outcastes

danda – stick, sometimes used by holy men

darshana (darśana) – philosophical system, viewing a deity

Das (Dās)– servant, name used by some Vishnu holy men

Dashanami (Daśanāmi) – group of Shiva holy men

dāsya – devotional attitude of service

devatas – name for guardian spirits

Devi – name for the Goddess

dhama – place of pilgrimage

dhārana – concentration

dharma – moral order, righteousness, law, religion

Dharmaśāstras – law books

dhyāna – inner meditation

Dravidian – culture and language system mainly in south India

Durga (Durgā) – name of goddess

dvaita – duality as in Dvaita Vedanta

Ganesha (Ganeśa) – elephant headed deity, son of Shiva and Parvati

Gāyatrī – daily invocation to the sun at sunrise, gāyatrī mantra

ghat (ghāt)– steps leading down to a river

gopi (gopī) – milkmaids associated with Krishna

gopura – temple gateway

grāmadevatā – village goddesses

Grihya Sutras (*Gṛhya Sutras*) – texts on Hindu rites of passage

Guru – teacher, spiritual master

Harijan – Gandhi's term for outcastes meaning people of God

Harivamsha (*Harivaṁśa*) – sacred text centred upon Krishna

Hindutva – 'Hinduness' as a right-wing sense of Hindu identity

Ishta-devata (Ishta-devatā) – one's chosen deity

Jaggarnath – Krishna as Lord of the World pulled in temple carts at the Puri festival

jala – holy water

jāti – sub-castes within the caste system

jiva (jivā) – the living self of humans, not as deep as the ātman

jivanmukti (jīvanmuktī) – release while alive from the round of rebirths

jnāna – knowledge

Kali Yuga – the fourth, last and weakest of the four world ages

Kalkin (Kalki) – tenth avatara of Vishnu who will wind up Kali Yuga

kāma – erotic love; name of deity of love; kāma sūtra

karma – good or bad works done in life

karma yoga – way of works done without thought of reward

kirtana (kīrtana)– group devotional singing

Krishna (*Kṛṣṇa*) – avatara of Vishnu, devotional deity in own right

Kshatriya (*Kṣatriya*) – second caste of warriors and rulers

kumari (kumāri) – maiden, Brahmā Kumaris – maidens of Brahmā

kundalini (kundalinī) – human and cosmic form of divine power

kurma – tortoise, classically the second avatara of Vishnu

Lakshmī – Hindu Goddess

līlā – play of humans or deities

linga, lingam – phallic symbol of Shiva

loka – world, sphere

mādhurya – sweetness, love, highest degree of bhakti

Mahābhārata – Hindu Epic, longest epic in world history

Maharshi – great seer, sage

Māhātmya – eulogy, Devi Māhātmya text praises the Goddess

mandala – geometric diagram used in meditation or Tantric worship

mandapa – hall within a large temple

mantra – word or formula often intoned

Manu – mythical ancestor and lawgiver as in the Law Book of Manu

marga (mārga) – path, way of salvation via knowledge, devotion or action

matha – monastic institution

matsya avatāra – fish, classically the first avatara of Vishnu

maya (māyā) – magical, creative, or illusory power

mela – fair, assembly, as in the largest one of all the Kumbha Mela

mleccha – barbarian or non-Hindu

moksha (mokṣa) – liberation

mudrā – gesture usually of the hand, often present in divine images

muhallah – assembly of huts often in villages

mukti – release from rebirth, similar to *moksha*

mūrti – images of deities used in ritual

nāga – snake, naked, Naga cult, Naga people

Narasimha – man-lion, classically the fourth avatara of Vishna

Nataraja (Nātarāja) – lord of the dance, as in Krishna Nataraja images

nirguna – without attributes, used of *Brahman* as impersonal Absolute

niyama – restraint shown in devotion or in yoga

Paraśurāma – Rāma with the axe, sixth avatāra of Vishnu

pasu (pasū) – cattle, or soul

pasupati – lord of the cattle, or lord of the soul, name of Shiva

prana (prāna) – life, breath

prapatti – act of surrender to deity

prasāda – grace, food offered in a temple to deity

pratyahara – inward turning and withdrawal of the senses

prema – love, intense love for deity

pūjā – worship generally and before images in temples

pūjāri – priest

Purānas – class of authoritative texts on deities and much more

rājadharma – the *dharma* of kings

rākhī – amulet often tied on wrists as in festival of Rakshā Bandhan

Rāma – seventh avatara of Vishnu and deity in his own right

Rāmayana – epic based upon the story of Rāma

Rāmarājya – kingdom of Rāma

Rāmlīlā – the play of Rāma, Rāmlīlā festival

rasa – emotion, especially in a religious sense

Rig Veda (*Rg Veda*) – first part of Veda and fountainhead of scripture

Saccidananda (Saccidānanda) – *Brahman* as Being, Consciousness, and Bliss

sādhu – Hindu holy man or saint

saguna – godhead with attributes, not nirguna without attributes

sakhyā – devotional attitude of friendship

samādhi – deep concentration

Sampradāya – religious order or tradition

samsara (samsāra) – wheel of rebirth, world process

sanatana (sanātana) – eternal

Sarvodaya – welfare of all, Gandhi's motto

sat – being, existent, real

satī – wife dying on funeral pyre with her husband

satya – truth, reality

Satyagraha – Gandhi's non-violent action for truth

seva – service to the deity and humans

Shilpaśāstras – treatises on sculpture

shikhāra – temple tower

Shiva (Śiva)– major deity

shruti (śruti)– what is heard and revealed, Hindu scripture

Shudras (śūdras) – fourth, servant caste

siddhi – spiritual power, unusual yoga accomplishments

Smārta Brahmins – worship five deities ecumenically

smriti (smṛti) – Hindu sacred texts remembered and handed down

Surya (Sūrya)– the sun

swadharma – one's own *dharma*

Tantras – sacred texts relating mainly to Devi, esoteric and specific

trimarga (trimārga) – three ways: knowledge, devotion, faithful works

trimūrti – three forms: Brahmā (creator), Vishnu (preserver) and Shiva (destroyer)

upanayana – initiation by receiving sacred thread

Upanishads (Upaniṣads– end part of Vedic scripture, thus promoting Vedanta (end of the Veda)

Vaishyas – third caste of artisans, traders

Vāmana – dwarf avatāra of Vishnu

varada (varadā)– giving of a gift, a famous hand gesture (mudrā)

Varāha – boar avatāra of Vishnu

Varanasi (Banaras) – premier holy city on the river Ganges

varna – general term for caste and the caste system

Vastushastras (*Vastūśāstras*) – treatises on architecture

Veda – basic text including *Vedas, Brahmanas, Aranyakas, Upanishads*

Vedanta (Vedānta) – premier philosophical system, end of Veda, based on the Upanishads

vina – musical instrument

Vishnu (Viṣṇu) – major deity, the Preserver, who sends forth avataras

Vyuha (Vyūha) – part, manifestation of Vishnu

yakshas – goblins, tree spirits, benevolent or malevolent

yama – self-restraint, part of yoga

yantra – mystical diagram

yoga – yoke, philosophical system, mode of spirituality

yoni – source, female sexual organ, symbol of goddess

yugas – four world eras covering vast amounts of time

Further Reading

Short introductions to Hinduism (Chapter 1): Hiltebeitel in Eliade (ed.) (1987); Sharma in Sharma (ed.) (1993); Weightman in Hinnells (ed.) (1997). *Short introductory books*: Klostermaier (1998); Knott (2000). *Longer introductory books by Indians*: Chaudhuri (1979); Dandekar (1979); Madan (ed.) (1991); Rambachan (1992). *Longer introductory books by westerners*: Flood (1996); Klostermaier (1994); Lipner (1994); Michaels (2004).

History of Hindu Tradition (Chapter 2): Basham (1959, 1989); Brockington (1996); Hopkins (1971); Klostermaier (2000) Panikkar K. M. (1962). *Early history*: Bryant (2001); Feuerstein, Kak, Frawley (1995); Parpola (1994); Thapar (1994).

Hindu deities (Chapter 3): *General* – Brockington (1996); Klostermaier (2000); Narayan (1990). *Krishna* – Archer (1957); Kinsley (1979). *Rāma* – Brockington (1984); Whaling (1980). *Shiva* – O'Flaherty (1981). *Devi (Goddess)* – Hawley and Wulff (eds) 1996. *Kali* – Mookerjee (1988). *Folk deities* – Fuller (1992).

Ritual (Chapter 4): Das,Veena (1982); Eck (1983, 1985); Fuller (1992, 2003); Lipner (1994); Rambachan (1992).

Hindu Traditions (Chapter 5): *General* – Brockington (1996); Embree (ed.) (1988); Klostermaier (1994, 1998, 2000). *Tantra* – Bharati (1975); Rawson (1973). *Shakti* – Woodroffe (1959). *Swaminarayan* – Williams (1984). *Bauls* – Openshaw (2002). *Kabir* – Vaudeville (1993). *Hare Krishnas* – Shinn (1987). *Shiva tradition* – Flood in Flood (ed.) (2005). *Vishnu tradition* – Colas in Flood (ed.) (2005).

Social and Political Involvement (Chapter 6): *General*: Dumont (1970); Fuller (1992); Mayer (1960); Srinivas (1996). *Modern situation* – Assayag and Fuller (2005); Baird (ed.) 2001; Chatterjee (1989); Das (2002); Deshpande (2003); Joshi (ed.) (1984); Jurgensmeyer (1982); Leslie (ed.) (1991); Ludden (ed.) (1996); Nandy (1998); Rajagopal (2001); Sharma (1996); Singer (1972); Smith (2003); Sontheimer and Kulke (eds) (1991); Vanaik (1997); van der Veer (1994). *Hinduism outside India* – Burghart (ed.) 1987; Fenton (ed.) 1988; Tinker (1977); Vertovek (2000); Williams (ed.) 1992.

Scriptures (Chapter 8): Bazaz (1975); Brockington (1984, 1998); Dimmit and van Buitenen (eds) (1978); Embree (ed.) (1988); in Flood (ed.) (2005) see Witzel (*Veda and Upanishads*), Rocher (*Dharmaśāstras*), Brockington (*Sanskrit Epics*), Matchett (*Purānas*), Cutler (*Tamil*), Freeman (*Malayalam*) and Martin (*Hindi devotional literature*); Minor (1986); O'Flaherty (1975,1988, 1991); Olivelle (1998); Surya Kanta (1981); Thomas (1987); Zaehner (1966, 1975).

Hindu Aesthetics (Chapter 9): Eck (1985); Elgood (1999); Kramrisch (1954, 1977); Michell (1988); Wulff (1984); Zimmer (1955).

Hindu Spirituality (**Chapter 10**): Eliade (1969); Feuerstein (1982); Panikkar. R (1979); Sivaraman (ed.) (1989); Werner (1993); Worthington (1989). *Mirabai –* Alston (1980); Martin (2002). *Ramakrishna –* Kripal (1995). *Ramana Maharshi –* Osbourne (ed.) (1964). *Sur Das –* Hawley (1984). *Kabir –* Vaudeville (1993).

Hindu Concepts and Philosophy (**Chapter 11**): Carman (1974); Halbfass (1991); Hiriyanna (1958); King (1999); Krishna (1996); Naravane (1964); Radhakrishnan (1923, 1927, 1932, 1939, 1967); Radhakrishnan and Moore (1967); Richards (1985); Sharma (1996, 1998); Smart (1964); Zaehner (1962). *Gandhi*: Copley and Paxton (eds) (1997); Gandhi (1993); Parekh (1997). *Dayanand Saraswati –* Jordens (1978). *Radhakrishnan –* Minor (1987). *Aurobindo –* Bruteau (1971).

Index